EXTREME SCOPING™

An Agile Approach to Enterprise Data Warehousing and Business Intelligence

first edition

Larissa T. Moss

Published by:

Technics Publications, LLC

2 Lindsley Road

Basking Ridge, NJ 07920 U.S.A.

www.technicspub.com

Edited by Carol Lehn

Cover design by Mark Brye

This book is printed on acid-free paper.

ISBN, print ed.   978-1-935504-53-5

ISBN, Kindle ed.   978-1-935504-54-2

ISBN, ePub ed.   978-1-935504-55-9

First Printing 2013

Library of Congress Control Number: 2013944206

ATTENTION SCHOOLS AND BUSINESSES: Technics Publications books are available at quantity discounts with bulk purchase for educational, business, or sales promotional use. For information, please email Steve Hoberman, President of Technics Publications, at me@stevehoberman.com.

 # Praise for Extreme Scoping™

As data warehousing has matured, the methodologies and the development approaches for the building of the data warehouse have also matured. This book by Larissa Moss – *Extreme Scoping™* – represents the evolution of methodology. Larissa is absolutely correct in saying that the development approach for data warehouse is fundamentally different from the development approach for applications. There is much wisdom in this book. I highly recommend it.

Bill Inmon

For over a decade, one voice has consistently called for the use of agile methodology for BI and Data Warehousing. Larissa Moss has written several books and given numerous public classes on this topic. Organizations that have taken heed have benefited from her guidance. Organizations that have disregarded agile methodology continue to struggle. This new book gives even greater insight into the successful implementation of the agile method.

Derek Strauss, Chief Data Officer, TD Ameritrade

Extreme Scoping is a methodology and approach to enterprise data warehousing and business intelligence that is perfect for 21st century organizations of any size or industry. By combining the foundations of data management and data analysis with the agile methods of rapid releases and user-centric delivery for business intelligence, Larissa Moss has given new life to the development path for any decision support initiative. Written from the perspective of an industry expert and practitioner who has delivered many successful EDW/BI projects, Ms. Moss' *Extreme Scoping* combines the best aspects of many other methodologies into one manageable and proven approach to meeting business needs with data warehousing and business intelligence. This book is a valuable addition to the field, and should be used by all DW/BI professionals.

Anne Marie Smith, Ph.D., Enterprise Information Management Consultant

A wonderful Practitioner's Guide, chock-full of great tips to help make your data warehouse projects successful. I learned some great new ideas, and reinforced lessons I had learned. A must read!

Bonnie K. O'Neil, Data Architect and co-author, Business Metadata

The dilemma faced by BI project managers is the pull from the business that wants speedy delivery and, on the other side, the requirement to follow an IT methodology that does not lend itself to a fast and furious BI delivery schedule, as well as the need to develop solutions that are enterprise-wide. In *Extreme Scoping*, Larissa Moss provides some breakthrough methods and reasoning that should satisfy both the business and the IT methodology auditors.

Sid Adelman

Can data be agile? Or more specifically, can data projects produce the same types of cost, schedule, functionality, and risk benefits that Scrum and XP have brought to the software development world? That is the question that Larissa Moss tackles in this important new book. Without spoiling a thoroughly enjoyable read - the short answer is yes. The co-author of the *Business Intelligence Roadmap* has done an excellent job describing how to bring agility to data-driven BI projects. If you are under pressure to speed up the time it currently takes to deliver data value - this book is a must read.

Peter Aiken, President DAMA International

In a world that no longer has patience to wait for the next solution to be developed; where selection is usually based on the religious "I believe ...."; where too many mistakenly use "The Agile Agenda" as an excuse for every team to do as they see fit; Larissa differentiates data integration projects from software development projects and identifies the strengths and weaknesses of many methodologies as the foundation for a new toolkit which is both robust and highly customizable. Easy to read, this insightful book is "a valuable must read" for any who want or need to understand where and how different methodologies deliver best value and optimal risk – those in IT, finance, and most project stakeholders and team members. Students and teachers of IT disciplines will find the book a valuable investment, and I expect that many of the comparisons will surface as exam questions. Above all – consultancies, that promote a particular methodology, need to be prepared to also offer *Extreme Scoping* or face challenges by customers that have read Larissa's masterpiece.

Kenneth Hansen, Analytic Domain Group, Australia and UK

This book is an important contribution to our industry. It alerts readers, who are perhaps ready to get on the agile bandwagon a bit too fast, about the unique hazards associated with managing data-centric BI/DW project efforts. It tackles the subject of how to reduce risk through ensuring that a data management perspective is explicitly baked into "agile" BI/DW development efforts.

Nancy Williams, Vice President, DecisionPath Consulting

As usual, Ms. Moss offers insightful advice to BI professionals through her latest book. *Extreme Scoping* is – as are all of her books – quite readable. "Enjoy" is not a term I generally use for such works, but her books are the most enjoyable of all that I've read on the subjects of Data Warehousing and Business Intelligence. The chapters are well organized, the information is useful, and her approach is real world. My current team is new to BI and we are struggling with a pre-delivered warehouse. This book provides the direction and approach that we've been lacking and will be on everyone's performance plan to read. I'm excited to use *Extreme Scoping* to manage our next project.

Donna Welch

I found Larissa's book a wonderful collection of insightful nuggets all based on experience and wisdom. How appropriate and logical that organizations that seek data-driven wisdom, action, and performance, need to employ data-driven project methods. *Extreme Scoping* is extremely logical in that regard. I also totally agree that data analysis is a critical project step. It brings data realities and context to the project and is critical to understanding what is possible. Otherwise, it is too easy for business executives to dream far beyond the capabilities of their data. Project leaders and stakeholders should expect to be constantly finding balance between business, data, technical and project concerns. I find that BDTP Balance™ is an effective way to describe the essence of this challenge.

Don Frederiksen

To my "big sister" Tamara

Contents at a Glance

Contents

Acknowledgments

The idea for this book started to germinate even before my *Business Intelligence Roadmap* book was published in 2003. Since then, I have been trying out and refining my agile Extreme Scoping™ approach with numerous clients. I wish to thank all of them for their contributions.

Without my mentor, colleague, and good friend Sid Adelman, who persuaded me to write books in the first place and invited me to co-author his books *Data Warehouse Project Management, Impossible Data Warehouse Situations,* and *Data Strategy,* this book would have never been written. Thank you, Sid. It's been great working with you.

I am grateful to Dave Wells, former director of education at the Data Warehousing Institute, Günter Fuhrmeister of Sigs-Datacom GmbH Germany, Giovanni Modica of Technology Transfer Italy, Kurt Häusermann of BI Consultants GmbH Switzerland, as well as numerous other seminar and conference organizers in the US, Europe, and Asia, who repeatedly gave me a platform to present my methodologies in a public forum.

All of my colleagues around the globe have, in one way or another, knowingly and unknowingly, influenced and shaped my ideas, in particular Bill Inmon, Claudia Imhoff, Wayne Eckerson, Steve Hoberman, John Zachman, David Marco, Larry English, Danette McGilvray, Derek Strauss, Shaku Atre, Michael Scofield, Anne Marie Smith, Michael Brackett, Nancy Williams, and many others. I extend my thanks to colleagues and clients across the pond: Ken Hansen in the UK, Gerd Hay and Frances d'Silva in Norway, Torben Westergaard in Denmark, Zuzana Bednarova in the Slovak Republic, and Markus Fricke in Germany.

Many thanks to my loyal proof reader and significant other Donald Sherman, who doesn't always understand what I write about, but who is determined to catch my long and awkward "German" sentences, which at times span a paragraph. He also corrects my grammar and sentence structure before I submit my manuscripts to the publishers, and takes our dog Pepper for long walks while I am locked up in my "cave" (basement office) writing epics. I thank Pepper for keeping my feet warm in my cave.

I want to thank Wayne Eckerson and Dave Wells for writing the flattering forewords. In addition, many thanks to Anne Marie Smith, Bill Inmon, Peter Aiken, Sid Adelman, Bonnie O'Neil, John Murphy, Ken Hansen, Donna Welch, Nancy Williams, Derek Strauss, and Don Frederiksen for their feedback and suggestions for the book.

I have an enormous amount of appreciation for Steve Hoberman, my publisher. Steve, I am very grateful that you decided to branch out into the publishing business. I believe it was Graeme Simsion who remarked that "many more-established publishers could learn from [you]" and I whole-heartedly agree. My publishing experience with you was a delight.

Finally, I wish to thank Carol Lehn, my editor, Mark Brye for the cool book cover, and the entire publishing staff that transformed my draft manuscript into a well laid out book that pleases the eye.

About the Author

Larissa Moss is founder and president of Method Focus Inc., a company specializing in enterprise data warehousing and business intelligence. She has over 30 years of IT experience, and for over 20 years, her focus has been on data management, project and program management, and methodologies. She is a world renown speaker at conferences in the US and Europe on the topics of data warehousing, business intelligence, master data management, agile enterprise data warehouse project management, spiral data warehouse/business intelligence methodologies, enterprise information management, data governance, and data quality.

Ms. Moss is a widely published author. In 1991, she self-published her first methodology, *RSDM 2000, Relational System Development Methodology, Volumes I & II*. Since then, she co-authored the books *Data Warehouse Project Management*, *Impossible Data Warehouse Situations*, *Business Intelligence Roadmap*, and *Data Strategy*. She has published dozens of articles in Cutter IT Journal, Teradata Magazine, TDWI Journal of Data Warehousing, TDWI Flash Point, DM Review (now Information Management), and EIMInsight Magazine (www.eiminstitute.org). Her white papers include *Organizational and Cultural Barriers to Business Intelligence*; *Developing BI Decision-Support Applications: Not Business As Usual*; *Data Quality is Not Optional*; *The Importance of Data Modeling as a Foundation for Business Insight*; *Extreme Scoping*: *An Agile Approach to Enterprise Data Warehousing and BI*; and *The Role of A Chief Data Officer in the 21st Century*.

Her present and past associations include Teradata 3rd Party Influencers, the IBM Gold Group, the Cutter Consortium (Data Insight & Social BI Practice), The Data Warehousing Institute (TDWI), Data Management Association (DAMA) Los Angeles Chapter, the Relational Institute, and Codd & Date Consulting Group. She was a part-time faculty member at the Extended University of California, Polytechnic University Pomona, and has been lecturing for the Cutter Consortium, TDWI, MIS Training Institute (MISTI), Professional Education Strategies Group, Inc. (PESG), IRM UK Strategic IT Training Ltd. and Technology Transfer Italy. Ms. Moss can be reached at methodfocus@earthlink.net. Her Website is www.methodfocus.com.

Foreword by Wayne Eckerson

I've read many books about data warehousing and business intelligence (BI). This book by Larissa Moss is one of the best.

I should not be surprised. Larissa has spent years refining the craft of designing, building, and delivering BI applications. She has many battle scars from doing hand-to-hand combat in the BI trenches, both as a BI practitioner and consultant. (I love the story she tells in the preface of her first data warehousing development experience.) Over the years, she has developed a keen insight about what works and doesn't work in BI. This book brings to light the wealth of that development experience.

Best of all, this is not some dry text that laboriously steps readers through a technical methodology. Larissa expresses her ideas in a clear, concise, and persuasive manner. She effortlessly captures the essence of an issue and reinforces key themes throughout the book to keep the reader on track. I highlighted so many beautifully written and insightful paragraphs in her manuscript that it became comical. I desperately wanted the final, published book rather than the manuscript so I could dog-ear it to death and place it front-and-center in my office bookshelf!

The bottom line is that I learned a lot reading this manuscript. And I think you will, too. For those of you who spend most of your time in the BI trenches, the book will both challenge and validate your own experiences and serve as a handy reference guide during the planning, design, and development phases of a BI project. For business and technical executives, the book makes a compelling case for investing in the creation of an integrated set of enterprise data.

Given the continuous parade of new tools, technologies, and methodologies, it's easy to forget the ultimate mission of BI. Larissa reminds us that the real value of BI comes from delivering a reusable corporate asset that consists of clean, consistent, and integrated data. And best of all, she shows us how to do it!

Wayne Eckerson

BI thought leader and consultant
Author of *Secrets of Analytical Leaders*
Hingham, Massachusetts

Foreword by David Wells

Extreme Scoping is a timely book and one that will make a difference for those who are serious about implementing mature, sustainable, and adaptive Business Intelligence. BI has become increasingly challenging for anyone trying to keep up with the pace of change in business, data, and technology. The demand for information and analytics continues to grow, and the current "big data" craze further raises the stakes. Business wants more, they want it faster, and they want to believe the "magazine cover magic" of industry press.

Under the pressure of increasing demands for more results and higher speed, it is quite natural that BI teams look to agile development methods. The trouble is that there are substantially more teams who attempt agile than who succeed with agile. I can't offer numbers to support that assertion – only compelling anecdotal evidence of conversations with and observations of the many BI professionals that I meet.

Larissa Moss has captured the essence of the difficulties with Agile BI. In short, there is a natural tension between *agile* and *enterprise* that is difficult to overcome. When done well, BI is enterprise focused; agile is, by definition, user focused. Agile is predicated on "better ways of developing software", yet managed data is more significant than software development for effective BI programs. Making BI and agile work together is a complex and ambitious undertaking. Yes, there are successful agile BI projects, but they are rare and seem to be out of reach for many.

Larissa itemizes many of the tensions between BI and agile methods. The intent of the book and the method, however, is not to itemize problems but to offer solutions. Some of the key concepts among the solutions include:

- Frequent delivery
- Managed releases
- Managed dependencies
- Balance of competing priorities
- Parallel development
- Milestone management

A first impression when viewing these solutions as a simple list is that there's nothing new here. All of these concepts have been around for years and applied in many different contexts. Release management, for example, is a core part of the Rational Unified Process (RUP) that is a proven scope containment technique. Milestone management is a very practical way to shift project focus from tasks and activities to deliverables – a nod to the old saying that warns us to not confuse furious activity with progress.

But Extreme Scoping is not simply a list of concepts. The newness is in the unique combination – weaving together many proven techniques into a rich tapestry that is a new way of thinking about BI projects. The magic is in the interaction and dynamics among the concepts. Extreme Scoping is not invention; it is innovation – using existing concepts and techniques in new ways that create a powerfully different approach to enabling BI capabilities.

Extreme Scoping is not a methodology so much as a set of principles and techniques that you can overlay onto whatever methodology you use. The book is rich with advice and guidance for virtually every aspect of BI projects from planning and requirements to deployment and from back-end data management to front-end information and analytics services.

Some will argue that Extreme Scoping is not "true" agile. If agile implies Scrum, then they may be correct. That debate, however, is a pointless semantics argument of little value. Call it what you like – agile, nimble, spry, or quick BI. Extreme Scoping is a valuable contribution to the field.

I'm honored that Larissa asked me to write this foreword. She is a friend and a colleague from whom I have learned much over the years. She challenges conventional wisdom, and her sometimes contrarian ideas are always thought provoking. Larissa is both a pragmatist and an independent thinker. Those qualities come through in the style of this book.

Extreme Scoping is a well-written book that is easy to absorb. It is not full of surprises. It is filled with a lot of common sense and lessons learned through experience. Perhaps most important, it recognizes that BI development is a human process and that attention to people and culture is critical.

Dave Wells

BI Mentor, Guide, and Consultant
Kirkland, Washington

Preface
Why I Wrote This Book

I always start my seminars and conference presentations with a true story of how I stumbled onto *agile*. I remember the many "death march" (mission impossible) data warehouse projects I had worked on in the mid-1990's. One such project was at a mortgage loan company. IT management had heard about this new type of system called a data warehouse. The idea that management had at the time was to take their three major mortgage loan systems and merge them into the data warehouse: loan origination, loan servicing, and loans sold on the secondary market. Anyone who has ever worked in a mortgage loan institution will recognize immediately that these three systems combined contain the majority of all the data in the company. In other words, standardizing and integrating most of the data in the company in one fell swoop is no small feat. However, we were too naïve to realize that at the time.

Our team was made up of about a dozen developers, some with mainframe skills and others experimenting with a brand new online analytical processing (OLAP) tool, which also ran on the mainframe. In addition, there was a systems analyst, a data modeler (me), a very experienced technical trouble shooter, and a project lead. We all reported to a department manager in IT who had already promised to senior management that we will deliver this data warehouse with merged data from all three systems within nine months, without ever checking with the team first. He saw this project as nothing more than a mapping exercise between three old flat file structures into one relational database. Needless to say, it was much more involved than that.

When we analyzed the three operational systems, we found several additional files we had to consider. We quickly realized that the data across all the files was inconsistently named and populated, and the data was full of mistakes. The users of the three systems had completely different views of the data. They disagreed on the meaning and usage of the data. They used different codes, and they reused different data elements for various other purposes with multi-layered REDEFINE (COBOL) statements. We were given half a dozen code translation books to help us define and standardize the data. Unfortunately, half the values in the data we analyzed did not exist in any of the code translation books, and the users did not know what they meant. As soon as we put a stake in the ground and defined some of the data as best as we could, several of the users would disagree. When we changed the definitions to include these users' views, other users would disagree. When we tried to get all the users into one room to resolve their differences, they refused to come. Soon the users stopped talking to us all together, while our department manager was getting more and more anxious about our slow progress. It had been over six months and we were still in the "Analysis Phase" when, according to our 40-page project plan, we were supposed to be coding already.

Even though the systems analyst on our team was extremely knowledgeable about the mortgage loan industry, it was practically impossible to get the business people to review, much less approve, our work and equally impossible to get consensus among them. Our project lead kept telling us to do our best, and so we worked 16 hours a day, six (sometimes seven) days a week for months. More than once, the department manager would come to our cubicles and berate us for being incompetent. I remember one incident when he showed up furious, red in the face and veins bulging in his neck, yelling at our systems analyst, who was one of the best systems analysts I have worked with in decades. At that confrontation, he threatened to fire all of us if we didn't get this project done. He didn't want to hear our explanations or excuses, much less try to help us resolve our roadblocks – we were to simply complete the project, otherwise he would look bad in the eyes of his senior management.

In the meantime, the systems analyst, the technical trouble shooter and I have become a very close-knit group. At a two-hour lunch, which was more liquid than solid, we decided we had nothing to lose in light of our impending termination, so we may as well try to turn our fragmented and incomplete data models into a semi-cohesive data warehouse structure.

Our first agreed upon task was to ceremonially burn our useless 40-page project plan in a metal dust bin in the parking lot, which got us into more trouble with security. It was obvious that the saying "plan the work, then work the plan" was a complete joke on this particular project, not that it had ever worked all that well on any previous projects. The methodology we were forced to use was a development methodology from the 1970's. It had no data-related tasks at all, no time for data analysis, data profiling, data modeling, data transformation, data standardization, data cleansing, or data dispute resolution.

Our second decision was to work by the seat of our pants. We expanded our little group to include one full-time developer, and we met every morning for as long as it took to review what we had done, decide what needed to be done next, discuss and resolve issues we had, and delegate work to one another. We also decided to team up on all our tasks to minimize errors and delays if one person was out sick, and to spread as much knowledge among us to keep the project going. To our amazement, both the project lead and the department manager did not challenge our new approach and just ignored us for three months. To the amazement of management and the rest of the staff, the four of us took our imperfect and incomplete data warehouse into production at the end of the three months.

Shortly thereafter, I left the company and swore to never work on a data warehouse project again. I had concluded that all data warehouse projects were "death march" projects and completely unmanageable. As fate would have it, shortly after this experience, I was invited to join the Cutter Consortium's Business Intelligence practice (now called Data Insight & Social BI practice) in Massachusetts. During my first attendance at a Cutter Consortium Summit (conference), I learned that their most established IT practice was Agile Product and Project Management. As I was listening to a young man give a presentation on a radically new software development method called Extreme Programming (XP), I thought to myself in disbelief, "Oh my God, there is a method to this madness." He was describing a project dynamic very similar to ours on that dreadful "death march" project. He was talking about daily stand-up meetings, self-organizing project teams, short delivery cycles, and so on. That was very similar to what we ended up doing on our project. The same day of the presentation, I briefly met with this young man to discuss my experience with him and solicit his advice. Of course, this young man turned out to be Kent Beck, and unbeknownst to him, our conversation led to my decision that I should take the lessons learned from that dreadful project and turn them into meaningful contributions to the industry.

The first lesson was that data warehouse projects are not like traditional operational system development projects. They have to be organized and managed differently. This led to the book *Data Warehouse Project Management*, which I co-authored with Sid Adelman, followed by the book *Impossible Data Warehouse Situations* by Sid Adelman, with contributions from eight additional data warehouse consultants.

The second lesson was that data warehouse projects are primarily enterprise-wide data integration initiatives. This means that a data warehouse cannot be built in one big bang; instead it evolves incrementally. In addition, and more importantly, the project teams must follow a data-driven methodology, not a development-driven methodology. This led to the data warehouse specific methodology *Business Intelligence Roadmap*, which I co-authored with Shaku Atre.

The third lesson was that data warehouse projects are larger and take longer than traditional operational system development projects because of the necessary data standardization and data integration activities. Unless you are building departmental stovepipe solutions, you cannot avoid the data work. The conundrum is that business people expect shorter delivery times while the project scopes are getting larger due to the increasing amount of data, which requires more and more time to be analyzed, modeled, standardized, cleansed, transformed, and integrated. This leads to one conclusion: we must cut the scope of projects into smaller releases that can be developed, deployed, and refined incrementally. This *Extreme Scoping* book is about such an agile approach.

Scrum and XP

I feel compelled to say a few words about other popular agile methodologies, such as Scrum and Extreme Programming (XP). If you are already an agile practitioner, it is likely that you have been trained, either formally through seminars or informally on a project, to use Scrum or XP, especially if the training occurred on an operational system development project. My experience over the last decade has been that Scrum/XP practitioners struggle with alternative agile methods that do not follow the exact same structure and terminology as Scrum or XP. On the extreme side, some agile practitioners insist that a methodology is not agile unless it is Scrum or XP. Webster's New World Dictionary definition is "agile and nimble both imply rapidity and lightness of movement." This can be achieved in ways other than Scrum or XP, especially when the environment in which the methodology is applied is so different from the environment where Scrum and XP are successfully applied. I will even go out on a limb and wonder if it isn't possible that, had Scrum and XP been developed by data warehouse professionals for enterprise-wide data integration projects specifically, these methodologies might have looked different.

As I pointed out earlier, a data warehouse project is completely different from a traditional operational system development project. The emphasis in data warehouse projects is on the data, while the emphasis in system development projects is on coding. Data warehouse projects must be led by data management professionals, while system development projects can be led by technicians. The users of a data warehouse are *all* employees of a company, and potentially their customers and suppliers, while the users of a system are usually confined to *one* business unit.

A data warehouse is *not* an assortment of independent, customized BI applications for different business units. The primary goal of a data warehouse is to deliver a pool of consistent, clean, standardized, integrated, and trustworthy data, while the primary goal of a development project is to deliver functionality. In data warehousing, we do have functional deliverables called BI applications and reports, but those are not separate and independent from the data warehouse itself – at least they shouldn't be because the data warehouse is the engine of BI. Therefore, it is my opinion that agile methodologies, which were invented by developers for other developers to streamline their development process of turning requirements into working code, are not appropriate for data management professionals who organize and manage enterprise-wide data integration initiatives, such as a data warehouse, customer relationship management, or master data management. In the same vein, Extreme Scoping, which is a data warehouse and BI specific agile method, is not appropriate for system development projects that focus solely on delivering functionality as quickly as possible. I explain my position further in Chapter 5.

Who Should Read This Book

Every data warehouse project has at least two tracks or teams: (i) the back-end data management and database development team and (ii) the front-end BI application and report development team. The back-end team is heavily staffed with data management professionals, such as data analysts, data modelers, data quality analysts, data administrators (now called enterprise information management professionals), database designers or database architects, and ETL developers, who physically move data from operational source systems into enterprise-class target databases. The front-end team is heavily staffed with developers who use the data in the target databases in their queries, reports, applications, and other analytics delivery mechanisms to the users. There could be third and fourth tracks, such as metadata administration, data mining, and others. These teams must all work together cooperatively and harmoniously because they all work toward the same goals and deliverables. Because Extreme Scoping is based on a robust soup-to-nuts data warehouse specific methodology (Business Intelligence Roadmap), all teams and all types of work activities are under its umbrella. Therefore, all team members and users who work on or participate in the evolution of an enterprise-class data warehouse with its dependent data marts and BI applications should read this book.

IT managers, project teams, and data management professionals of other enterprise-class data integration initiatives, such as master data management (MDM), customer relationship management (CRM), customer data integration (CDI), etc., will benefit from applying Extreme Scoping to their projects. In addition, C-level executives and business managers will get an appreciation of the inherent complexities of EDW/BI projects by reading Part I, Part II, and Part IV of this book.

How This Book Is Organized

This book is divided into four sections. I encourage the reader to read all sections sequentially to fully appreciate my perspective and to understand my reasons for creating a new agile methodology, which is specifically designed for data management professionals who organize and manage enterprise-wide data integration initiatives.

Part I: Setting the Stage – gives the reader insight into my data management background and my philosophy. It is an introductory section that explains why traditional waterfall methodologies are inappropriate for enterprise-wide data integration initiatives.

Part II: Going Agile – contrasts traditional waterfall methodologies with spiral (iterative) methodologies, and introduces the reader to agile principles and popular agile development methodologies like Scrum and XP. In this section, I also elaborate on when Scrum and XP can be used on a data warehouse project, and when these methodologies should be replaced by Extreme Scoping.

Part III: Extreme Scoping Planning Process – is the largest section of the book. It describes the seven-step planning process in detail, using the data warehouse specific Business Intelligence Roadmap methodology as an example. There is no need to buy the *Business Intelligence Roadmap* book because it should be easy for the reader to substitute the methodology used in their company and to follow the seven-step process without undue complication.

Part IV: At the Program Level – concludes with a discussion of scaling the Extreme Scoping method from a project to a program level. I describe the necessary infrastructure that should be in place, and I mention the long-term cultural changes that have to take place in a company. Finally, I use the BI Maturity Model, published by Wayne Eckerson in his book *Performance Dashboards*, to position Extreme Scoping next to other agile methodologies on the evolutionary path of data warehousing.

Appendix A: Business Intelligence Roadmap Things to Consider – contains additional things to consider when reviewing the Business Intelligence Roadmap methodology or your own methodology before deciding which development steps to select or drop during the Extreme Scoping Planning Process.

Appendix B: Business Intelligence Roadmap Activities – describes the high-level activities in the sixteen development steps in the Business Intelligence Roadmap methodology. Compare them to your own data warehouse methodology to ensure you are not missing important activities.

Appendix C: Glossary – contains additional definitions for terms I use in the book.

References – contains references for additional reading materials that pertain to data warehousing, business intelligence, enterprise information management, data governance, and agile practices.

Giving in to the time pressures and ignoring quality is a time trap in which many organizations are caught. It is a vicious cycle, because the more redundant the data, the more inconsistent it is, the less users trust it, and the more they end up building their own customized stand-alone solutions. I call that the "Sinatra way", based on Frank Sinatra's song "I did it my way" … and you did it your way. Figure I illustrates that as redundancy increases, data quality gets even worse, and user satisfaction decreases even more.

Figure I The Time Trap

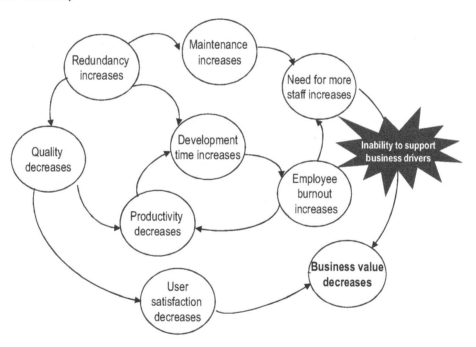

At the same time, maintenance of the redundant systems increases, which leads to a need for more staff. Development time also increases because it takes longer to sift through the pool of redundant databases and applications. Because time is still of the essence, employees work longer and harder, which leads to employee burnout, and that, in turn, leads to decreased productivity, and so on. Being seduced by the time trap leads to decreased business value and can potentially result in the inability to support the organization's business drivers – and thus put a company out of business.

Chapter 1
Business Intelligence and Data Warehousing

Business intelligence (BI) does not refer to a product you can buy or to a system you can build. Instead, it is a new way of delivering and managing the decision support function in an organization. BI uses data like a strategic asset of the company, which, when turned into information and applied as knowledge, gives the company an advantage over its competitors. For data to become a strategic asset, each unique data element must be carefully managed and reused to provide maximum return on asset. Think about how other assets are managed in a company, for example, inventory, cash, buildings, personnel, and accounts receivable. Data is just as critical to running the business as are these other assets and should therefore be managed the same way.

Business Intelligence

I define business intelligence as *"cross-functional disciplines* and an *enterprise architecture* for creating an *integrated collection* of operational as well as decision support applications and databases, which provide the business community *easy access* to their business data, and allows them to make *accurate business decisions."* It is a definition that goes beyond the common definitions published in our industry. It is what I hope BI will mean in the future. Let us parse my definition to understand all of its components.

Cross-functional disciplines refer to a common way of creating and using data and processes across the entire organization. That includes the use of a common infrastructure, common data-driven methodology, common standards, common policies and procedures, and common roles and responsibilities.

Enterprise architecture is a collection of models and matrices depicting all data, processes, and resources (e.g., hardware, software, human, fixed assets, financial, etc.) of a company. It is the blueprint of a company. Each model is supported by metadata, which is detailed information about all of the components of the enterprise architecture. Of particular importance to BI and data warehousing is the enterprise information architecture (EIA). John Zachman refers to it as the "what" column or the data column in his Zachman Framework. In other words, EIA refers to data models, such as conceptual data models, project-specific logical data models, physical database models, the "single version of the truth" enterprise data model, and on the physical side, the data definition language for a database or the data declaration section in a programming language. Enterprise architecture and cross-functional disciplines are intertwined because all architectural components are governed by those disciplines.

Integrated collection of operational as well as decision support applications and databases needs to be parsed even further. Integrated in this context refers to unique and distinct components that are reusable. Examples are unique data elements and common program subroutines (code). When talking about data, many people confuse data integration with data consolidation. Consolidating data simply means gathering data elements that describe the same business entity (e.g., customer data or product data) from multiple sources and storing them in one target data store (e.g., file or table). Integrating data goes far beyond that to achieve the "single version of the truth" because, in addition to consolidating data, integration enforces data uniqueness. Data uniqueness means there are no synonyms and no homonyms. Every data element is defined only once and is reused (not redefined) in multiple systems. That requires four actions during logical data modeling:

1. Examine the definition, the semantic intent, and the domain values of each logical attribute to find potential duplicates of a business entity that would otherwise not be discovered because the entities are known under different names in the source systems.

2. Ensure that each entity instance has one and only one unique identifier (primary key), which, in turn, is never reassigned to a new entity instance even after the old instance expired and was deleted from the database.

3. Use the six normalization rules to put "one fact in one place". The six normalization rules are: first normal form (1NF), second normal form (2NF), third normal form (3NF), Boyce-Codd normal form (BCNF), fourth normal form (4NF), and fifth normal form (5NF). The word "fact" in the phrase does not refer to its new meaning of "measures in a *fact* table in a star schema", but to its old meaning of "one *attribute* in one, and only one, owning entity." This means that an attribute can be assigned (or placed) into only one entity as either an identifier of that entity or as a descriptive attribute of that one, and no other, entity. This modeling activity ensures that each attribute is captured once and only once, and that it remains unique within the data universe of the organization. Hence, the "single version of the truth."

4. The last, and most important, activity of integration is to capture the business actions (transactions) that connect the business entities in the real world. The results of these business actions are shown as data relationships among the entities. It is paramount to capture them from a logical business perspective (not from a reporting pattern or data access perspective) because these relationships are the basis for all potential database access patterns, known and unknown, now and in the future. Business people will never ask for information about two completely unrelated business entities because any such information would be irrelevant, if not nonsensical.

"Single" version of the truth refers to unique, standardized, and integrated entities and attributes. There are no synonyms or homonyms, every attribute belongs to one and only one entity, and every non-key attribute is fully functionally dependent on the key, the whole key, and nothing but the key.

This does not mean that the "version of the truth" never changes. Changes in the business affect data, data relationships, and data policies. However, there always should be a "single" version of the truth, as opposed to multiple versions, at any one time.

Another misunderstanding of what "single" version of the truth means is that you must browbeat all users into agreeing on one, and only one, definition of customer. Wrong! Customer is a data subject area with a complex multi-tier supertype/subtype structure. The entire supertype/subtype structure represents the "single" version of the truth.

Currently, all companies still see BI and data warehousing as separate in organization and function from their operational systems. However, I see these two worlds converging in the distant future, which is why I include operational as well as decision support applications and databases in my definition. As I frequently tell my audience, I think that data warehousing is the biggest, albeit currently still necessary, crutch IT has ever invented. Once we standardize and minimize our operational systems, and with the technology already available, data warehousing the way we know it today should some day become unnecessary and obsolete. For example, if master data management were implemented centrally, and if all transactional databases were reduced to transaction data only (with keys linking to the master data), and if we stored history for both master data and transaction data in the operational databases, we could simply run BI tools against the operational databases, or against an exact duplicate of them so as not to affect operational performance. This scenario assumes that there would be no uncontrolled data redundancy (data chaos) and that data quality would be pristine in the operational databases, neither of which are reality today.

Easy access in my definition of BI refers to a standardized platform (e.g., hardware, software, databases, database gateways) which enables users to easily access, merge, and analyze their data. This has evolved into self-service business intelligence (SSBI). SSBI enables business people to access and analyze their data without the involvement of IT, once IT has created and populated the enterprise data warehouse (EDW) target databases, provided a populated metadata repository for reference, and installed the user BI tools.

Accurate business decisions are only possible if the data is accurate. That means that data quality is a big part of BI. Data quality activities, such as profiling source data, creating a logical data model of the business data, and merging models into the enterprise data model need to address data quality. Since the activity of logical data modeling is a solely business-focused data analysis activity, it includes the validation of the logical data model components (i.e., entities, attributes, data relationships) and of the business metadata (i.e., definitions, domains, business rules, etc.) against the existing operational data in the source systems. The validation activities include asking probing questions, applying normalization rules to put "one fact in one place" and scrutinizing definitions, domains, and semantic meanings of all entities and all attributes to ensure their uniqueness. Performing this type of data archeology during logical data modeling will inadvertently expose data quality problems that would otherwise never have been detected during database design activities because database designers/architects neither have the time nor the responsibility to perform such validation activities while they are trying to design an efficient database.

Role of an Enterprise Data Warehouse

The term data warehouse, also known as enterprise data warehouse (EDW), has had many definitions over the years. Bill Inmon called it "a subject-oriented, integrated, non-volatile, time-variant collection of data organized to support management needs." Ralph Kimball considered it "nothing more than the union of all the constituent data marts." The Data Warehousing Institute (TDWI) defined it as "a data structure that is optimized for distribution. It collects and stores integrated sets of historical data from multiple operational systems and feeds them to one or more data marts. It may also provide user access to support enterprise views of data." Regardless of definition, I think all experts would agree that the EDW is an important building block in BI. It is the "under-the-hood engine" of BI. BI applications and BI tools require consistent, clean, and integrated data in order to generate accurate information upon which business executives and managers can act. Data warehousing provides that basic pool of consistent, clean, and integrated data because of its two major objectives: data management and data delivery.

Think of these two objectives as a residential duplex. In a duplex you have two separate units under the same roof, as illustrated in Figure 1.1. If you were to physically separate the units, you would no longer have a duplex, but two single family residences. Similarly, a data warehouse is only a data warehouse as long as it addresses both objectives: data management and data delivery. If you remove either one of the objectives, it is no longer a data warehouse. It may be a data governance initiative, which addresses data management, or a stand-alone data mart development activity, which addresses data delivery, but not a data warehouse.

Figure 1.1 The Duplex

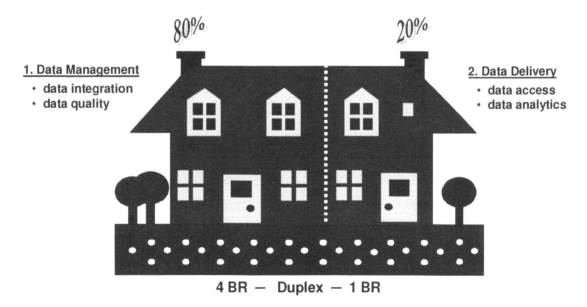

Note that in Figure 1.1, the size of the two units in the duplex are not the same. Data management is like a four bedroom unit taking 80% of the development effort, while data delivery is like a one bedroom unit taking only 20% of the development effort.

Yet, most organizations concentrate almost all of their efforts on data delivery and pay little – if any – attention to data management. There are several reasons for this:

- Project schedules are very tight and there is no time for data management activities;
- Data administrators (EIM professionals) are not effectively embedded within EDW/BI projects;
- The old, traditional system development lifecycle methodologies don't demand data management activities;
- Departmental users don't care about enterprise-wide data integration, especially if it slows down their projects or impacts their budgets.

TDWI BI Components Framework

The Data Warehousing Institute (TDWI) provides one of the best definitions for BI and data warehousing, as well as of the relationship between them, in its BI Components Framework. Figure 1.2 illustrates the three layers in this framework: the business layer, the administration and operations layer, and the implementation layer.

Figure 1.2 TDWI BI Components Framework

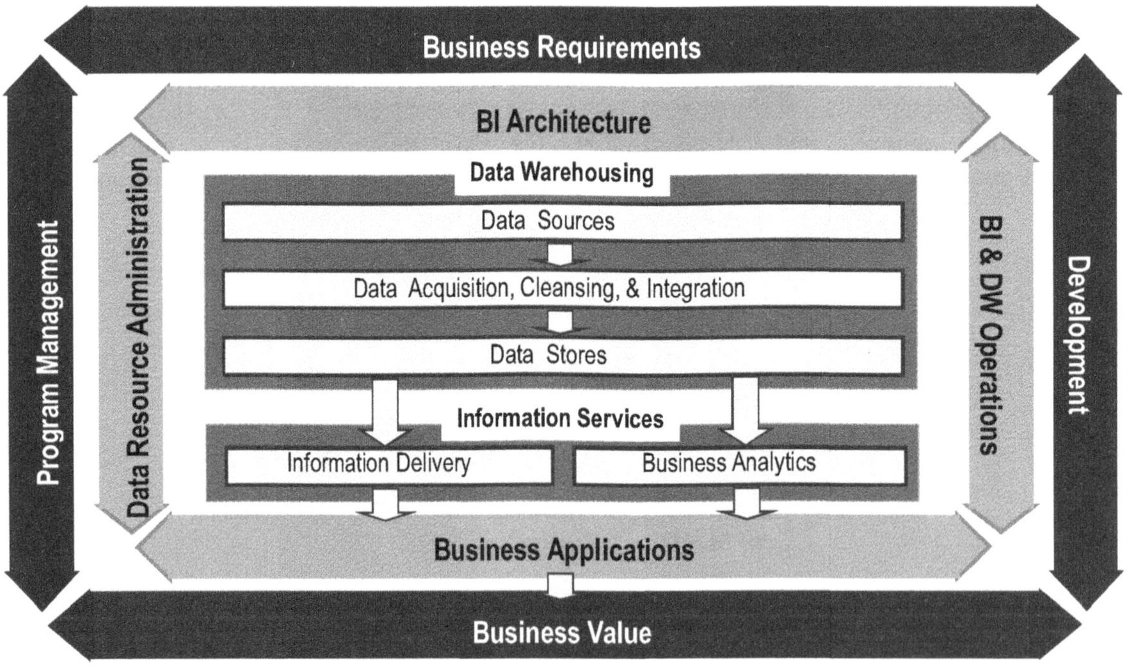

Based on the original TDWI BI Fundamentals Seminar, © 2005–2013 by TDWI. Used by permission of TDWI (tdwi.org).

BUSINESS LAYER

The business layer contains four components that frame the entire BI initiative. It is the layer that involves the business people as owners of the initiative.

1. **Business requirements** for information about the business and requirements for analytic capabilities are, of course, the very reasons for a BI initiative. Companies have hundreds, if not thousands, of reporting requirements. Some requirements are no more than to replace existing operational reports without adding new data or functionality. It is not unusual to see companies that have many more operational reporting requirements, which typically provide the lowest return on investment, than strategic analytical requirements, which could greatly impact the company's bottom line. The EDW/BI teams often struggle with the prioritization of all requirements, which leads to the second component.

2. **Business value** are the benefits anticipated from, or achieved by, BI including such things as increased revenue, improved profit margins, risks mitigated or avoided, reduced costs, and so on. It is important that business people negotiate the priorities for EDW/BI projects among themselves. The EDW/BI teams are often overwhelmed with the number of new project requests, and sometimes they are forced to prioritize based on a user's seniority or importance within the company, on his or her strong personality or family ties with the chief executive officer (CEO).

3. **Program management** is the ongoing activity of managing the interdependent components of the BI initiative or BI program for maximum business value. Interdependencies exist among resources, skill sets, code modules, databases, and so on. I often refer to the EDW/BI environment as one giant kettle of soup with many cooks. If one cook puts salt into the soup, another cook better not do the same or else you can no longer eat the soup. Part of program management is establishing infrastructure, cross-functional disciplines, enterprise architecture and standards, synchronizing multiple and parallel projects, realigning the requirements with changing business needs, etc.

4. **Development** refers to the project activities that create and deploy EDW/BI databases and applications. Part of managing development includes the use of a common methodology, decomposing service requests into multiple releases, funding the projects, staffing them appropriately, identifying project success measures, etc. Some people are surprised to see development in the business

layer because they are so used to IT traditionally having this responsibility. That was true in the days when business people abdicated all involvement in anything that had to do with technology, which over the decades created an adversarial "us versus them" relationship. Fortunately, the relationship between IT and the business has been changing slowly into a co-managed and collaborative association, with business people accepting their role of ownership.

The business requirements and the prioritization of those requirements based on business value are the sole responsibilities of business people. Program management and development are shared responsibilities between business people and IT – or at least they should be.

ADMINISTRATION AND OPERATIONS LAYER

The administration and operations layer contains components that connect the technical aspects of EDW/BI with the business aspects. This layer also has four components.

1. **BI architecture** includes frameworks, models, standards, policies, procedures, guidelines, and conventions that describe the EDW/BI components and the relationships among them. There are different types of architectures, such as business architecture (strategic goals and objectives, business drivers), data architecture (enterprise data model, database design schemas), technology architecture (platforms), organizational architecture (roles and responsibilities, organizational charts), and project architecture (project plans, release plans).

2. **Business applications** are the way BI is utilized in the company. They are business processes that access or receive data from the EDW/BI environment through reports, ad-hoc queries, analytics applications, business scorecards, dashboards, and so on. Business managers use that information to better manage their department, and business executives act on that information to change the direction of the company.

3. **Data resource administration** is also known as data administration or enterprise information management (EIM). They create and manage policies, procedures, and processes for data governance. Earlier, I referred to this as the 80% data management work effort. The responsibilities of EIM include data profiling, data modeling, metadata management, collaborating with data owners and data stewards, helping business people resolve their data

disputes, and other custodial responsibilities, such as helping developers with data mapping and validating data transformation and cleansing test results.

4. **BI & DW operations** refer to executing all extract, sort, merge, cleanse, transform, and load processes, as well as running and monitoring BI applications and reports. Efficient operations ensure that acceptable quality, availability, security, and performance of the EDW/BI environment are maintained.

IT and the business people collaborate on BI architecture and data resource management activities, while IT is responsible for EDW/BI operations, and the business people manage and use their business applications.

IMPLEMENTATION LAYER

The implementation layer contains all of the technical components that are needed to extract the source data, cleanse and transform it, load it into the target databases, and deliver that data to the business people. This is considered the "plumbing" behind BI. This layer has two major functions: data warehousing (data storage) and information services (reporting and analytics), or as Claudia Imhoff, Founder and CEO of Intelligent Solutions, likes to call it: "get the data in" and "get the data out."

1. **Data warehousing** is a collection of programs (code), processes, and procedures that extract and integrate data and then store the data. I call it the pool of consistent, clean, standardized, and trustworthy data that will be accessed by the information services and delivered to the users for analysis.

2. **Information services** are the applications, processes, and procedures that turn data into information, and deliver that information to the business people in two ways. The *state of the practice*, and the original way of delivering information, includes managed query and reporting services and using an OLAP tool. The *state of the art*, and more recent way of delivering information, includes business analytics applications such as dashboards and scorecards.

Since this is the technical layer of EDW/BI, IT carries most of the responsibility for developing the solutions. However, the business people must actively participate in all analysis, design, prototyping, and testing activities.

Final Thought

The goal of EDW/BI is to turn the data chaos we have created in our operational systems world over the last five decades into an architected and integrated set of databases and applications with maximum reusability of data and processes. This requires a new approach to developing our applications. Refusing to comply with enterprise data standards (if they exist) and building customized stand-alone solutions, with duplicate and inconsistent data, stored on a multitude of heterogeneous platforms, are no longer acceptable practices because it takes too long to extract critical and trustworthy business information from them.

Chapter 2
Why Traditional Methodologies Don't Work

As you are managing an EDW/BI project, you draw upon your past experience as a project manager. But to your dismay, you find that in spite of your experience, your EDW/BI project is unusually difficult to manage. The requirements appear to be a "moving target." Communication between staff members takes too long. Assigning tasks in a traditional way seems to result in too much rework. Using a traditional methodology simply does not work. To top it all off, the business people are pressuring you for quick deliverables (90 days or less), while they are still "fine-tuning" their requirements. As the project team scrambles to meet those expectations, data standardization is skipped, testing is cut short, documentation is not done, and quality is compromised. The end result is often an independent data mart – always accompanied by the promise to consolidate it later with the other stand-alone data marts (and data warehouses). However, regrettably this rarely happens.

Waterfall Methodologies

The traditional system development lifecycle methodologies simply do not support EDW/BI goals and objectives. Instead, they support stand-alone system development. Waterfall methodologies were created in the 1970's to help developers successfully turn requirements from individual users or departments into customized solutions. The concepts of data governance and data integration did not exist in those days. Therefore, these methodologies were not designed to deliver enterprise-wide standardized solutions that all business people in the organization could use because they do not include the extensive data activities that are required for enterprise-class solutions.

Looking at the phases of these methodologies, shown in Figure 2.1, we notice that they are not data-driven. The first phase assumes that some well-defined business need exists; in other words, that the requirements can be clearly defined and have a certain finite scope. Of course, this is rarely true for EDW/BI requirements, which can be very fuzzy and have an almost infinite scope for data requirements. One scorecard can have hundreds of metrics, which need to be sourced by and calculated from many hundreds of source data elements.

Figure 2.1 Waterfall Methodologies

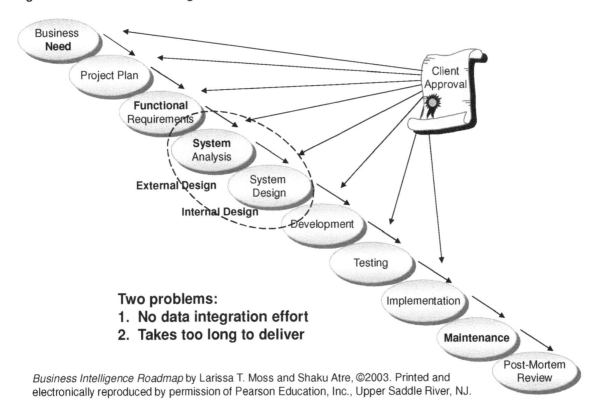

Business Intelligence Roadmap by Larissa T. Moss and Shaku Atre, ©2003. Printed and electronically reproduced by permission of Pearson Education, Inc., Upper Saddle River, NJ.

The second phase requires the team to put together a project plan. Assuming that one project is much like another, project managers often copy the project plan from their last project and then spend a few hours to change the details of the plan, such as resources, budget, milestones, deadline, and so on. Rigorous source data analysis is not defined as a project planning activity in these old development-driven waterfall methodologies. Yet, without analyzing the source data for quality, conformity, consistency, and redundancy, there is no way of estimating the effort and duration of an EDW/BI project!

Once the project manager and the team commit to a project plan, which is happily accepted by the user as "cast in concrete," they proceed with requirements definition, specifically defining the *functional* requirements. This time, the IT project team happily accepts the requirements document signed off "in blood" by the user. Both sides are now locked into battle: business people will not allow changes to the deadline, and IT will not allow changes to the requirements. There are two more things wrong with this picture. Using the 80/20 rule, the amount of and complexity between data requirements and functional requirements on EDW/BI projects are 80% data effort compared to 20 % coding effort. Yet, these old waterfall methodologies do not have any tasks or estimates for data analysis because these methodologies are meant to be used for developing brand new systems where data does not yet exist. The second thing wrong with it is committing to a project deadline before studying the requirements.

Now the work can proceed to analysis, more precisely *system* analysis. There is a big difference between system analysis and data analysis. Webster's New World Dictionary defines analysis as "a separating or breaking up of any whole into its parts, esp. with an examination of these parts to find out their nature, proportion, function, interrelationship, etc." The activity of breaking up and examining the functional requirements, which is being performed during system analysis, is geared toward producing a potential design for the system to be built. The activity of breaking up and examining the data requirements, which is being performed during data analysis, is geared toward integrating and standardizing data, as well as understanding and correcting existing defects in the data, irrespective of any system design, database design, or implementation method. In other words, *data* analysis is a *business*-focused activity, not a system-focused activity, and it is completely missing in old waterfall methodologies. This is a major problem when using a development-driven methodology because data management tasks are by far the most important and most labor intensive activities on EDW/BI projects.

After the analysis phase comes the design phase. However, I see more developers performing one combined analysis/design phase than two separate analysis and design phases. On EDW/BI projects, I even see data modelers merging data analysis and database design activities. That indicates to me that business data modeling is not being performed, and that all data modeling activities have only one goal, which is to design a database. When analysis and design activities are performed from a purely technical perspective, the desire to combine both activities is understandable. A technician might think that if system analysis is the thought process that turns requirements into a potential design for a system, and system design is exactly the same thought process, why not combine them? However, if you understand that analysis is a business-focused activity and design is a system-focused activity, you would not be combining those two disciplines. In the 1970's and 1980's, we were much more precise with our definitions and development processes, and we called these two phases: external design and internal design. Notice the word *design* in both phases!

Here is my point: Several decades ago, writing code was the most important IT activity, and the data just came along for the ride. Today, data standardization and integration is the most important EDW/BI activity, and the coding just comes along for the ride. EDW/BI projects are business projects, not technical projects! Yes, we do design and write some code, although we mostly use tools and products for the extract/transfer/load (ETL) process and for reports and BI applications. However, writing code is not the most important activity on EDW/BI projects.

The next phase in a waterfall methodology is development. Finally! For months, we had "wowed" the users with fancy models, charts, graphs, and metadata, which they reviewed and approved, often without fully understanding them or seeing any errors in them. These approved documents are now turned over to the developers, who spend days trying to understand the coding instructions, often scratching their heads and going back to the users for clarification. I even witnessed some developers ignoring the specification documents all together and starting from scratch with the users.

After performing and signing off on all the different test runs that are required according to company policy, it can take a few more weeks to put the system into production and to turn over the code, as well as all the documentation, to the maintenance team. Unless there is a problem with the system, which requires a post-mortem review, the project team is done. As the term post-mortem implies, we usually only take time to review the development process of a system when it "dies" shortly after implementation. Since the system is done, it is too late to apply any lessons learned. By the time we are into the next system, we have forgotten the lessons learned.

To summarize, the activities and tasks in all phases of the old waterfall methodologies are geared toward developing customized stand-alone applications. These development-driven methodologies contain no cross-functional activities that would involve additional business people from other departments to be engaged in data standardization, data integration, or data governance activities. In addition, each phase must be completed before the next phase can start. As indicated in Figure 2.1, this results in two major problems when developing enterprise-wide data integration solutions:

1. The tasks focus on turning individual user requirements immediately into customized stand-alone applications. These methodologies do not have any tasks for in-depth data analysis, business data modeling, data standardization, data cleansing, and data integration (as I defined it).

2. As we know, reconciling and rationalizing data across the enterprise takes much longer and involves many more users from other departments than

simply coding a customized application for one user or one department. Therefore, it takes much too long to develop EDW/BI deliverables.

Waterfall methodologies were very popular because they organized the development activities into distinct phases. Each phase had to be completed and signed off before another phase could start. The thinking behind this was that mistakes can be caught early in the development process when they are still much less costly to fix. This approach worked well for the old operational systems because we did not have modern development tools where code could be changed relatively easily. In addition, operational systems had well defined requirements, a relatively small scope, and they were confined to one user or one department. The underlying technology platform was usually known and proven (we were on mainframes), and data volumes were relatively small. Finally, the process was more or less repeatable because the development activities were almost the same on each project. None of this applies to EDW/BI projects!

Industrial-Age Mental Model

To make things worse, many business people are still stuck in the industrial-age mental model. I will explain what I mean by describing an exercise I like to do with business people during my consulting engagements. I draw a blank matrix. There are five columns and an arrow across the top indicating priorities from 1 to 5 (1 being highest and 5 being lowest). On the left are five blank rows to be filled in with five 3M self-adhesive labels, which I had already marked with the words PEOPLE, BUDGET, QUALITY, SCOPE, and TIME. These five words represent the common constraints on all projects. I then ask the business people to think about their projects and to prioritize these five constraints from 1 to 5. They have to choose what is most important to them and what is least important to them. For example, is getting a deliverable in two months most important? Or is it more important that all of the requested data and functionality is delivered, regardless of how long it takes? Is budget an issue or will they give IT a blank check? At first, many business people list all of the constraints in the first column as their highest priority, as shown in Figure 2.2. They don't realize the contradiction when they assume that they can get all of their requirements (scope) in the shortest amount of time with 100% quality on a fixed budget with limited resources. These expectations are quite unrealistic, but they are still very common.

Figure 2.2 Constraint Prioritization Matrix (1)

highest to lowest priority →

Project Constraints / Priority	1	2	3	4	5
PEOPLE	✓				
BUDGET	✓				
QUALITY	✓				
SCOPE	✓				
TIME	✓				

EVERYTHING IS PRIORITY ONE !

The second try with this exercise, usually yields the result shown in Figure 2.3. This result is very much tied into the traditional development approach, which emphasized automation of manual business processes as cheaply and as quickly as possible. Twenty years ago, this model would have shown scope as the highest priority on a project. In other words, business people expected to have the entire new system built in one big bang project with all of its requested functionality delivered at the end of the project. In today's business environment, time is the highest priority on projects, immediately followed by scope. Budget and people are usually a distant third and fourth priority. That leaves quality in the lurch. Some business people won't even put the last label into the priority 5 column because they know intuitively that putting quality last is not a good reflection on their values when prioritizing the natural constraints on their project. However, since time and scope are more important, and budgets and resources are often fixed, there is no other place for quality to go – but last.

Figure 2.3 Constraint Prioritization Matrix (2)

highest to lowest priority →

Project Constraints / Priority	1	2	3	4	5
TIME	✓				
SCOPE		✓			
BUDGET			✓		
PEOPLE				✓	
QUALITY					✓

Cost-based value proposition →
- Cheaper, faster, better
- Automate as quickly as possible

Business Intelligence Roadmap by Larissa T. Moss and Shaku Atre, ©2003. Printed and electronically reproduced by permission of Pearson Education, Inc., Upper Saddle River, NJ.

When using this industrial-age mental model, the return on investment (ROI) calculations are purely cost-based, i.e., comparing the business value of automating a unique, customized process to the cost of building it. Since operational systems were built independently of each other, the concept of reusability of data and processes never entered into the equation.

The problems with this old mental model are clear to everyone today. Data is duplicated hundreds, sometimes thousands, of times with totally inconsistent values. Reports are produced with inconsistent totals that must be explained to business executives after weeks of researching and reconciling. Historical data is not easily accessed and integrated because file structures changed and archived data ended up being stored on different storage devices. Worst of all, data is still not integrated between the silos. At best, bridges are built between systems. Now these bridges have to be maintained, which requires additional staff for additional costs.

Final Thought

As disheartening as the situation is with our existing operational systems, it is very discouraging to see – and difficult to believe – that many companies continue to build applications, even BI applications, in the same customized stand-alone manner as always. They are only adding to the data chaos! The old traditional development approach discussed in this chapter is definitely not a framework for cross-functional data integration, which, after all, is one of the main goals of data warehousing. As long as we don't change our mental model as well as our development approach from building customized stand-alone solutions to building an integrated enterprise-class EDW/BI environment, we will continue to add to the current data chaos, regardless of what we call the new databases or what new technology we use. Resolving the chaos is one big reason to embrace enterprise information management (EIM) and to incorporate EIM activities into EDW/BI projects.

Wasn't it the author Rita Mae Brown (in her book Sudden Death) who defined insanity as "doing the same thing over and over again but expecting different results?"

The lesson should be obvious. It is completely illogical to expect the outcomes to be different if we continue to use the traditional development approach to produce them, as shown in Figure II.

Figure II Traditional Development Approach

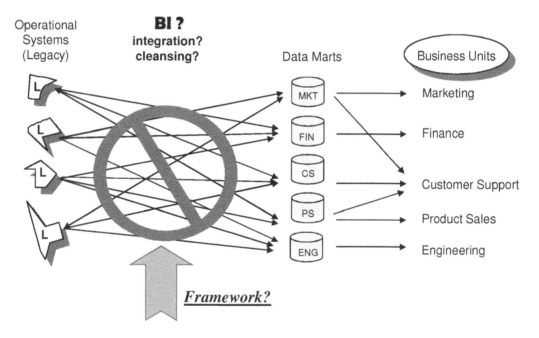

There are common root causes for why we have data chaos today. Once we know these root causes, it is up to us to remove them and to change our behavior in terms of our development process. It is high time that we treat data as the valued business asset that it is. This is the data management part of any data warehouse – and it is the foundation for BI.

In the Preface, I stated that my first lesson in data warehousing was to learn very quickly that data warehouse projects are not like traditional operational system development projects. My second lesson was to realize that EDW/BI project teams must follow a data-driven methodology, not a development-driven methodology. The reason is that our primary deliverable from EDW/BI projects must be clean, consistent, trustworthy, and reusable data. What the business is looking for is information. How we get the information is of lesser importance to the business. As I said before, the ETL processes and BI applications come along for the ride. In order to make the transition in our development approach, we have to start by changing our mental model.

Information-Age Mental Model

We have to replace the industrial-age mental model with the information-age mental model, illustrated in Figure 3.1.

Figure 3.1 Constraint Prioritization Matrix (3)

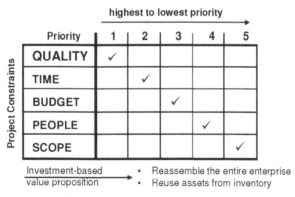

This new mental model emphasizes the ability to reassemble the entire organization (i.e., build new data marts and BI solutions) from reusable components, especially reusable data. This model demands that the quality of our reusable components be as pristine as practical, and it puts quality on the top of the constraint priority matrix, followed immediately by time. People and budget are still a distant third and fourth priority, with scope being last.

When using this new information-age mental model, the ROI calculations include computations for return on asset (ROA). ROA calculations are investment-based (asset-based). While ROI calculations compare the business value of automating a process to the cost of building it, ROA calculations compare the business value of the newly automated solution to the cost-savings (lifetime value) achieved through reusing some or all of its components. Let's use a simple example to illustrate the difference. When a company purchases a new server for a specific purpose, and it receives the expected benefit from this purchase, it is ROI. When the company is then able to reuse the same server for a second and third purpose, the savings from not having to buy two more servers for the second and third purpose is ROA.

> To take the ROA concept a step further, discussions are currently taking place among some EIM professionals and a few certified public accountants to devise a method for placing data as an asset on the company books.

The same ROA principle is used by object-oriented developers who deliberately build reusable code components. They have two reasons for building reusable objects. One is to increase the lifetime value of the code they write, and the other is to standardize their routines (code modules). The same has been true for agile developers on the operational systems side. Yet, when EIM professionals want to apply this principle to standardizing data so that it can be reused and shared, there is resistance from both IT and the business. The reason for the resistance is that standardizing data slows down the development process. But wait – not standardizing data has led to the current data chaos, which in turn has cost many companies millions, if not billions, in technology and development dollars to "fix." I contend that it is cheaper, much cheaper, in the long run to make the investment in time and effort to standardize data once and then reuse it and share it as often as possible. This is the whole concept behind master data management and the governance of data. It should also be an embraced concept in EDW/BI.

Cross-Functional Development Approach

The previous discussion leads to one obvious conclusion. In our EDW/BI environment, we must not use a customized development approach, but a coordinated, cross-functional development approach. I call it *cross-functional* because the deliverables are developed with an enterprise perspective, not with the perspective of one user's tunnel vision.

Figure 3.2 Cross-Functional Development

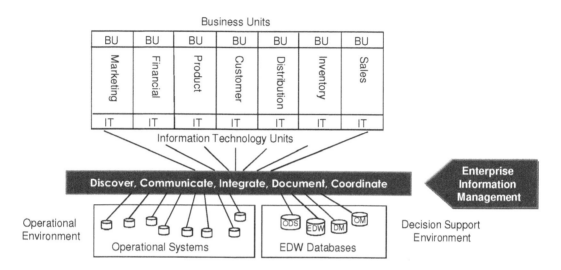

Figure 3.2 shows that this approach includes tasks and resources to discover, communicate, integrate, document, and coordinate all interdependent project activities under one BI program umbrella. This will ensure standardization and reusability of data and processes across the enterprise. The tasks include creating an enterprise architecture, i.e., an inventory of reusable data and process components, as well as collectively architecting databases and applications with special attention to quality. Collectively architecting means reusing data and process components wherever possible, as opposed to building silo solutions. As previously stated, this will require some fundamental changes to our system development habits, including the involvement and assistance of a centralized EIM group that is tasked with data governance. This group is also known under the older names of data administration (DA), data resource management (DRM), and information resource management (IRM).

My guidelines for instituting a development approach with a cross-functional focus, i.e. establishing data governance for data warehousing, are:

1. The company must decide to manage data as a strategic asset, and that decision is an expressly stated and accepted business principle in the

organization. Therefore, data integration and data standardization tasks are embedded in the methodology.

2. All business requirements and the development of multiple BI applications for different users or departments are prioritized and coordinated under a BI governance program.

3. EIM resources are made available to support and coordinate the cross-functional activities.

4. Standards, policies, and procedures for cross-functional integration are developed and published, and all EDW/BI project teams are expected to follow them.

5. These policies are enforced. Enforcement can take different shapes. It can be a proclamation that stand-alone solutions will no longer be allowed to be put into production. It can also mean that there is a mandate to go through a common coordinated staging area, or a mandate to reconcile all databases. Compliance can be encouraged by tying it to people's performance appraisals, promotions, salary increases, and bonuses.

Spiral Data Warehouse Methodologies

Some EDW/BI managers who have a strong data management background understood early on, that four fundamental changes had to be adopted:

1. Most importantly, they had to stop thinking of EDW/BI as a project. EDW/BI had to be treated as a program with many interdependent projects.

2. Equally important, they recognized that data had to be managed as a business asset, which required creating a centralized EIM function and embedding EIM staff in every EDW/BI project.

3. They had to modify their methodologies and development approaches to include cross-functional activities that would lead to enterprise-wide data standardization, data integration, and data governance in general.

4. Finally, they had to invent a development methodology that would allow the different EDW/BI project teams to coordinate their activities with each other in order to avoid building independent customized BI solutions.

These methodologies are called spiral data warehouse methodologies. Two examples are the Business Intelligence Roadmap and the BI Pathway Method by DecisionPath Consulting (http://www.decisionpath.com).

Spiral (iterative) data warehouse methodologies are based on a common enterprise infrastructure with technical and non-technical components. The non-technical components are activities and tasks that address cross-functional business value, data reusability principles, governance, resources, policies, and enforcement of those policies. Figure 3.3 shows the reason why these types of methodologies were popularly called "spiral" methodologies. It is because these methodologies supported building the EDW in iterations, one BI application at a time.

Figure 3.3 Spiral DW Methodologies

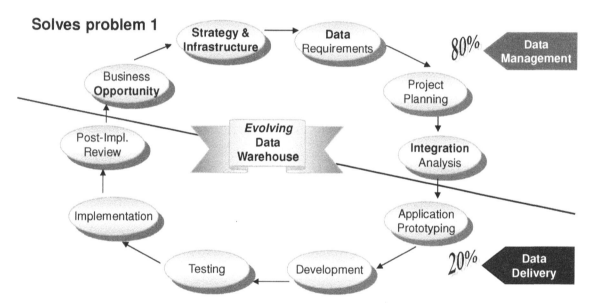

Iterative Development = One BI application at a time

Business Intelligence Roadmap by Larissa T. Moss and Shaku Atre, ©2003. Printed and electronically reproduced by permission of Pearson Education, Inc., Upper Saddle River, NJ.

Spiral data warehouse methodologies do not presume to build independent customized BI solutions for individual users or departments, where project teams work independently from each other. Instead, they support building an evolving and expanding EDW/BI environment for an integrated collection of reusable databases and applications. In other words, they solve problem 1 of traditional waterfall methodologies, which is "no data integration effort."

The first change in a spiral data warehouse methodology is the assumption that the business requirements are based on undiscovered business opportunity, not on a specific functional business need. That usually translates into requirements like this: "I need all the data from these 20 or 50 operational systems" and "I don't know yet what I will do with all that data until I start using it." Needless to say, requirements like these are very fuzzy and the data scope is very large. Translation: these are high-risk projects! While the functional scope is very small, the data scope is huge. That means it will probably take a long time to standardize and integrate the data (remember my "death march" project). During that time, it is quite likely that the user will change the requirements; maybe add another five operational systems or a few external feeds into the requirements. Scope creep of this kind would affect other business people who are waiting in the wings with their EDW/BI projects.

Since BI is a program with many interdependent projects, a strategy and a common infrastructure must exist. The strategy must include architectural components, such as:

- Types of target databases (e.g., EDW, data marts, operational data store (ODS), exploration warehouse)
- Developer tools (e.g., ETL tools, report writers)
- BI user tools (e.g., OLAP, dashboards)
- Metadata repository (MDR) (e.g., data dictionaries, databases storing contextual information)
- Platform (e.g., servers, disk arrays, network protocols)

The common infrastructure has two components: technical and non-technical. I just listed examples of technical infrastructure. Non-technical infrastructure components include many aspects of enterprise information management and data governance:

- Enterprise standards
- Naming standards
- Common methodology
- Roles and responsibilities
- Business, technical, process, and usage metadata
- Enterprise data model

The next difference in these methodologies is to spend some time to study the data requirements to understand how much effort will be needed to model, standardize, map, cleanse, transform, and integrate source data into the target databases. Until you know what the data effort will be, you cannot create a project plan and commit to any deadline.

Planning EDW/BI projects is not as simple as copying the project plan from the last project and simply changing a few items on it like name of user, budget, resources, and schedule. Every EDW/BI project is different, and there are many things to consider.

- How involved will the users be? What tasks will they participate on?
- How much source data chaos exists that has to be standardized?
- Do you have sufficient resources with the right skill set?
- Are there any dependencies you have to be aware of? Example: another team is working on the same ETL code that this team needs to modify.
- Are there architectural issues to consider?
- Does a metadata repository already exist?
- Will load statistics, error statistics, and reconciliation totals be loaded into the metadata repository?

The most important development step in a spiral data warehouse methodology is integration analysis. This step does not exist in traditional development-driven waterfall methodologies because there was nothing to integrate when these methodologies were popular. In the EDW/BI environment almost everything is integrated. Remember that my definition of "integrated" includes uniqueness and reusability of data and processes wherever possible. In order to keep track of all EDW and BI architectural and physical components, an inventory of them must be maintained in a metadata repository. This inventory must be consulted or updated each time new data, new functionality or new BI applications are added to the EDW/BI environment. Many times, a new service request can be accommodated by reusing an existing data mart or BI application after making some modifications to it.

> Do *not* automatically jump on building a customized stand-alone solution for every BI service request.

The next step is prototyping. With today's sophisticated developer tools, it is not necessary to spend weeks on design activities before coding can start. Most often, system analysis, design, and coding activities are all rolled into one prototyping activity. This is especially true for front-end BI application development and report writing. In companies that strictly enforce their current methodology, which has an explicit development phase, project teams can designate the last iteration of a prototype to be the final development activity where all the "i"s are dotted and all the "t"s are crossed.

Following development and before going into production, do as much testing as you would do on operational systems, such as integration testing, regression testing, performance testing, quality assurance testing, and user acceptance testing. These are executed under formal test plans that outline the purpose for each test, the test cases, in what sequence the tests are run, expected and actual test results, and so on. Since EDW/BI is an evolving and growing environment, it is important to save the test bed with all the test data for future regression testing.

After the new EDW/BI project is implemented in production, the project team performs a post-implementation review, regardless of whether the project was successful or not. It is important to learn lessons from every project so that the project team can streamline its development approach by avoiding unnecessary tasks or including tasks that are omitted in their methodology, changing roles and responsibilities, improving communication, getting better at estimating, identifying gaps in infrastructure, and defining critical success factors for the next project.

Using the 80/20 rule, the first half of these development steps can be loosely considered to fall into the 80% data management objective of data warehousing, and the second half of these steps support the 20% data delivery objective, as illustrated in Figure 3.3. A final observation about spiral methodologies is that, although they are designed to build an EDW/BI environment in iterations, one application at a time, the development steps within each iteration are executed in a sequential waterfall way. I call spiral methodologies "yo-yo" methodologies because you drop through all development steps – top to bottom – multiple times before you're finished.

Final Thought

Spiral data warehouse methodologies solve problem 1 of traditional waterfall methodologies, namely "no data integration effort." Fixing that problem created an unintended consequence: the development lifecycle takes even longer now than on traditional projects because of the additional enterprise-wide data management effort. At the same time, BI vendors promise the business people that they can build a data mart in 30 days using their products. Sure they can – if they use the traditional development approach and build a stand-alone BI solution, which is only the 20% effort of data delivery, and completely ignore the 80% effort of data management. Remember that a data warehouse is not a data warehouse if you don't address both objectives: data management and data delivery. Since data management involves standardizing and integrating data from multiple operational sources, the data analysis effort alone can easily take up 30 days or more.

Chapter 4
Agile Development Approaches

Agile methodologies were specifically invented to solve problem 2 of traditional waterfall methodologies, namely "it takes too long to deliver something to the user." Many agile authors and practitioners are either project managers or senior developers, each with decades of experience in developing stand-alone operational systems – most written with reusable object-oriented code. Individually, and collectively, they have compiled volumes of evidence why traditional waterfall methodologies do not work, not even on operational systems, and why those methodologies should be abandoned. They have applied and refined their agile techniques since the mid 1990's and officially created and published the Agile Manifesto in 2001 (http://www.agilemanifesto.org), which reads:

> We are uncovering better ways of developing software by doing it and helping others do it. Through this work we have come to value:
>
> **Individuals and interactions** over processes and tools
> **Working software** over comprehensive documentation
> **Customer collaboration** over contract negotiation
> **Responding to change** over following a plan
>
> That is, while there is value in the items on the right, we value the items on the left more!

Release Concept

If you want to stay true to building a standardized and integrated EDW/BI environment and not revert back to building stand-alone BI solutions, and if you want to deliver something tangible to the users in a reasonably short amount of time (30-120 days), you need to break each EDW/BI service request into multiple releases. By doing so, you solve problem 2 of traditional waterfall methodologies, which is "it takes too long to deliver something to the user."

There are a few more advantages to this approach. The scope is smaller and the project is less complex, and thus less overwhelming and easier to manage. In addition, you learn an incredible amount about the new EDW/BI components as you are building them. You can apply that knowledge to improve the deliverables as you progress through the releases. The business people see tangible pieces of their new EDW/BI request and have the opportunity to hone their requirements instead of asking for everything because they are not sure what they need or want. Sometimes, business people even cut out a requirement when they see the hurdles and complexities that surface during the project. They decide it's not worth spending the time to conquer those hurdles and complexities because that particular requirement is not so important in the first place.

Think of each release as being a mini-project, as illustrated in Figure 4.1.

Figure 4.1 Release Concept

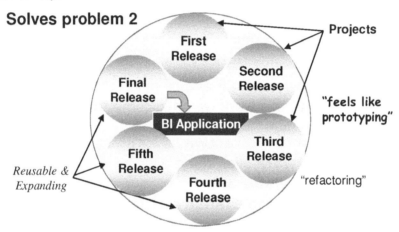

Business Intelligence Roadmap by Larissa T. Moss and Shaku Atre, ©2003. Printed and electronically reproduced by permission of Pearson Education, Inc., Upper Saddle River, NJ.

The project team members sit down with the user, and they brainstorm on how to break a large service request into smaller, more manageable pieces. Keep in mind that maybe some of the data or processes already exist and can be reused. By talking through the requirements on the service request, it is not that difficult to negotiate what the first deliverable should be. The first release is usually a fundamental piece of the final deliverable upon which other pieces depend. It can be the skeleton of a BI application, such as:

- A table populated with current-month data
- Sample reports from a temporary prototype table

- One simple dial on a dashboard

Building each of these partially-functioning deliverables feels like prototyping, but these are not throwaway prototypes. Each release produces a production-worthy deliverable, regardless of whether the decision is made to put it into production or not. The goal is to develop the highest-quality deliverable based on the knowledge you have at that point in time. However, as we all know, the first time something is delivered, it is not always the best. How often do people say "had I known this at the beginning, I would have done it differently." When we build systems in one big bang, we do not have the luxury at the end of the project to improve it, unless the user pays for additional enhancements. The beauty of using releases is that you *can* improve what you created in the previous release. This is referred to as *refactoring* in agile vernacular. In other words, you can continue to improve what you've already created as you are adding more data and more functionality with each release.

Some of you may think that your business people will never accept the release concept. I have heard users insist that their service request is the "minimum required" scope. Some insist that Sarbanes Oxley and Basel regulations prohibit their service request to be broken into releases. These are all excuses for not wanting to change the old habit of turning one's "wish list" over to IT and then walking away from it until it's time for user acceptance testing, with the exception of answering a few questions here and there. These companies still operate under the "us versus them" model where business people "contract" with IT to develop something for them. I call it a master-slave relationship. Business is the master with the purse strings and IT is the slave. This model has never worked very well; in some companies it has led to an antagonistic relationship between business and IT. It is time to change the old model to a new collaborative model where business people "partner" with IT and even co-manage projects.

I entertain my seminar and conference audiences by play acting a silly made-up story to illustrate the old model versus the new model. Imagine a young man living in Beverly Hills who does not need to work for a living. He manages a lucrative family business and spends most of his time designing and driving custom-made fancy cars. One day, he goes to his favorite car maker who only makes customized cars. He has a detailed drawing in his hands, which he calls "requirements" for a new car, and hands this drawing over to the car maker with the question, "How long will it take you to build it and how much will it cost?" The car maker looks at the drawing, thinks about it long and hard, scribbles some numbers on paper, and says "based on my experience with other similar designs, about 12 months and one million dollars." While the car maker is studying the drawing, he also immediately recognizes that he was not handed a list of requirements by his customer, but a detailed design. Sound familiar? I have observed business people handing over terribly inefficient table designs (basically flat files in a table) to a DBA with the command "just build this for me." Unless business people are trained in relational database design by their DBMS vendor, they should not be designing databases!

The eagle eye of the car maker also sees some problems with the design; after all, he is the expert, and this has happened before on a prior car. The car maker knows that, if he follows the handed-over design specifications (not "requirements"), he will end up delivering a car to his customer in 12 months that will be unacceptable and very costly to modify later. However, knowing his customer from past projects, the car maker knows it is futile to challenge the customer's design. Instead, he suggests to the customer that he will start by building a prototype car frame, and that he would like the customer to come back in three weeks to review and approve it. The rich, young man gets very indignant about this suggestion and exclaims, "This is *your* job not mine. I have a business to run." Sound familiar? I have heard business people say something similar to this to a developer or an analyst.

Nevertheless, the car maker persuades his customer to return to his shop in three weeks to look at the car frame prototype. The prototype is only a frame with hood and trunk, made out of Styrofoam. It is propped up on boxes where the wheels will go, and has an apple crate inside to serve as a seat. The car manufacturer motions his customer to step inside and sit on the apple crate to "test drive" his car prototype. At first the spoiled young man objects to this ridiculous situation, but then relents and follows the car maker's invitation. He steps inside, looks straight ahead, fidgets a little, and stretches his neck to better see over the hood. "Hm" he thinks to himself. "Something is wrong. I can't see the road. I bet he (car maker) didn't follow my instructions." He steps out of the Styrofoam frame and immediately accuses the car maker of making a mistake. Sound familiar? I have been witness to more than one argument between a user and a developer about who was at fault for the "wrong" deliverable.

The car maker is very patient. He pulls out the requirements/specifications he received from the customer and looks for a measuring tape. He slowly measures every section of the frame and compares his measurements to the requirements. It all matches to the millimeter. The cause for the "wrong" deliverable is a flaw in the "requirements." The customer reluctantly admits it, and asks the car maker what it would take to change it. The car maker gives him a new price and a new deadline. Now the customer has to make a decision whether to change/correct one of his requirements or to let the car maker proceed with the original design. How fortunate that the car maker insisted on an early inspection of a prototype! From this point forward, the rich, young customer gladly comes periodically to inspect the progress on his new car.

The lesson is to demonstrate to the business people that they are better off with the release concept because it offers visibility of the project, ongoing verification of requirements, ability to accommodate minor requirements changes, stability of each release, as well as accuracy and consistency of the deliverable.

Agile Methodologies

Agile methodologies are unique in many respects, as illustrated in Figure 4.2.

Figure 4.2 Agile Methodologies

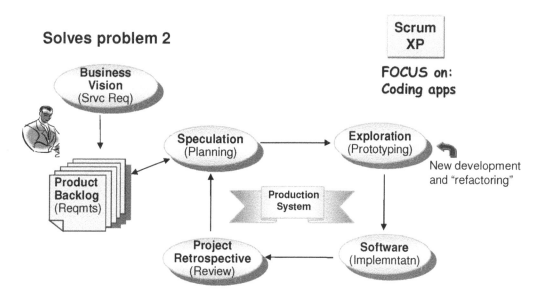

Agile practitioners do not recognize a service request for a new system to be the final set of business requirements that the project team has to deliver on a committed date. Instead, they view the request as a *business vision* for a system that may or may not end up looking exactly the same when it is finally completed. With the participation of the user, the developers convert the requirements into desired *features* or *user stories*, which are put on a *product backlog* stack. The users control their product backlogs. They can add requirements to it and they can remove requirements. They are also responsible for prioritizing the requirements.

The developers then select features from the stack for their first (or next) release. Rather than come up with estimates for the entire service request that the business people habitually consider to be cast in concrete, the team *speculates* how long it will take to turn the selected features into working code based on what is known to them at that point in time. Development is called *exploration* and occurs in *sprints*. A sprint is a predetermined period of time during which development work has to be completed and made ready for user review. The predetermined period of time occurs in constant intervals, or in a rhythm, called *cadence.*

Each deliverable is production-worthy software for the selected features. In other words, it is a partially-functioning system that is being built iteratively. Before the next cycle (sprint) is started, the team takes one day to perform a *project retrospective.* They take half a day to review lessons learned and the other half to plan the next release.

Progress is measured by the number of features delivered and not by the number of tasks performed. Any task deemed necessary can be performed anytime by anybody as often as needed during exploration (prototyping). Instead of using Gantt charts for progress reporting, the developers use burn-down charts, which show the total number of effort-hours (Y axis) plotted on a timeline (X axis). The chart reflects the effort estimated versus the effort spent. If the trajectory on the burn-down chart indicates that the deadline cannot be met, the scope is immediately adjusted or the work is stopped and renegotiated.

PRINCIPLES OF AGILE METHODOLOGIES

It is helpful to recap some of the important differences agile methodologies bring to the development process. The first important principle of agile development is to recognize that the initial set of requirements is seldom what the users really want. It's what they think they want when they submit a service request. But almost always, they change their own requirements during the development process. Therefore, the initial set of requirements is called nothing more than the initial business vision, which is expected to change.

Since the term *estimating* has become to mean "I guarantee these dates," the term *speculation* is used instead. And instead of following the waterfall phases of requirements definition, analysis, design, coding, and testing, all of these phases are combined into the concept of exploration, which I call prototyping.

Another important agile principle is to insulate the project team from management interference and interruptions. The team members alone decide what tasks to perform and how and when to perform them. Daily stand-up meetings replace the weekly status report meetings and keep the project team on target.

The principle of pair programming is based on sharing the responsibility for quality control of the code that is written. The role of the project manager is redefined as a ScrumMaster who acts as a facilitator for the project team. This person has an in-depth understanding of the agile Scrum methodology and has specific responsibilities and duties. Users are called product owners because they pay for and own the system (product) being built for them.

Another agile principle is to start coding as soon as possible, rather than take months to document the requirements and design the system on paper. The requirements document is replaced by the concept of user stories, or features, on backlogs, which are controlled by the users. The users can reprioritize, add, or remove requirements from their backlogs at will.

A detailed traditional project plan for the entire set of requirements is replaced with time-boxed development increments. The predetermined time span for the time-box is always the same, which is why it is called a rhythm or cadence. That rhythm is 29 days in Scrum, and as short as ten days in Extreme Programming (XP). After each such cycle (sprint), a portion of the requested system is ready for demonstration and potential implementation in production. While an increment is being worked on, its scope is frozen.

The principle of KISS (keep it simple stupid) emphasizes the importance of writing clean, uncomplicated, modularized, and reusable code. Another important agile principle is to put quality before quantity (referring to code quality and system quality). Refactoring is the concept of refining and enhancing a system over time. Another way to say it is to let the system "evolve." This is accomplished through frequent releases of a small number of features, rather than delivering all requirements of a finished system all at once. Another agile principle is to discard the lengthy, cumbersome, and complicated PERT charts and Gantt charts, which require hours in front of a project management tool to maintain. Instead, simple burn-down charts are used, which plot hours estimated versus hours burned (used) to date.

There are additional agile principles well documented in a plethora of publications, but this will suffice to demonstrate the major differences between traditional waterfall methodologies, spiral data warehouse methodologies, and current popular agile methodologies. Since Extreme Scoping is neither Scrum nor XP, I will not be using their terminologies.

Final Thought

Just like the traditional waterfall methodologies, agile methodologies also support the belief that mistakes should be caught early in the development process when they are still much less costly to fix. But instead of breaking the project "horizontally" into traditional development phases with strict sign-offs for each phase (e.g., requirements, analysis, design, coding), agile methodologies achieve the same result by breaking the project "vertically" into multiple releases.

Keeping the scope of each release extremely small gives you the same control for a high-quality deliverable because the requirements can be implemented in small increments. Each partial deliverable is a usable, albeit incomplete, portion of the final system. This approach allows the users to solidify their requirements as they learn more about the capabilities and limitations of the system. In addition, the new technology components can be tried and tested in increments as well. Breaking an application into several small releases gives you the opportunity to establish an efficient repeatable development process. Finally, there are two additional benefits to using the release concept instead of trying to complete a BI application in one long project:

1. The quality of each release deliverable is much higher because you have time to address quality rather than rush to meet an impossible deadline to deliver the whole system all at once.

2. You have the chance to review the development approach (tasks, schedules, procedures, skills, staffing, etc.) after each release and improve it. That means that your development process will get faster and faster.

Chapter 5
Agile BI versus Agile EDW

Let us agree that we need to make some fundamental changes to our out-dated, and in some cases harmful, development habits. I suggest we begin our makeover with the following four affirmations. Remember that affirmations are like commandments – violate them at your own peril.

1. We will stop building customized stand-alone solutions, especially silo BI solutions.

2. We will manage data as a business asset, which requires a centralized enterprise information management (EIM) function, and we will embed EIM staff in every EDW/BI project.

3. We will modify our methodology and development approach to include cross-functional data management activities that will lead to data standardization and integration.

4. We will sharply reduce the scope of projects and develop applications using the release concept. The smaller the scope, the more time can be allocated to data management activities.

Affirmation 1: I explained why our old development habits are harmful to a company. It is up to business executives and IT senior management to decide whether and when they will stop building customized stand-alone solutions. In my definition of BI, I call for "an *integrated* collection of operational as well as decision support applications and databases." It may take many more years to get to the operational systems side, but let's at least begin with our EDW/BI projects.

Affirmation 2: Until recently, companies have considered data management to be an IT responsibility. However, in the last few years, the data governance practice has been embraced by many business people as their responsibility. The pendulum has swung from one end to the other, and now it must settle in the middle. IT and business must work together to share the three aspects of data governance: authority, accountability, and administration.

1. **Authority** resides with the data owners who are business executives with the power and expertise to make business policy and set business rules for data assets.

2. **Accountability** lies in the hands of data stewards who are subject matter experts in the various lines of business. It is their job to enforce the data policies and business rules and to periodically audit the data under their control.

3. **Administration** is the responsibility of a specialized EIM group that is staffed by data management professionals and is currently reporting to an IT manager at some level. There is a movement in the industry to create a new executive position called Chief Data Officer to whom EIM will report. I describe this position in Chapter 12. The management of all enterprise-wide initiatives like data governance and enterprise-class development like EDW/BI projects should be moved under this new CDO position. Many books have been written and will be written in the future on this subject. Several of them are listed in the reference section of this book.

Affirmation 3: It may or may not be up to the EDW/BI project team to decide which methodology and development approach they want to use. Many companies already use some form of spiral data warehouse methodology. However, some older companies have rigorous IT standards and will require all project teams to use their current waterfall methodology, even to the detriment of the project outcome. Some younger companies have no methodology at all. They rely on their young, and frequently less experienced, developers to remember all potential tasks relevant to an EDW/BI project. The Business Intelligence Roadmap methodology has over 900 tasks to remember! Clearly, nobody does. These are political and cultural issues that need to be worked through by each company in their own way.

Affirmation 4: While most companies recognize that focusing on data management activities is very important for EDW/BI projects, they still struggle with becoming more agile at the same time. Project teams are caught in the dichotomy of these two approaches.

1. If they include comprehensive data management activities, the project takes too long.

2. If they adopt one of the popular agile methodologies, it usually results in focusing on development activities and dropping, reducing, or moving data management activities out of the project.

That brings us to the next questions: Can agile be used for BI applications? Can agile be used for EDW? What is the difference?

Can Agile Be Used for BI?

There are a growing number of companies that profess to be using agile methodologies on their BI projects successfully, in particular Scrum and XP. My research shows that those companies restrict their development effort to stand-alone BI solutions, very similar to the development of stand-alone operational systems. In other words, the BI teams work with one user or one department, they do not go through an EDW, and they don't deal with data standardization and integration – or at least, not very effectively, and definitely not from an enterprise perspective.

BI WITHOUT AN EDW

Figure 5.1 shows two scenarios of BI without EDW.

Figure 5.1 BI without EDW

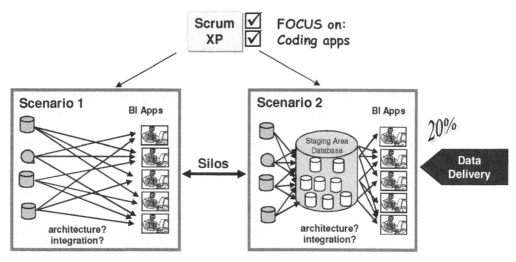

BI team solves problem 2

In the first scenario (on the left), many customized stand-alone BI applications are being developed simultaneously by multiple different BI solution architects (developers). This group of BI developers is sometimes referred to as the BI competency center. This can be one centralized organization in the company, or it can be "virtual," made up of people from different departments spread out across all lines of business. Each BI application is sourced directly from the source systems, and each BI application has its own ETL process, its own databases, and its own user(s). There is practically no sharing of data and processes.

The second scenario (on the right) looks different from the first, but is actually very similar to it. The BI developers insist that they are going through a data warehouse, but upon closer inspection of what they call a data warehouse, it becomes apparent that it is nothing more than a centralized staging area database. These databases are usually partitioned either by source systems, departments, BI applications, or BI groups, to support the independent ETL processes. The tables in the partitions are often nothing more than exact copies of operational files. Simply calling such a database their "data warehouse" does not make it so, because the database does not contain standardized, integrated, and unique sets of enterprise data. A true data warehouse is a set of collectively architected databases that reflect the "single version of the truth," after data from multiple source systems has been standardized and integrated (remember my definition of *integrated*, as opposed to *consolidated*). Collectively architected means that before new data marts are added to the environment, the database architects review the inventory of existing EDW target databases and determine whether or not they can be reused or expanded. This activity is omitted in scenarios one and two.

Both scenarios only solve problem 2 of waterfall methodologies, namely "it takes too long to deliver something to the user." Neither scenario addresses the enterprise data management objective; that is, neither scenario addresses problem 1 of waterfall methodologies, namely "no data integration effort." Any BI group that develops customized stand-alone BI solutions for their users, with or without a central staging area database, will have no difficulty at all using today's popular agile methodologies like Scrum or XP. The only difference between stand-alone BI applications and stand-alone operational systems is the additional coding of ETL processes. In other words, these are development-driven silo BI solutions, which can use development-driven agile methodologies.

BI WITH SEPARATE EDW

At first glance, Figure 5.2 looks like a perfect text-book EDW/BI implementation with a truly standardized and integrated data warehouse database from which dependent data marts are populated in support of BI applications. However, this figure also shows that only the BI developers are using agile methodologies to code their BI applications once the data has been loaded into the EDW target databases. A different EDW team uses a traditional methodology to do the heavy lifting of standardizing and integrating the source data. Many companies have gone so far as to separate the EDW team from the BI team and have both teams report to different managers. Frequently, BI teams report to business managers in the various lines of business, and the EDW team reports to a manager in IT. This not only disrupts the cohesion of the work effort for each service request, but also creates an unfair competition (not comparing "apples" to "apples") and significant animosity between the teams.

Figure 5.2 BI with Separate EDW

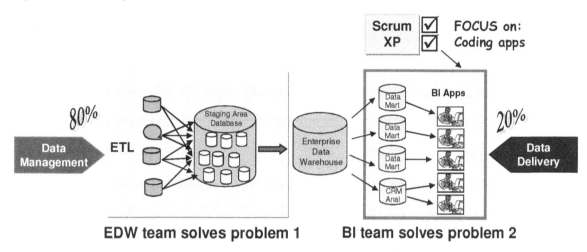

EDW team solves problem 1   **BI team solves problem 2**

There is another problem with this scenario. Some of the BI teams are told to wait for the data to be ready in the EDW before they develop their BI applications, often using XP 10-day sprints because that type of front-end effort can often be accomplished within days or weeks. Other BI teams cannot wait for the data to be ready in the EDW, so they revert back to developing their BI applications by going directly against the source systems (as shown in Figure 5.1), often using Scrum 29-day sprints, which gives them a little more time to deal with data issues in the ETL process.

This agile scenario – separating the supporting EDW data activities from BI application coding – still only focuses on writing software, namely the BI application, and not on standardizing, integrating, modeling, cleansing, and documenting the data across all functional lines of business. The 80% of data management activities are delegated to a separate EDW team with the unrealistic expectation that they can keep up with the pace of the BI application developers who are only responsible for 20% of the overall development effort. In fact, I often hear complaints in these companies that the data is the "problem" and that the EDW staff is too slow, incompetent, and unwilling to be agile. Clearly these companies do not understand that data management is the most important aspect of EDW/BI and not data delivery. In addition, anyone who accuses the EDW staff of being too slow, incompetent, and unwilling to be agile has no understanding of what their data activities entail, and how these activities are executed.

Once again, the focus of the BI team in this scenario is to solve only problem 2 of waterfall methodologies, namely "it takes too long to deliver something to the user," while a separate EDW staff is solving problem 1, namely "no data integration effort." It is very disturbing that some companies that implement this scenario do not appreciate and support their EDW staff, but often chastise and revile them. Separating EDW from BI is not the solution! EDW and BI are not two separate initiatives but one, where EDW is the foundation of BI as is clearly defined by the TDWI BI Components Framework described in Chapter 1.

Can Agile Be Used for EDW?

That leaves us wondering if agile can be used for the data management effort of EDW. If it is not a good idea to separate the EDW team from the BI teams, then obviously it is not a good idea to split a service request in two and manage requirements for BI applications separately from managing requirements for the supporting EDW components. EDW and BI are inseparable (remember the duplex).

Figure 5.3 shows the most mature scenario of BI, which *includes* constructing the underlying EDW components that are necessary to support the BI application, and having that effort be part of the same project that delivers the BI application. If you want to apply agile principles to planning and managing the entire end-to-end solution (including all data management activities necessary for the EDW), then – in my opinion – using current popular agile methods like Scrum or XP will not work the way they were designed, but Extreme Scoping will.

Development-driven agile methodologies like Scrum and XP were not designed by data management professionals for data-centric enterprise integration projects. They were designed by developers for other developers of code-centric stand-alone systems. In other words, they do not address problem 1 of waterfall methodologies, namely "no data integration effort." Some people argue that these methodologies can be adapted and made to work. Of course, all methodologies, even waterfall methodologies, can be adapted and made to work, but then you are no longer using the methodology in its original form as intended, because adaptation means breaking many of their rules.

Using the 80/20 rule again, 80% of the combined EDW/BI development effort is on the back-end data management side, and only 20% of the effort goes into building the front-end BI applications. To make things more complicated, while BI applications are often separate and independent pieces of software, a collectively architected ETL process is not. That makes the ETL architecture as well as the ETL software extremely complex, not to mention the collectively architected EDW target databases (including data marts).

Figure 5.3 BI Including EDW

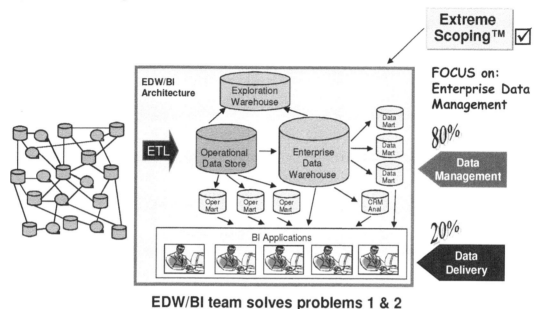

EDW/BI team solves problems 1 & 2

By their own admission, agile practitioners concede that the more complex the system architecture and the software are, the more "thinking" (architecting) has to be done before coding. On EDW projects, the architecting alone can sometimes take weeks to avoid omissions and errors in the collective architectures, which later could result in massive rework measured in months. This is the primary reason why companies that use Scrum or XP either build silo BI solutions (each with their own ETL process) or separate their front-end BI activities from back-end EDW activities. In my opinion, that is the wrong solution! The right solution is to use an agile method that is designed to include all EDW data activities in the agile process, such as:

- Standardizing the data across the enterprise
- Agreeing on common data definitions
- Modeling the data from an enterprise business perspective
- Integrating the data according to the enterprise data model
- Fully qualifying data names based on the data definitions
- Standardizing and ratifying business rules
- Collecting business metadata
- Analyzing source data
- Defining data cleansing rules

These data activities are the most crucial and the most time consuming of the back-end data preparation process for the EDW, and they must be performed diligently for every BI application that requires new source data. It is important that these activities be performed by trained EIM professionals (not developers or database architects) with the participation of data owners, data stewards, and information consumers from multiple lines of business. These activities will determine the total effort and time needed to develop EDW/BI solutions.

Since the development-driven agile methodologies currently on the market were created neither by nor for EDW professionals, they do not consider all of the tasks and complexities inherent in EDW/BI projects. Therefore, if you are developing enterprise-class EDW/BI solutions as described in this section, consider using Extreme Scoping, which is an EDW/BI-specific agile method that merges as many agile principles as apply to EDW with a robust spiral data warehouse methodology, as shown in Figure 5.4.

Figure 5.4 Spiral Merged With Agile

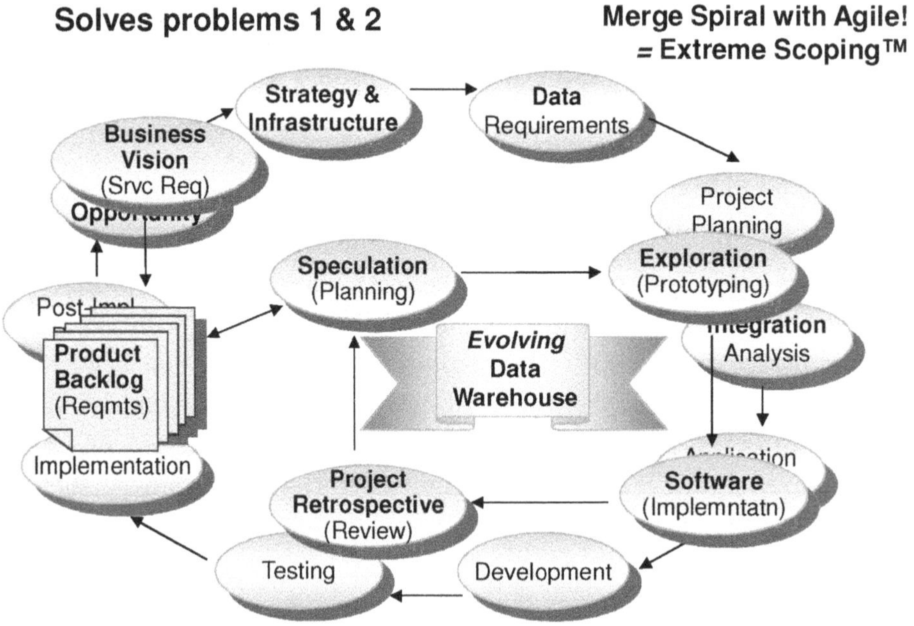

AGILE PRINCIPLES THAT WORK FOR EDW

There are many agile principles that apply to the more mature EDW/BI projects where EDW is considered part of and not separate from BI. They are:

- Treating the initial requirements as a business vision rather than cast-in-concrete requirements.

- Not committing to estimates, which are nothing more than best-guess speculations, anyway.
- Exploration (prototyping with continuous refinements) makes much more sense than trying to get the whole EDW/BI service request right from the start.
- Giving the project team full authority over their work, without interference from anyone outside the team, including the users and IT management.
- Nobody should work alone; all tasks and deliverables should be co-owned and co-created (similar to pair programming).
- EDW/BI project teams should also place more importance on physical deliverables than comprehensive documentation, and make frequent deliverables their primary goal.
- The agile decree of "ability to respond to change is valued over following a plan" is even more important to EDW/BI projects than operational systems because EDW/BI requirements change constantly.
- With EDW/BI project scopes being as large as they are, breaking the projects into releases makes a lot of sense.
- All releases must be time-boxed into weeks or months – not years.
- Nothing is cast in concrete – everything can be renegotiated.
- Quality comes before quantity and is applied primarily to *data* quality in EDW/BI projects.
- Since the EDW/BI environment evolves one release at a time, the developers can "refactor" (refine, redesign, simplify, improve) all deliverables with each release, and the data modelers can refine their business data models with each release as they learn more about the data.

AGILE PRINCIPLES THAT DON'T WORK FOR EDW

On the other hand, there are some agile principles that do not apply to EDW/BI projects. For example, we don't have the luxury to simply "freeze" the scope because our EDW/BI releases are too large. We must allow scope changes on releases that take three or four months, as long as we perform impact analysis and do not allow scope creep.

The responsibilities and duties of a ScrumMaster are inappropriate in enterprise-class BI initiatives for two reasons. First, if Scrum is not the chosen agile methodology, then there is no need for a person who is certified in the methodology to mentor the project team on how to use it. Second, a developer, even a seasoned one, does not have the combined expertise in the areas of business value, data effort, technical considerations, and knowledge of project constraints and interdependencies that are necessary to manage mature enterprise-class EDW/BI projects. It is imperative to have a project management team that collectively possesses such balanced expertise, which I call BDTP Balance™. BDTP stands for business value, data effort, technical considerations, and project constraints and interdependencies. I expand on this concept in Chapter 7.

Referring to a user as the product owner is not applicable because the EDW and the BI applications are not owned by any one user or one department. Instead, they are owned by the organization, which is represented by the BI steering committee. In other words, each project would, in effect, have to have many product owners who would have to agree on all strategic and tactical decisions, which is the responsibility of the BI steering committee. It is the BI steering committee that prioritizes the sequence of EDW/BI projects from various users and departments. It is the BI steering committee that decides whether or not a project deadline can be extended to include additional requirements from one user. Making the BI steering committee the product owner of all EDW/BI requirements from all users is also not feasible. Executives do not work at that level of detail. Moreover, intermingling user requirements from different business people is unmanageable and surely not acceptable to any business person. In addition, project backlogs would be tied into the overall program backlog. Therefore, one user or one product owner cannot indiscriminately and continuously monopolize the backlog without eventually affecting other business people who are waiting for the EDW/BI team to work on their service requests.

The scope and deliverable for any EDW/BI release is not and should not be based on how much code can be written in a specific time period. Instead, the scope and deliverable for each EDW/BI release is totally dependent on and defined by the BDTP Balance, with business value being the driver, but data effort being the determinant.

Cadence is another principle that cannot and should not be enforced on EDW/BI projects. Because of the vastly different data effort that is required to deliver different BI functions, it is entirely possible that some releases will take months to complete, while other releases can be finished in a few weeks. On EDW/BI projects, data effort is the determining factor in defining the length of a time-box, not how much code can be written.

The KISS (keep it simple stupid) principle is somewhat applicable to EDW/BI projects, but must be vastly expanded to include the data. One EDW/BI complexity that does not exist on stand-alone operational systems is that EDW target databases and the ETL process are collectively architected in order to be reusable. That limits how uncomplicated the code can be.

Burn-down charts are popular with developers, but they appear to be unpopular with business managers and executives who prefer to see Gantt charts. However, there are several issues with Gantt charts on agile projects. Not only are they too detailed, too long, and take too much time to maintain, but the main issue with Gantt charts is the tracking of tasks: when a task is started, how much of it has been completed, when it was completed, and by whom. Measuring progress by the number of delivered features, instead of measuring what tasks were performed by whom and how often, is just as applicable on EDW/BI projects as it is on operational system development projects. However, instead of using burn-down charts, an acceptable alternative is to replace the traditional Gantt chart with a simple milestone chart.

Extreme Scoping has the following release guidelines:

1. Always trust your instincts.
2. Change any methodology (including this one) to fit your needs and your culture.
3. Deliver something tangible to the users every one to four months (give or take).
4. Make your data scopes as small as is practical without losing business value.
5. Time-box all your releases, but forget about cadence.
6. Involve the business representative as much as possible (it will go faster).
7. Establish enterprise standards as soon as possible.
8. Don't ignore metadata!
9. Let the EDW and the BI applications evolve.
10. Manage user expectations, and manage your own and your staff's expectations.
11. Nothing is cast in concrete; everything is renegotiable.
12. Apply change control procedures to minor requirements changes and hurdles.
13. Defer large requirements changes and roadblocks to future releases and the BI steering committee (that's why they're there).
14. Have fun with your project (life's too short not to).

Final Thought

I am asserting that today's popular agile methodologies were not developed for enterprise-wide data integration initiatives, and are therefore not appropriate for mature EDW/BI projects. However, that does not mean that EDW/BI projects are condemned to use traditional waterfall or spiral data warehouse methodologies. It is entirely feasible to apply agile principles to a spiral data warehouse methodology and to achieve similar short delivery timeframes that developers of operational systems achieve with Scrum and XP. Extreme Scoping is such an agile method. It does not compel or result in the back-end data management team and the front-end data delivery team to be split into two distinct groups that report to different managers and use different development methodologies. On the contrary, it keeps all EDW and BI components together in one project.

The Extreme Scoping planning process is comprised of seven steps, as shown in Figure III.

Figure III Extreme Scoping Planning Process

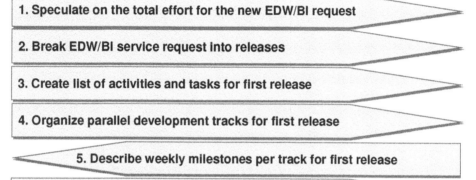

1. Speculate on the total effort for the new EDW/BI request
2. Break EDW/BI service request into releases
3. Create list of activities and tasks for first release
4. Organize parallel development tracks for first release
5. Describe weekly milestones per track for first release
6. Schedule work assignments across weekly milestones
7. Create milestone chart for progress reporting

The first step is a diligent review of the entire soup-to-nuts spiral data warehouse methodology to select the appropriate development steps for the entire set of initial requirements of a new EDW/BI service request. The second step is to break the new EDW/BI service request into releases by carefully balancing business value, data effort, technical considerations, project constraints and interdependencies. The third step begins with another review of the selected development steps, and this time the appropriate activities, tasks, or subtasks are selected for the first release only. In the fourth step, the release activities can now be organized into the appropriate number of development tracks for the first release only. In the fifth step, each development track team determines their weekly milestones. They start with the deadline and work ***backwards*** using the list of activities, tasks, or subtasks as a guide. The sixth step is to schedule all the selected activities, tasks, and subtasks for each development track team across the weekly milestones, and to create a micro plan for internal use by the core team members to manage the release. The seventh step is to create a macro project plan, which is an aggregated milestone chart, for reporting progress to management.

In a traditional waterfall approach, the project manager reviews the system development lifecycle (SDLC) methodology and extracts the activities and tasks that are needed to build the system. The project manager then uses the work breakdown structure as a guide to create a detailed project plan in the form of a Gantt chart, critical path method (CPM) algorithms and a PERT chart. The project team then uses these project plans to track progress for the development phases of requirements definition, analysis and design, coding and testing, and implementation. The detailed project plans show all the tasks to be performed, the persons assigned to the tasks, start and end dates, estimated time frames and task dependencies. They are used to guide the day-to-day work activities, the change control process, and progress reporting. That's the traditional way.

The Extreme Scoping approach does not utilize Gantt charts, CPM algorithms, or PERT charts. These documents take days to develop, many hours every week to maintain, and they become inaccurate after the first couple of weeks into a project. However, in the first step of the Extreme Scoping approach, the core team members do start out in a similar way to traditional project teams by discussing the development steps in their methodology and selecting those that are needed to deliver the entire BI application with all of its supporting EDW components. I am using the Business Intelligence Roadmap methodology, shown in Figure 6.1, as an example, to demonstrate how all development steps are considered. You will be using your own methodology in a similar way.

The core team members review the objectives and artifacts of each development step and determine whether or not a development step is necessary for the entire new EDW/BI service request. Together, they decide which development steps have to be performed and which ones can be dropped. They also use their traditional estimating techniques to guess how long it would take to deliver the entire new EDW/BI service request if they were to build it in one big bang – the traditional way.

EDW/BI projects have many different development steps, similar to phases in traditional waterfall methodologies. Not every project will need to perform all steps. In fact, few do. Methodologies typically list the steps in sequence across the engineering stages of justification, planning, (business) analysis, design, construction, and deployment, indicating the dependencies among them. However, on

EDW/BI projects these steps are rarely executed in the order they are presented. Depending on the project, the type of work to be performed, and the resources available, some steps can be skipped, some can be combined, some can be executed out of sequence, and some can be performed partially or repeatedly.

Figure 6.1 Business Intelligence Roadmap

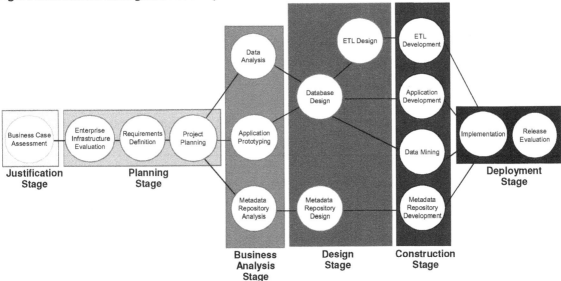

Business Intelligence Roadmap by Larissa T. Moss and Shaku Atre, ©2003. Printed and electronically reproduced by permission of Pearson Education, Inc., Upper Saddle River, NJ.

> The core team functions as the project management team. This team includes a hands-on project manager or project lead, a business representative, an experienced EIM professional, and a technical expert. I describe the reasons for this particular core team composition in more detail in Chapter 9.

In this first step of the Extreme Scoping approach, shown in Figure 6.2, we do not yet concern ourselves with how the work will be organized. The core team members simply want to understand the scope of the entire new EDW/BI service request and how big of a project it is. They can do that by reviewing the development steps of an EDW/BI methodology and by examining the typical artifacts produced for each step. They must decide which development steps apply to the new EDW/BI service request and what type of work artifacts they are required to produce. All they want to know at this point is: Are we being asked to build an elephant, a tiger, or a mouse? If this new service request were to be developed in a big-bang way, would it be a multi-year project, a one-year project, or a three-month project?

Figure 6.2 Extreme Scoping Step 1

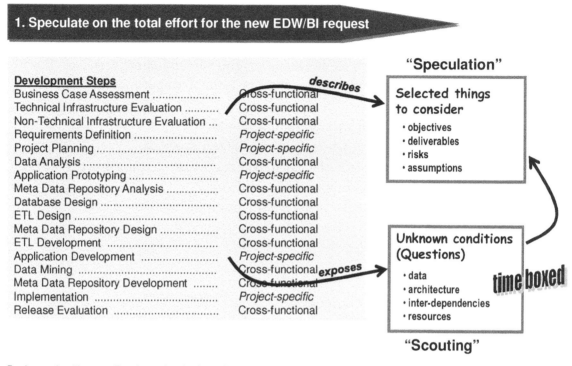

Using the Business Intelligence Roadmap methodology as an example, let's review its sixteen development steps across the six common engineering stages of justification, planning, business analysis, design, construction, and deployment. Additional things to consider about all sixteen development steps are described in Appendix A.

Justification Stage

Nothing is ever built without a reason. The reason could be an analytical business need, a compliance issue to be addressed, a problem to be solved, or a business opportunity to be realized. Every project must have a justification, especially when the project is enterprise-class, such as EDW/BI, master data management (MDM), customer relationship management (CRM), customer data integration (CDI), and so on. The justification stage has one major development step: business case assessment. At the beginning of a BI initiative, this step is often performed as a separate project. Once an EDW/BI environment exists, a smaller version of this step is performed for each new EDW/BI service request.

BUSINESS CASE ASSESSMENT

As shown in Figure 6.3, the focus in this step is on describing the business needs in terms of:

- Business drivers, such as increased revenue or customer retention
- Executive sponsorship, which should be collective sponsorship from business executives
- General business information requirements
- Return on investment, which is a cost-benefit analysis
- Return on asset, which is the calculation of future savings due to reusability of data, processes, and resources
- Organizational readiness to determine how much business people understand about BI

Figure 6.3 Business Case Assessment

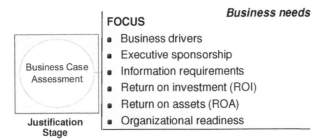

Business Intelligence Roadmap by Larissa T. Moss and Shaku Atre, ©2003. Adapted, printed and electronically reproduced by permission of Pearson Education, Inc., Upper Saddle River, NJ.

If business executives at the highest level in the organization do not perceive any business pain from the current data chaos, business sponsorship for EDW/BI projects is frequently limited to departmental reporting databases (data marts) that are often built in the same old traditional silo fashion. Therefore, assessing the business needs as well as the organizational readiness for an enterprise-class BI initiative and for each new EDW/BI service request is an important step.

Artifacts for a business case assessment typically include an assessment report that summarizes your findings, points out issues and opportunities, and makes recommendations for solving the business need or quest for business opportunity. It is very important to tie the business value of the proposed solution to the business drivers behind the business pain in order to get buy-in and full support from the BI steering committee.

Consider the risk of not performing this development step before you decide to drop it. A major risk is to build a BI solution that is not tied to a strong business driver and does not support a strategic business goal. This can result in a lack of trust by the business community and potentially a cut in funding at the end of the project. No matter how valuable the BI application is to one user or department, it may not have the highest business value to the business community at large.

Planning Stage

Planning is usually the process of preparing for the work to be done. It involves taking stock of the existing infrastructure, the resources, the skills available versus the skills needed, the budget, and the expected date for delivery. Since the entire Extreme Scoping approach replaces the planning process of a methodology, you will only review and discuss those aspects of project planning that are beyond organizing the project, such as skills, training, critical success factors, assumptions, constraints, measures of success, and so on.

The planning stage has three development steps: enterprise infrastructure evaluation (technical and non-technical), requirements definition, and project planning. In traditional methodologies, requirements definition follows project planning. However on EDW/BI projects, the planning process cannot be completed until the requirements are understood, especially the data requirements. Therefore, I recommend that the requirements definition step be part of the planning stage.

ENTERPRISE INFRASTRUCTURE EVALUATION

Part of organizational readiness is an assessment – or gap analysis – of the infrastructure necessary to support enterprise-wide initiatives. Infrastructure comes in two flavors: technical and non-technical. Both are equally important, but non-technical infrastructure is often ignored. You cannot implement an EDW/BI environment without hardware, software, a network, and tools. And you should not implement an EDW/BI environment without standards, procedures, architecture, and methodology.

> The entire infrastructure does *not* need to be in place before embarking on EDW/BI projects; it can be built over time. However, you need to know the major gaps up front.

Technical Infrastructure Evaluation

For adequate performance, it is very important to have sufficient "horsepower" and scalability with technical infrastructure components. As shown in Figure 6.4, the focus in this step is on identifying the technology gaps for:

- Hardware, such as processors and other physical devices
- Network, such as broadband lines and protocols
- Middleware, such as database management systems (DBMS) gateways
- DBMS, such as relational or columnar databases, and DW appliances
- Tools, such as ETL tools and OLAP tools
- Utilities, such as DBMS backup and load utilities

Figure 6.4 Technical Infrastructure Evaluation

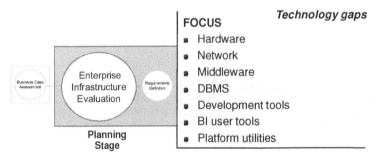

Business Intelligence Roadmap by Larissa T. Moss and Shaku Atre, ©2003. Adapted, printed and electronically reproduced by permission of Pearson Education, Inc., Upper Saddle River, NJ.

Artifacts for technical infrastructure evaluation typically include a technical infrastructure gap analysis report that outlines the gaps and limitations in your current platform and justifies the need to expand it. The second deliverable is the selection and eventual installation of new products.

Consider the risk of not performing this part of the enterprise infrastructure evaluation before you decide to drop it. A major risk is a drop in performance in a growing EDW/BI environment. Therefore, it is mandatory to assess and upgrade the hardware, middleware, DBMS, and tools from time to time. If you don't pay attention to your technical infrastructure, performance could degrade to such an extent that the EDW/BI environment becomes unusable. It is also important to stay current with the existing technology because technology advances occur every few months. That does not mean that the platform must be upgraded every few months, but it is important to be up-to-date with new products and vendors.

Non-Technical Infrastructure Evaluation

A non-technical infrastructure needs to be put into place to prevent the EDW/BI environment from becoming as fragmented as the operational systems environment. As shown in Figure 6.5, the focus in this step is on identifying the procedural gaps in terms of:

- Standards
- Guidelines
- Procedures
- Enterprise data model, i.e. architectural standards
- Metadata repository strategy and solution
- Methodology

Figure 6.5 Non-Technical Infrastructure Evaluation

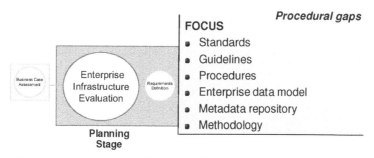

Business Intelligence Roadmap by Larissa T. Moss and Shaku Atre, ©2003. Adapted, printed and electronically reproduced by permission of Pearson Education, Inc., Upper Saddle River, NJ.

To create this non-technical infrastructure involves project activities, such as:

- Collaborating with business people from many lines of business
- Resolving age-old disputes among business people about data definitions, data domains (valid values), and data usage
- Standardizing data names and data values based on business rules across the enterprise
- Creating a regular forum where business people review and maintain enterprise standards, business rules, and business policies on a regular basis.

Artifacts for non-technical infrastructure evaluation typically include a non-technical infrastructure gap analysis report that outlines existing shortcomings and justifies the need to improve your current standards, policies, procedures, and guidelines. The second artifact is a set of requirements to improve the non-technical infrastructure either as part of your EDW/BI project or as a completely separate project.

Consider the risk of not performing this part of the enterprise infrastructure evaluation before you decide to drop it. A major risk is to build customized stand-alone BI solutions instead of a collectively architected EDW/BI environment. BI is an enterprise-wide initiative that needs cross-functional standards, policies, procedures, and guidelines. Therefore, if you don't address non-technical infrastructure, you run the risk of perpetuating silo BI solutions with different standards, different transformations, and different analytic results.

REQUIREMENTS DEFINITION

On EDW/BI projects, the traditional phase called requirements definition is often not executed as a separate development step; instead, it is folded into project planning, data analysis, and prototyping. As shown in Figure 6.6, *data requirements* are most important and are on the top of the list:

- Data requirements
- Functional requirements for ETL, BI application, data mining, and reports
- Technical as well as non-technical infrastructure requirements
- Metadata repository requirements
- Historical requirements, which will affect the data effort
- Security requirements
- Performance requirements

Figure 6.6 Requirements Definition

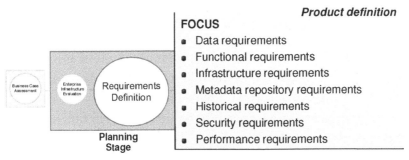

Business Intelligence Roadmap by Larissa T. Moss and Shaku Atre, ©2003. Adapted, printed and electronically reproduced by permission of Pearson Education, Inc., Upper Saddle River, NJ.

The common artifact for a requirements definition step is a requirements document, which describes all the detailed requirements for the EDW/BI project based on the service request, the technical and non-technical gap analysis findings, and preliminary results from source data profiling. The user also conveys the desired service level agreements, which, at this stage in the project, are more like general user expectations for performance, availability, timeliness, and quality.

Consider the risk of not performing requirements definition activities before you decide to drop them. Requirements definition activities can be, and often are, combined with data analysis or with application prototyping activities. That's OK on small projects, but here are some risks in totally skipping separate requirements definition activities on larger projects. When data modelers get into the weeds (details) too soon, it often results in analysis paralysis. When the BI application developers start prototyping too soon, it often results in scope creep. Other risks include: missing functionality or data, lax or no security, and too many un-prioritized requirements.

PROJECT PLANNING

Project planning is the familiar activity of coming up with a game plan for the project. As shown in Figure 6.7, the focus in this step is on:

- Business involvement
- Data management activities
- Overall project scope
- All types of requirements
- Staffing and skills required and available
- Risks and assumptions

The difference on EDW/BI projects is the focus on the work effort for data requirements as opposed to functional requirements. Data management activities such as data modeling, data standardization, data profiling, and data cleansing, take four to five times more effort than code-related activities such as producing reports, queries, applications, or even scorecards and dashboards. Another difference is the team structure. EDW/BI projects work best when co-managed by the members of the core team and executed by parallel development track teams, which I describe in Chapter 9.

Figure 6.7 Project Planning

Business Intelligence Roadmap by Larissa T. Moss and Shaku Atre, ©2003. Adapted, printed and electronically reproduced by permission of Pearson Education, Inc., Upper Saddle River, NJ.

An important artifact for project planning (in addition to the project plan) is a project charter that describes the negotiated agreement for the project, such as:

- EDW/BI goals and objectives aligned with business goals and objectives
- Proposed solution(s)
- Cost/benefit analysis
- Scope assessment (functional and data)
- Infrastructure gap analysis (technical and non-technical)
- Historical requirements
- Number and condition of source files
- User responsibilities
- Assumptions
- Constraints
- Risks

Consider the risk of not performing these additional planning activities before you decide to drop them. You should never build an EDW/BI deliverable by the "seat of your pants." You may as well take a dart, throw it at a calendar, and commit to the date that was hit by the dart. There are over 900 potential tasks to remember. Nobody can remember 900 tasks! Therefore, several risks exist: deadlines are missed, you are over budget, the wrong solution may get implemented, or you may never get to the implementation.

Business Analysis Stage

The traditional engineering stage of (system) analysis evolved into business analysis or integration analysis in spiral data warehouse methodologies. Business analysis results in an in-depth understanding of the existing inventory of shared databases and reusable processes in the EDW/BI environment. The ability to share data and reuse processes is the primary goal of a mature EDW/BI environment.

The business analysis stage has three development steps: data analysis, application prototyping, and metadata repository analysis. (In most methodologies, writing detailed requirements definitions is also considered an analysis activity, but I recommend you spend time analyzing the requirements during the planning stage.)

DATA ANALYSIS

The most important development step in the business analysis stage is data analysis. Traditional methodologies have – at best – a system analysis phase where requirements are immediately "turned into" a design. Data analysis, on the other hand, yields a comprehensive understanding of the data requirements and the operational business context (business process) that originates, manipulates, or uses the data. As shown in Figure 6.8, the focus in this step is on data integration, addressing such things as:

- Logical data model, which documents the business view of the data requirements as business metadata in the metadata repository
- Enterprise data model enhancement to include new entities, attributes and data relationships, and to update existing structures
- Source data analysis to find dirty data, such as data domain and data integrity violations
- Data cleansing specifications to repair poor-quality data

Figure 6.8 Data Analysis

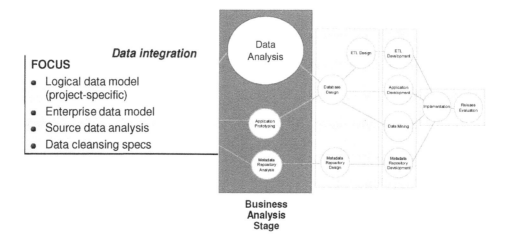

Business Intelligence Roadmap by Larissa T. Moss and Shaku Atre, ©2003. Adapted, printed and electronically reproduced by permission of Pearson Education, Inc., Upper Saddle River, NJ.

During this process, data anomalies, misunderstandings, and disagreements about the data surface among users. These have to be resolved as data elements are rationalized, standardized, and defined. This is the single most significant step for any enterprise-wide data integration initiative, such as EDW/BI, MDM, CRM, CDI, and so on.

The first artifact for data analysis is a project-specific logical data model, which is a fully normalized entity-relationship diagram showing:

- Entities
- Data relationships
- Cardinality (one or many)

- Optionality (zero or one)
- Unique identifiers
- All attributes

The second artifact is the business metadata that describes the entities and attributes of the logical data model in terms of their:

- Business names
- Business definitions
- Cardinality rules
- Unique identifiers
- Data types
- Data lengths
- Domains (valid values)
- Business rules
- Business policies
- Data sources
- Data owners
- Data stewards

The third artifact is a document that describes the cleansing logic that must be applied to the source data in order to bring it into compliance with technical data conversion rules, data domain rules, and data integrity rules. The fourth artifact is an expanded enterprise data model.

Consider the risk of not performing data analysis activities before you decide to drop them. Whenever you are loading data into an enterprise-class EDW/BI environment, this is a mandatory step! The most important objective of EDW/BI is to clean up the redundant, inconsistent, and incorrect operational source data before loading it into the EDW target databases. You can only achieve that through rigorous top-down business data modeling and bottom-up source data analysis. The risk of not performing this step is to load redundant, inconsistent, and incorrect data into the EDW target databases and let business people make strategic business decisions based on this data.

APPLICATION PROTOTYPING

With today's multitude of sophisticated development tools, BI solutions (e.g., BI applications, reports, queries, dashboards, scorecards, etc.) can be most effectively built using the prototyping approach. As shown in Figure 6.9, this step is about demonstrating the feasibility of the new EDW/BI service request with focus on:

- Performing system analysis
- Designing and coding the BI application and reports
- Designing and coding the user interfaces
- Testing the technology
- Finalizing the requirements

Figure 6.9 Application Prototyping

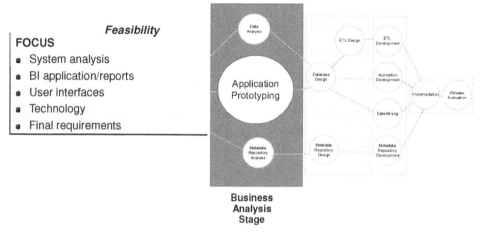

Business Analysis Stage

Business Intelligence Roadmap by Larissa T. Moss and Shaku Atre, ©2003. Adapted, printed and electronically reproduced by permission of Pearson Education, Inc., Upper Saddle River, NJ.

There are several types of prototypes, each with its own rigor and life expectancy.

A *show-and-tell* prototype can be used to obtain budget approval. The functionality of a show-and-tell prototype is limited to displaying the most important screens to get user buy-in. There is no real coding involved, and it is a throwaway.

A *mock-up* prototype is used to clarify the application requirements and to try out some of the proposed functionality, as well as the user interfaces. There is little real coding behind a mock-up prototype, and it is a throwaway.

A *proof-of-concept* prototype is developed to explore uncertainties and risks in order to decide whether to proceed with the project. The scope is usually very narrow and no user interfaces are built or demonstrated. Only enough coding occurs to make a Go/No-go decision. This is also a throwaway.

A *visual-design* prototype is ideal for designing and testing the user interfaces for the BI application, and should result in interface specifications. The code generated during this type of prototype may survive and be reused for the real BI application.

A *demo* prototype is used to demonstrate functionality to business people. This type of prototype is not fully functional, but it is more than just a collection of code stubs.

Code developed for a demo prototype may survive and be reused for the real BI application.

An *operational* prototype is equivalent to a production-worthy release. The purpose of this prototype is to iteratively build the selected BI application functions, reports, and queries and to obtain continuous feedback from the users who participate in the prototyping activities. This type of prototype is referred to as *exploration* in other agile methodologies.

There are potentially several artifacts for prototyping activities. The first artifact is a prototype charter, which is a mini version of a project charter describing the purpose, scope, and deliverables of the prototypes. The second artifact is a revised application requirements document. During prototyping, the original application requirements are often changed because the business people learn more about the capabilities of the BI tool. Another reason for the change could be that they realize they left out some important requirements or included some insignificant requirements that will only slow down the project.

The third artifact is a skills matrix showing the technical and business expertise of the various business people who will be using the final BI application. Another artifact may be an issues log showing problems encountered with the original application requirements. Design documents, such as report layouts, screen designs, algorithms for reports and queries, and design of an online help function (wizard), can usually be produced automatically by the prototyping tool.

Consider the risk of not prototyping before you decide to drop this step. There are two big risks. One is to build something that the user will not accept because the deliverable does not match what the user had in mind. Another is to underestimate the complexity of the requirements or the technology and thereby underestimate the time and money it will take to build the solution.

METADATA REPOSITORY ANALYSIS

Metadata is the contextual information about business data and business processes (collected during requirements definition and data analysis) and the corresponding technical IT components (collected during design and construction). Metadata is no longer the "dirty D word" as in documentation, but the "nice N word" as in navigation. Metadata helps business people locate, manage, understand, and use the data in the EDW target databases. Add "A" for the word administration, and you have metadata being the DNA of every EDW/BI environment. A metadata repository helps technicians maintain and administer all the components in an EDW/BI environment. As shown in Figure 6.10, the focus in this step is on defining the requirements for capturing contextual information:

- Metadata capture
- Metadata integration
- Metadata delivery
- Metadata usage
- Metadata security
- Metadata repository staffing

Figure 6.10 Metadata Repository Analysis

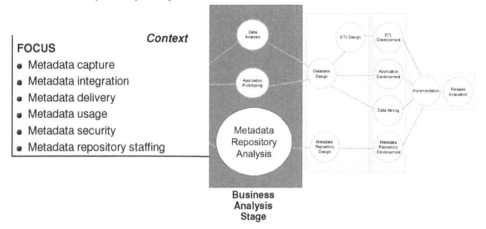

Metadata must be captured, linked (integrated), and maintained in a metadata repository to make the data in the EDW/BI environment fully useful to the business and technical communities. It will provide the necessary data lineage for the business people to help them navigate through the EDW target databases.

The first artifact produced for metadata repository analysis is a logical meta model, which is a fully normalized entity-relationship diagram showing:

- Entities (metadata components)
- Relationships among metadata components
- Cardinality (one or many)
- Optionality (zero or one)
- Attributes for metadata components

The second artifact is the meta-metadata that describes the entities (metadata components) and attributes of the logical meta model in terms of their:

- Names
- Definitions
- Relationships
- Data types
- Data lengths
- Origin (where it is captured)
- Business rules
- Business policies
- Metadata ownership

Consider the risk of not addressing metadata on your project before you decide to drop this step. Standardizing data implies that you will make many changes to the source data before you load it into the EDW target databases. Changes may include:

- Renaming the data based on its business definition
- Splitting one source data element into multiple target columns
- Populating one target column from multiple source data elements
- Translating cryptic codes into intuitive mnemonics
- Changing data values to make them conform to standards
- Filtering out inappropriate or invalid data

You need metadata to trace these changes. Without it, business people would have a difficult time finding and understanding the transformed data in the EDW target databases. The risk is that once business people think the EDW/BI environment is too difficult to use, or that the target data is unreliable because it no longer matches what is in the operational systems, they will stop using it, and the entire BI initiative could be perceived a failure.

Design Stage

Once the new requirements are understood, try to find opportunities for reusability. If any existing ETL processes or EDW target databases can be shared, then expand and/or re-architect them. Only if reusability cannot be achieved should you design new processes and databases, as appropriate. Designs can be documented either on paper or as partially-functioning prototypes that serve the purpose of functional analysis.

The design stage has three development steps: database design, ETL design, and metadata repository design. Designing the BI application is done during application prototyping and is not a distinctly separate development step.

DATABASE DESIGN

Data is stored in a variety of different types of databases in the EDW/BI environment (ODS, data marts, EDW database, exploration warehouse, etc.). The database design schema can be multidimensional or relational/non-multidimensional. As shown in Figure 6.11, the focus in this step is on data storage, which includes:

- Database design
- Access paths to the database
- BI tool requirements

Performance considerations not only influence the database design schema (physical data model), but also affect other physical database design components, such as:

- Dataset placement
- Partitioning
- Clustering
- Indexing strategy

Figure 6.11 Database Design

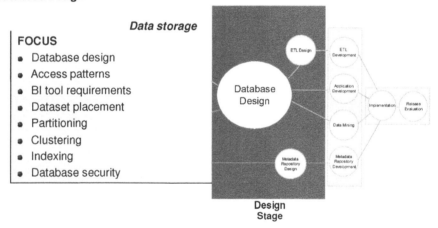

Business Intelligence Roadmap by Larissa T. Moss and Shaku Atre, ©2003. Adapted, printed and electronically reproduced by permission of Pearson Education, Inc., Upper Saddle River, NJ.

Artifacts for database design typically include the database design schema, which is documented as a physical data model. A physical data model shows tables, columns, primary and foreign keys, and indices. It is either a star schema, a snowflake schema, or a relational/non-multidimensional schema.

The second artifact is the physical design document, which describes dataset placement, index placement, partitioning, and clustering. The third and fourth artifacts are the script files, which include database data definition language (DDL) and data control language (DCL) statements.

Consider the risk of not performing database design on your project before you decide to drop this step. Database design is a special area of expertise that is required to be performed by trained database architects who understand the internal rules of the DBMS engine for which the databases are being designed. In other words, tables are not flat files in a database! They are not just a place to casually throw in some data. The risk of not performing this activity diligently and accurately results in poorly designed databases, with unacceptable performance.

> Many people call a relational/non-multidimensional schema a "normalized" schema or a "third normal form" (3NF) schema. However, physical databases are rarely – if ever – implemented fully normalized (5NF) or even in 3NF. Database architects always apply some degree of de-normalization during database design, such as collapsing two entities in a one-to-many relationship into one table, which then violates 1NF. Therefore, I prefer to call so-called "normalized" or "3NF" database designs relational/non-multidimensional schemas.

ETL DESIGN

Extract, transform, and load (ETL) is the most complicated process in an EDW/BI environment because it must coordinate the population of all EDW target databases. Source data will come from a variety of platforms. The purpose of the ETL process is to extract source data from these heterogeneous platforms and move it into the EDW target databases while, at the same time, standardizing and integrating the data. As shown in Figure 6.12, the focus in this step is on:

- Source to target mapping
- Data staging
- ETL tool and utilities
- ETL performance considerations
- ETL process flow
- ETL code

In addition, each ETL run will collect metadata, such as:

- Reconciliation totals
- Data error statistics
- Process error statistics
- Load statistics

Figure 6.12 ETL Design

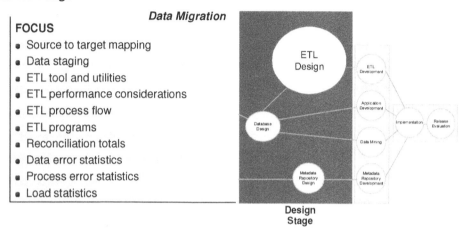

Business Intelligence Roadmap by Larissa T. Moss and Shaku Atre, ©2003. Adapted, printed and electronically reproduced by permission of Pearson Education, Inc., Upper Saddle River, NJ.

Two of the most important artifacts for ETL design are the source to target mapping document showing all data transformations, and the ETL process flow diagram showing all code modules, temporary and permanent work files and tables, and places where utilities will be used. A third artifact might be a program design document, which is broken up into code modules that can be given to different developers to code. When using an ETL tool, the program design document can be generated from the tool automatically.

> In an enterprise-class EDW/BI environment, we do *not* build a separate ETL process for each data mart or BI application. We build integrated enterprise-class solutions. Therefore, an EDW/BI project is *not* like a system conversion project, where you simply move data *"as-is"* from one technology platform to another. Instead, it is more like a system redesign project, where you want to *change* the data into a standardized format that is cleansed and enhanced for analytical reporting.

Consider the risk of not performing ETL design on your project before you decide to drop this step. Unless you are only writing reports against existing data in the EDW target databases, this is a mandatory step. The risk of not correctly designing an expandable ETL process can lead to a lot of costly redesigns in the future. If an ETL process is too inefficient, too complicated, or too cumbersome to enhance, the next project team may be tempted to bypass it and design their own.

METADATA REPOSITORY DESIGN

As shown in Figure 6.13, the focus in this step is on designing the solution for storing contextual information, i.e. metadata, which involves:

- Metadata repository solutions
- Metadata repository sources
- Metadata repository interfaces
- Metadata repository product capabilities
- Metadata repository design alternatives

There are a number of possible metadata repository solutions. A metadata repository can be custom-built or purchased. If the decision is made to build one, you have to design the metadata repository database as well as the migration programs that load and link the business metadata, technical metadata, process metadata, and usage metadata. In addition, you have to design the interface programs that communicate with the tools and the users, as well as a metadata online help function (wizard). If the decision is made to buy a metadata repository product, you have to evaluate, select, purchase, install, and test the product.

Figure 6.13 Metadata Repository Design

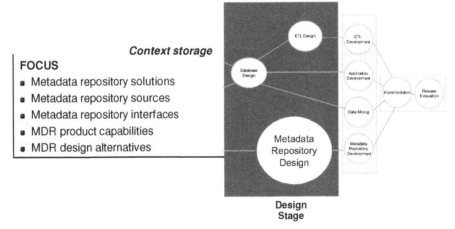

The first artifact for the metadata repository design step is a database design schema for your metadata repository database, which is documented as a physical meta model. This model shows tables, columns, primary and foreign keys, and indices. It is usually the same meta model produced during metadata repository analysis, unless you choose not to implement a fully normalized entity-relationship schema. The second and third artifacts are the database DDL and DCL statements. The fourth artifact is a set of metadata repository coding specifications for:

- Populating the metadata repository, which includes tool interfaces
- Delivering metadata either through people interfaces or reports and queries
- Online metadata repository help function (wizard)

Consider the risk of not performing the metadata repository design step on your project before you decide to drop this step. Building a metadata repository solution is like building any other system. It must be designed in such a way that it will have the desired functionality, performance, scalability, and maintainability. If you buy a metadata repository product, take the time to understand the requirements so that you buy a product that will meet your needs. If you do not take the time to design or buy a sustainable metadata repository solution from the start, you will end up with metadata strewn across various developer tools (e.g. ETL tool), BI tools (e.g. OLAP tool) and databases (e.g. SYSTABLES), and business people will not be able to make use of the metadata.

Construction Stage

This is the stage when the deliverables are physically built and tested. The user either accepts or rejects the product as the solution for the analytical business need, compliance issue, problem, or business opportunity. Development and testing are age old engineering disciplines used for building operational systems, and they are relevant in the same way to EDW/BI projects.

The construction stage has four development steps: ETL development, BI application development, data mining, and metadata repository development.

ETL DEVELOPMENT

Implementing the back-end ETL process is usually done through the use of an ETL tool. Depending on the age, location, and condition of your source files, the complexity of the required transformations and the functional limitations of the ETL tool, you may have to write some custom code to augment the ETL tool functionality. As shown in Figure 6.14, the focus in this step is on sourcing the EDW target databases by considering:

- Initial load process
- Historical load process
- Incremental load process
- Source data dependencies
- ETL process dependencies
- Database load dependencies
- Platform considerations

Being the most complicated process in an EDW/BI environment, the ETL code must be thoroughly tested under a formal test plan with:

- Test cases
- Expected test results
- Actual test results
- Detailed test log

Figure 6.14 ETL Development

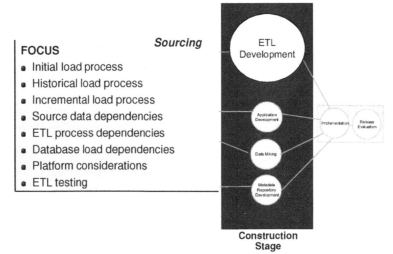

FOCUS
- Initial load process
- Historical load process
- Incremental load process
- Source data dependencies
- ETL process dependencies
- Database load dependencies
- Platform considerations
- ETL testing

Sourcing

ETL Development

Application Development

Data Mining

Metadata Repository Development

Implementation

Release Evaluation

Construction Stage

Business Intelligence Roadmap by Larissa T. Moss and Shaku Atre, ©2003. Adapted, printed and electronically reproduced by permission of Pearson Education, Inc., Upper Saddle River, NJ.

The first artifact for the ETL development step is the ETL code, which consists of three sets of ETL programs with three types of code modules, namely extract, transform, and load modules for the initial load, historical load, and incremental load. The second artifact is the formal test plan with detailed test cases and a test log that describes the expected test results. The test log also has a column for documenting the actual test results. In addition, test data is created with all the conditions required by the test cases.

Consider the risk of not coding new ETL modules on your project before you decide to drop this step. If you need to load new data into the EDW target databases, this step is mandatory. Without it, you do not have the data to support your functional deliverable.

APPLICATION DEVELOPMENT

As shown in Figure 6.15, the focus in this step is on delivering the BI functionality by focusing on:

- Prototyping results
- Code for the BI application and reports
- Application testing
- Development considerations
- User skills (training)

The front-end BI application and reports are often developed by extending and expanding the prototyping activities into a final release where all the "i"s are dotted and the "t"s are crossed. In other words, the operational prototype is turned into a production-worthy deliverable that is subjected to the same rigorous testing activities as the ETL processes.

Figure 6.15 Application Development

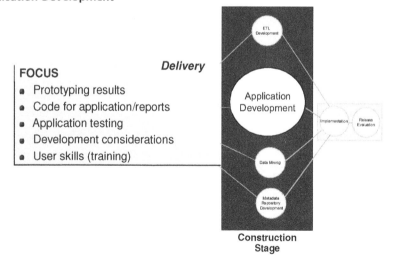

Business Intelligence Roadmap by Larissa T. Moss and Shaku Atre, ©2003. Adapted, printed and electronically reproduced by permission of Pearson Education, Inc., Upper Saddle River, NJ.

The first artifact for an application development step is the code for the BI application and reports. The second artifact is the formal test plan with detailed test cases and a test log that describes the expected test results, with a column for documenting the actual test results. In addition, test data is created with all the conditions required by the test cases.

A final potential artifact is a set of user training materials comprised of:

- Presentation slides
- Instructor notes
- Student workbooks
- Exercises
- Solutions to those exercises
- Other related handouts

Consider the risk of not coding the new BI application and reports before you decide to drop this step. Unless the EDW/BI service request does not ask for any new BI functionality, this step is mandatory. Without it, you are not delivering any new BI functionality.

DATA MINING

As shown in Figure 6.16, the focus in this step is on knowledge discovery. It involves:

- Data considerations (cleanliness, meaning, preparation)
- Data mining tool
- Analytical data models
- Staffing (statistician, DBA)
- Integration with other BI tools

Data mining is a unique application that involves a specialized data mining tool. The tool is run against a pool of data (usually the exploration warehouse), which is loaded for a specific data mining purpose. If the data does not need to be manipulated, the data mining tool can also run against any other EDW target database, or even operational files and databases.

Data mining operations are executed against that pool of data based on an analytical data model. The results are often displayed in a highly visual form, such as bar charts, pie charts, lift charts, decision trees, scatter plots, and histograms.

The first artifact for data mining is the evaluation and selection (and eventual installation) of a data mining tool. The second is the design of a data mining database (e.g., exploration warehouse). This database is populated with data from an operational system, an EDW target database, or a combination of both. Another artifact is the analytical data model, which is used by the algorithms of the data mining operations in the data mining tool.

Figure 6.16 Data Mining

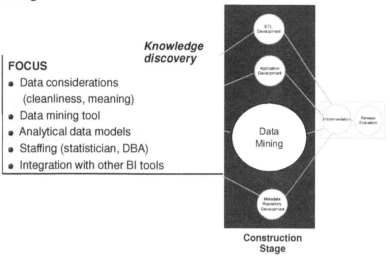

Business Intelligence Roadmap by Larissa T. Moss and Shaku Atre, ©2003. Adapted, printed and electronically reproduced by permission of Pearson Education, Inc., Upper Saddle River, NJ.

Consider the risk of not including data mining before you decide to drop this step. If your company expects to do extensive data mining, this step must be performed. Without it, the business analysts would not have the capability to discover unknown patterns in their data. These unknown patterns could give them insights into the buying habits of their customers, which they can exploit to increase revenue for the company. If your competitors benefit from data mining and you don't, you may lose customers to your competitors very quickly.

METADATA REPOSITORY DEVELOPMENT

Developing a metadata repository solution is much like developing a business application or installing a purchased package. As shown in Figure 6.17, the focus in this step is on context delivery and consists of:

- Metadata repository database/product
- Metadata repository programs/scripts
- Metadata repository testing
- Preparation for production
- ETL statistics

If you decide to custom-build a metadata repository solution, the development effort usually includes:

- Creating a database called a metadata repository
- Writing code to extract metadata from the tools where metadata is captured
- Writing code to deliver metadata to the users and technicians
- Writing code to provide an online help function (wizard)

Figure 6.17 Metadata Repository Development

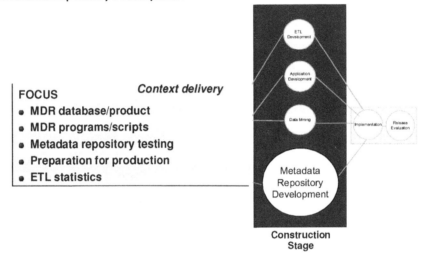

Business Intelligence Roadmap by Larissa T. Moss and Shaku Atre, ©2003. Adapted, printed and electronically reproduced by permission of Pearson Education, Inc., Upper Saddle River, NJ.

Another part of metadata repository development is writing ETL-specific metadata code modules that capture and store ETL load statistics, reconciliation totals, and error statistics that are produced during the ETL runs.

The first artifact for metadata repository development is the metadata repository database (built or purchased). The second artifact is a set of code modules and scripts to populate the metadata repository and to deliver the metadata. This includes all interfaces and the online help function. The third artifact is a formal test plan with detailed test cases and a test log with a column for the expected test results and a column for the actual test results. In addition, test metadata is created with all the conditions required by the test cases. Another potential artifact is a set of training materials for the business people who will be using the metadata repository.

Consider the risk of not providing a metadata repository before you decide to drop this step. If you are building your own metadata repository solution, then you have to perform this step. Without it, users would have to access each tool where metadata is captured to look up the metadata components they need. Most users are not technical enough to do that. A short-term solution may be to expand the dictionary of the data modeling tool or the ETL tool, but eventually, a bona fide metadata repository is the only solution.

Deployment Stage

After a system is built, it is moved to production and is made available for general use. Traditionally, we do not put a system into production until all of its functionality is built and tested by IT, and then approved and signed off by the user. Once in production, the system usually becomes the responsibility of a maintenance crew. That is not the case with EDW/BI projects. We do not build and test all of the requested functionality in one long EDW/BI project, and our users may choose whether or not to put a partially-functioning application into production. However, since a user may decide to put several releases into production, you have to understand and carefully estimate the activities in this step. The deployment stage has two development steps: implementation and release evaluation.

IMPLEMENTATION

As shown in Figure 6.18, the focus in this step is on rolling out the solution, which means:

- The production environment is prepared for rollout
- User training and ongoing support is planned and/or executed
- Database maintenance procedures are set up
- Plans are made to monitor utilization of resources
- Plans are made to manage growth

Figure 6.18 Implementation

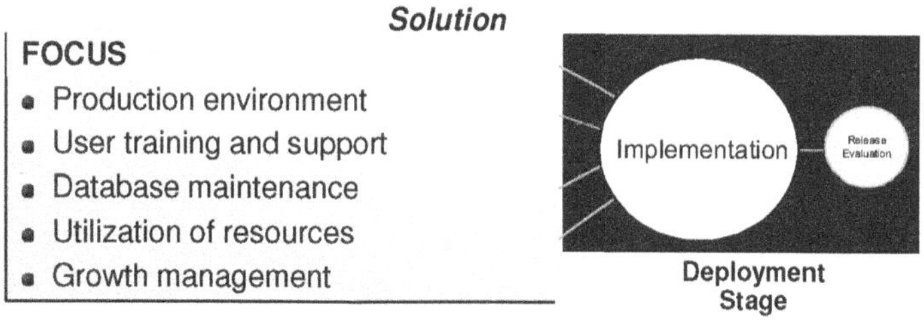

FOCUS
- Production environment
- User training and support
- Database maintenance
- Utilization of resources
- Growth management

Solution

Implementation Release Evaluation

Deployment Stage

Business Intelligence Roadmap by Larissa T. Moss and Shaku Atre, ©2003. Adapted, printed and electronically reproduced by permission of Pearson Education, Inc., Upper Saddle River, NJ.

The production databases are created as are the program libraries that will house the ETL and BI application and report programs. The metadata repository solution may also be moved into production, and all the EDW target databases are loaded with initial and historical data. All security measures are tested one more time, and the release is rolled out to the business community.

Artifacts for implementation include all physically installed EDW/BI components, such as production libraries for ETL code, BI application code, and potentially, the code related to the metadata repository (if it is moved into production). In addition, EDW target databases are created and populated with current and historical data from the source systems. If the metadata repository resides in production, it is fully populated with metadata from all the metadata sources, such as:

- Modeling tools
- ETL tools
- OLAP tools
- Spreadsheets
- DBMS system tables
- Data dictionaries
- Glossaries

Other artifacts include production documentation, such as operating procedures, monitoring procedures, and potentially, a reference guide or training manual.

Consider the risk of not going into production before you decide to drop this step. If the release does not have enough functionality or data to be useful to the user, it is possible to skip this step. However, since the goal is to produce releases that have immediate value for the user, you probably want to deploy them as often as possible. The risk of not performing this step is that business people will not be able to use the data and functionality that was developed in this release.

RELEASE EVALUATION

As shown in Figure 6.19, the focus in this step is about optimization. It is a very important last step in spiral data warehouse methodologies. A smaller version of this step is referred to as *project retrospective* in other agile methodologies. This step focuses on:

- Performing a post-implementation review
- Measuring success
- Planning for the next release
- Improving the development approach

Release evaluation is an expansion of the old post-mortem reviews, except that traditionally, post-mortems were only performed if the new system had severe problems that needed to be discussed to avoid similar problems in the future. EDW/BI application releases should always be reviewed and *lessons learned* should be discussed not only to prevent problems in the future but to streamline the project team's development process in order to run faster, with higher quality, and less waste on the next release. Release evaluation is also the forum to repackage dropped data requirements or functionality and to reprioritize them within the next several releases.

Figure 6.19 Release Evaluation

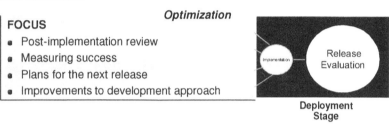

Business Intelligence Roadmap by Larissa T. Moss and Shaku Atre, ©2003. Adapted, printed and electronically reproduced by permission of Pearson Education, Inc., Upper Saddle River, NJ.

The first artifact for the post-implementation review step is the agenda for the meeting, which states the date, time, and place of the meeting. List all the project team members, as well as the users and other stakeholders as the invited attendees. Furthermore, itemize the topics and questions to be discussed, such as:

- Scope
- Schedule
- Budget
- User satisfaction
- Negotiation results
- Staffing
- Skills and training
- Project planning and progress reporting
- Development approach
- Use of contractors and consultants

The second artifact is a document of the meeting minutes, which should highlight all of the discussions, suggestions, and resolutions. The third artifact is an action item list, showing the names of the people to whom the action items were assigned.

Consider the risk of not performing a post-implementation review before you decide to drop this step. If you just finished a very small release without any problems, you can probably drop this step. However, on a larger release, a major risk is to miss an opportunity to learn valuable lessons. You may repeat costly mistakes in an EDW/BI environment that is growing rapidly and is affecting more and more business people with each release.

Completing the First Step

As the core team members review the objectives and artifacts of each development step, they agree on which development steps and which artifacts are necessary for the entire new EDW/BI service request to be completed. Before they proceed to estimating the total development effort for the entire new EDW/BI service request, they discuss the implications of cross-functional steps that will involve other stakeholders. They have to decide who the stakeholders are, how they will participate, when they will be available, and what input is expected from them.

CROSS-FUNCTIONAL STEPS

Figure 6.20 shows that most of the development steps have activities that address cross-functional disciplines, such as enterprise infrastructure, data standardization, enterprise data modeling, business rules ratification, coordinated ETL data staging, common metadata, collectively architected databases, and so on.

Cross-functional means that data and processes are collectively architected for maximum reuse, the existing inventory of data and processes is shared wherever possible, disagreements among business units are resolved, and the architected solution has an enterprise perspective instead of a customized individual user perspective. Only five development steps have a purely narrow project focus:

- Requirements definition
- Project planning
- Application prototyping
- Application development
- Implementation

However, for some EDW/BI projects, the steps of application prototyping and application development may also require a cross-functional focus if two or more departments have shared functionality or common reporting.

Notice also the extensive involvement of the EIM group, as indicated in Figure 6.20. Since they are involved in enterprise-wide data management activities, they have a cross-functional perspective by nature. Their job function is to create and consolidate project-specific logical data models, discover and communicate data discrepancies between projects, and help the users resolve those discrepancies.

Figure 6.20 Cross-Functional Steps

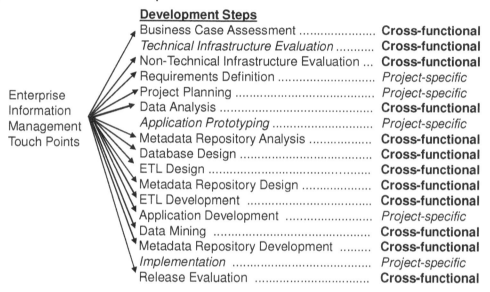

Development Steps	
Business Case Assessment	**Cross-functional**
Technical Infrastructure Evaluation	**Cross-functional**
Non-Technical Infrastructure Evaluation	**Cross-functional**
Requirements Definition	*Project-specific*
Project Planning	*Project-specific*
Data Analysis	**Cross-functional**
Application Prototyping	*Project-specific*
Metadata Repository Analysis	**Cross-functional**
Database Design	**Cross-functional**
ETL Design	**Cross-functional**
Metadata Repository Design	**Cross-functional**
ETL Development	**Cross-functional**
Application Development	*Project-specific*
Data Mining	**Cross-functional**
Metadata Repository Development	**Cross-functional**
Implementation	*Project-specific*
Release Evaluation	**Cross-functional**

Enterprise Information Management Touch Points

Business Intelligence Roadmap by Larissa T. Moss and Shaku Atre, ©2003. Adapted, printed and electronically reproduced by permission of Pearson Education, Inc., Upper Saddle River, NJ.

Cross-functional activities are tremendously important to avoid the following common scenario: The first EDW/BI project out the door gets to "define reality," i.e. naming conventions, definitions, sourcing, hierarchical relationships, tools and technology, etc. Users of subsequent projects get to argue and dispute these first definitions. As a result, the entire EDW/BI architecture and infrastructure is in question and often requires extensive modifications. If the first user doesn't agree to the modifications, and the subsequent users refuse to use the first definitions, you are right back to stovepiping again!

SPECULATION

Equipped with a thorough understanding of the work effort, and using their prior collective experiences with other EDW/BI projects as a guide, the core team members begin to *speculate* (come up with an educated best-guess estimate) on the total number of days it may take to complete each selected step. They take their identified risks and assumptions into account, as well as the knowledge that cross-functional activities will take longer.

As Figure 6.21 illustrates, the first attempt in coming up with high-level estimates usually fails because of a long list of unknown conditions and questions. I call that list the "shrug the shoulders" list, because the core team members usually look at each other puzzled, shake their heads, and shrug their shoulders. They simply don't have enough information to come up with a wild guess, much less an educated guess, for how long a step might take to complete. This gap in knowledge could be about:

- Unknown potential data sources
- Unfamiliar external data
- New technical complexity
- Unclear interdependencies with other EDW/BI projects
- Lack of skills
- Lack of resources

Figure 6.21 Initial Speculation

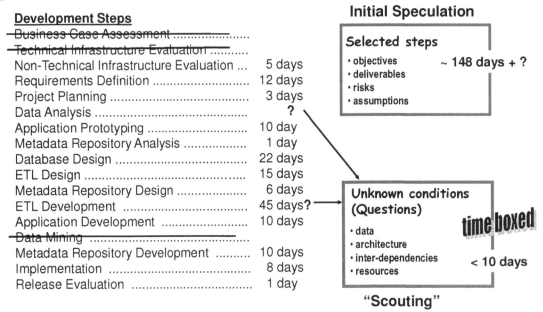

Before the core team can go any further with project planning, they must invest some time into researching the unknown conditions and questions on the "shrug the shoulders" list. One of my clients calls this activity a "scouting" exercise and the list a "scouting list."

SCOUTING

Scouting (researching) is a time-boxed activity of one to ten days. At the end of the allocated time, the core team members complete their speculation for those items that are now better understood. Any unresolved items that cannot be estimated are automatically out of scope until they can be resolved. Alternatively, the core team members may decide to extend the time-box for more scouting by another few days to remove the remaining unknown conditions and questions. All items that cannot be resolved are dropped from the scope, or at least deferred to a later release without any estimates or commitments.

A permanent scouting team can be created to continue the research while the core team proceeds with the planning and development of the EDW/BI service request. If the scouts are proactively scouting, there will be less guesswork involved in the planning of future releases. I have come across some companies that habitually have more questions than answers on most of their EDW/BI projects. They have a permanent scouting team in place that tries to stay ahead of upcoming projects with their research activities, such as:

- Proactive data profiling
- Proactive requirements gathering
- Proactive business value determination
- Proactive data modeling
- Proactive metadata gathering
- Proactive data architecture design
- Proactive capacity planning

Working with our example, let's assume that after five days of scouting, the core team members decide that they can comfortably estimate the time it will take to perform the data analysis step. They think it will take a total of 17 days. Based on their data research, they also determine that ETL development will take 15 days longer than previously estimated. They then raise their final speculation for the entire service request from approximately 148 effort days to a total of 180 effort days, as shown in Figure 6.22.

The core team then calculates elapsed days using their tried and true traditional method. For example, using a conservative estimate of six productive hours per day, the initial estimate would go up to 225 days. Using only four productive days per week, the team would raise their estimate again to approximately 56.25 weeks. Adding vacations and sick time, a more realistic estimate would be at least 60 weeks or 14 months of elapsed time to complete the entire service request. In other words, this looks like a tiger.

Figure 6.22 Final Speculation

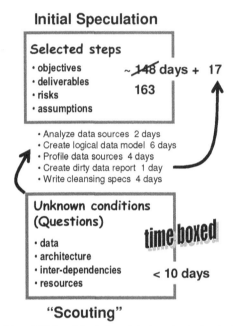

Business Intelligence Roadmap by Larissa T. Moss and Shaku Atre, ©2003. Adapted, printed and electronically reproduced by permission of Pearson Education, Inc., Upper Saddle River, NJ.

Final Thought

The purpose of this first step is not to come up with a precise and detailed project plan. It is only used to understand the overall effort, resources, cost, schedule, risks, and assumptions for the entire EDW/BI service request. Understanding whether you are dealing with an elephant, a tiger, or a mouse is vital to optimally break up the service request into the right number of releases, the right sequence of those releases, the right dependencies among the requirements, and thus, the right deliverable and scope for each release. Without this crucial step, the process of breaking a service request into releases would be completely arbitrary and could lead to a considerable amount of unexpected and undesirable rework.

Chapter 7
Scoping the Releases

The second step in the Extreme Scoping planning process, shown in Figure 7.1, is to carve out the optimum number of releases and their deliverables from the new EDW/BI service request.

Figure 7.1 Extreme Scoping Step 2

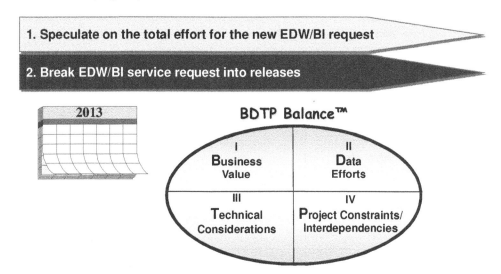

Unlike traditional projects that rely on the project manager to plan the project and assign tasks to individual project team members, EDW/BI projects are planned and co-managed by the entire core team. During speculation and scouting, the entire core team reviewed, discussed, and selected the applicable development steps of their data warehouse methodology. Now the entire core team deliberates and decides how to break the service request into multiple releases.

BDTP Balance™

Breaking a service request into multiple releases is not an arbitrary process, and it is not done by either the user or the project manager or a developer alone. Instead, the deliberation occurs among all members of the core team who have to balance business value, data effort, technical considerations, and existing project constraints and interdependencies. Using the total effort estimate from the previous step, the core team members discuss and decide on the best way to break up the scope of the service request into smaller deliverables. They go through the five-step process shown in Figure 7.2.

Figure 7.2 BDTP Balance

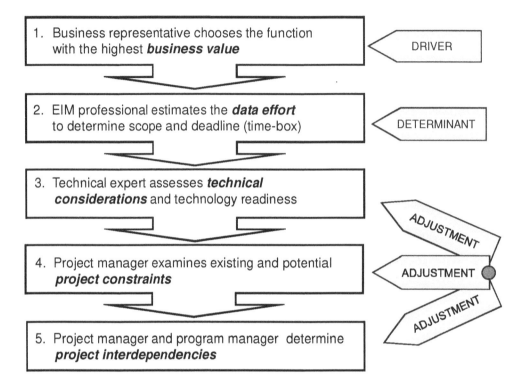

STEP 1: BUSINESS VALUE

Always start with the business representative prioritizing the functional requirements of his or her EDW/BI service request. Presumably, the business person will choose the function with the highest business value to be developed first. This function should be considered the *driver*. In other words, if it is at all possible to deliver this function in 120 days or less, it will be the scope of the first release. However, don't stop yet, because whether or not it is possible to deliver this function is not determined by the coding effort but by the data effort, which has to be examined next.

STEP 2: DATA EFFORT

The selected function must be balanced immediately with the data effort required to deliver it. It is the data effort that *determines* what scope is doable in what timeframe. The EIM professional on the core team analyzes the data requirements for the selected function, which involves:

- Reviewing EDW target databases to determine what existing data can be reused
- Identifying all potential new data sources
- Profiling the source data
- Spotting dirty data
- Determining the complexity of data cleansing
- Estimating the total data effort

It is entirely possible that a chosen function may require 80% of all the data that would be necessary to complete the whole EDW/BI service request. In that case, the scope for the selected function is much too large and the business representative is asked to break the selected functional requirement into several smaller sub-functions and choose one sub-function. If that doesn't work, a different functional requirement should be considered to be the first release, one that needs a smaller subset of the data.

The EIM professional may know of overlapping data requirements from other business people. If it becomes apparent that breaking up the functional requirements into something smaller that still has any business value is difficult, the EIM professional may propose to limit the deliverable from the first release to extracting, cleansing, transforming, and loading just the overlapping data into the EDW target databases. While this alternative may not provide immediate functional use to the users of the current EDW/BI service request, it is an acceptable alternative for two reasons:

- The data effort for a subset of the data that is required to support the functional requirements would be completed.
- Other information consumers benefit from that data immediately.

STEP 3: TECHNICAL CONSIDERATIONS

Once the core team members are comfortable with their decisions for the driver and the determinant, they still must take the opinions of the technical leads, especially the ETL architect, under advisement. In some cases, the data effort is doable from an EIM perspective, but not from an ETL architectural perspective. It is possible that the chosen subset of data requires a complete redesign of the ETL process flow, which would take too long and not fit into the 120 day window.

Other technical considerations may be that the current version of the ETL tool lacks a function that is needed to process the new source data, and the new version will not be installed in time. There may be performance issues with the current design schemas of EDW target databases, and some of the databases have to be redesigned in a major way before new data can be added. Installation of the BI tool that the user plans to use with the selected function is delayed by a few months, or a decision to migrate to a different DBMS is pending. All technical issues must be taken into consideration when choosing the scope and deliverable for the first release.

STEP 4: PROJECT CONSTRAINTS

The first three steps are the most important for scoping the releases. However, your decisions up to this point may be affected by two more factors. The first is any conflict due to some constraints within the project. For example, the core team members discussed organizing multiple teams to work in parallel but now realize that they cannot get enough resources. Other examples might be that the person with the required skills is not available at the time you need him or her, or the business representative who will work with the project team is unable to participate when needed. Let's assume that training the staff and hiring a consultant are prerequisites for the selected release scope, and that funding for both is still not approved or is even in question. That forces the core team to choose another scope for the first release, one that does not require training or the help of a consultant.

STEP 5: PROJECT INTERDEPENDENCIES

The last factor that may affect your scoping decisions is a potential conflict due to some interdependencies among multiple EDW/BI projects. For example, a different project team that is working on another EDW/BI project is already working on the same ETL processes and the same EDW target databases that you need to expand for your first release. Another example might be that the subject matter experts you need on your project are currently helping other project teams. It is even possible that someone from your own team is currently still finishing up another project, but this person is indispensable for working on the selected scope. The program manager may decide to participate in the process of defining releases and may try to influence the core team to select a specific scope and deliverable for the first release because it would benefit a high-ranking executive in the company.

Completing the Second Step

The core team members deliberate the five steps I just described and break the service request into multiple releases. They also determine the sequence of those releases using the same process. During this process, they use their best judgments to guess how long it will take to complete and deploy each release. This does not involve any formal estimating – only a guess from the gut that all members of the core team agree with. Each carved-out deliverable becomes a proposed release, and each release becomes an achievable project that is 30 to 120 days in duration and will produce a defined, tangible, and production-worthy deliverable.

Since the data effort is different for each release, some releases will take only 30 days to complete, while other releases will take 120 days or even a little longer. If the scope for your release does not include new source data, it is conceivable that you can complete a set of new reports in as little as ten days. On the other hand, if you have to bring in a new data source for your release, and that source has many dirty data elements, you may have trouble meeting the 120-day deadline because the data effort alone may take up most of that time. This is the reason why cadence does not apply to enterprise-class EDW/BI projects. Cadence is the ongoing rhythm of a predefined number of days when something is delivered, like every ten days in XP or every 29 days in Scrum. We cannot follow such a rhythm because we base our scope and development effort on the time it takes to profile, standardize, model, integrate, define, extract, cleanse, and transform the data, and not on the time it takes to code a module.

Remember that the aggregate time to complete all releases must add up to approximately the total elapsed weeks determined in the first step of the planning process. If we use our example from the previous step, then all proposed releases would have to add up to approximately 60 elapsed weeks or 14 months, as shown in Figure 7.3.

Figure 7.3 Release Plan

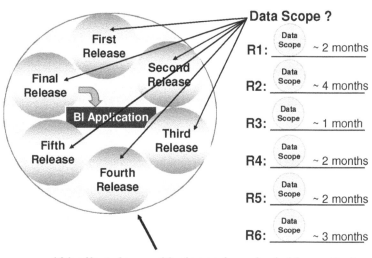

Business Intelligence Roadmap by Larissa T. Moss and Shaku Atre, ©2003. Adapted, printed and electronically reproduced by permission of Pearson Education, Inc., Upper Saddle River, NJ.

If the speculated (guessed) timeframes for all the releases from the second step do not approximate the total estimate from the first step, the core team must decide whether they underestimated the total effort in step one of the planning process or if they are overestimating the timeframes for each release. In either case, both steps have to be reworked.

Final Thought

Traditional project teams depend on the project manager to plan the project, to coordinate and assign tasks to individual project team members, and to track and report the progress of the project. A traditional project manager also reviews the work artifacts and makes project-related decisions. The individual project team members are responsible for their assigned work artifacts, which they hand off at the appropriate time. For example, the requirements analyst elicits the application requirements, which are then handed off to the data modeler who creates the logical data model, which is then handed off to the database administrator who produces the physical data model and builds the database structures, which are then handed off to the developer who codes the application. The only collaborative interaction that involves all team members at the same time happens once a week during the status review meeting. This traditional approach may have worked on very large, multi-year projects that use traditional methodologies and have dozens of members on a team, but it is completely ineffective for agile EDW/BI projects that must deliver in 30 to 120 days. Only a self-organizing core team composed of a business person, an EIM professional, an experienced EDW/BI technician, and a seasoned project manager can co-manage an agile enterprise-class EDW/BI project effectively.

Chapter 8
Defining the Work

In the third step of the Extreme Scoping planning process, shown in Figure 8.1, the core team members define the detailed activities they have to perform in order to build a production-worthy first release.

Figure 8.1 Extreme Scoping Step 3

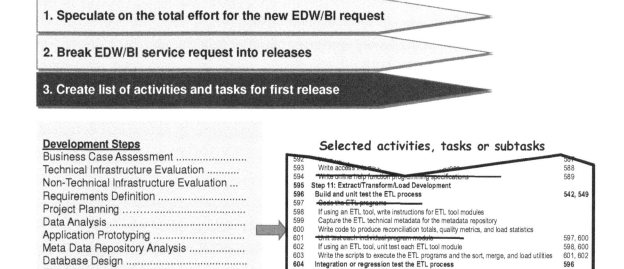

Business Intelligence Roadmap by Larissa T. Moss and Shaku Atre, ©2003. Adapted, printed and electronically reproduced by permission of Pearson Education, Inc., Upper Saddle River, NJ.

They do this for the ***first release only.*** In fact, steps three through seven of the Extreme Scoping planning process apply only to the first (or next) release and not to the entire EDW/BI service request. Note that unless you are only writing new reports against existing databases, the EDW portion is always part of the release scope.

Before deep diving into work activities, the core team members first review those development steps that they selected during speculation and scouting to determine whether all of those steps apply to the first release. More often than not, all of those steps are not needed for each release.

After the core team members eliminate those development steps that do not apply to building the first release, they proceed to review, discuss, and select activities from those development steps that do apply. Similarly, not all activities within a development step apply to all releases. It is entirely up to the core team members to choose the minimum number of activities that will produce the highest quality results.

EDW/BI Development Step Activities

While the core team analyzes only those development steps that apply to their first (or next) release, I will itemize all activities for all sixteen development steps in the Business Intelligence Roadmap methodology, which I am using as an example throughout this book. The high-level activities listed in this chapter are described in more detail in Appendix B.

BUSINESS CASE ASSESSMENT

The business case assessment step has nine major activities, as shown in Figure 8.2. The arrows indicate common dependencies between the activities.

Figure 8.2 Business Case Assessment Activities

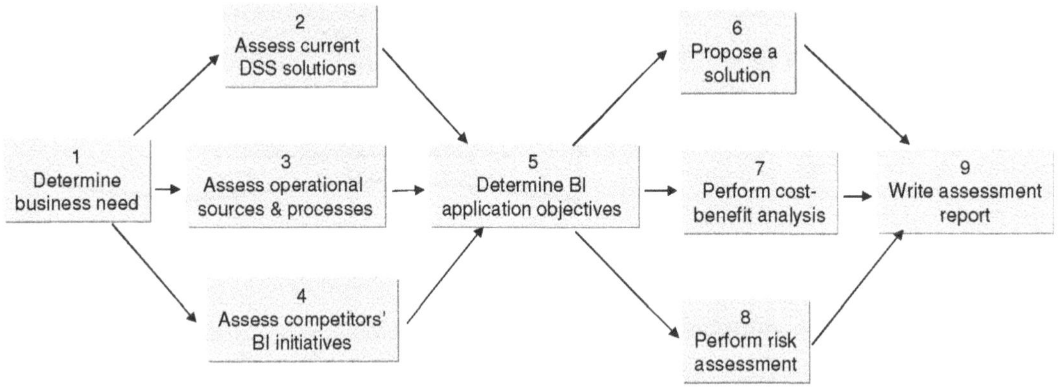

Business Intelligence Roadmap by Larissa T. Moss and Shaku Atre, ©2003. Printed and electronically reproduced by permission of Pearson Education, Inc., Upper Saddle River, NJ.

1. Determine business need – What is the business value of this EDW/BI service request?

2. Assess current decision support system (DSS) solutions – Why can't business people get this information today?

3. Assess operational sources and processes – What are the shortcomings in the operational systems and business processes?

4. Assess competitors' BI initiatives – What type of information do the competitors have that you don't have?

5. Determine BI application objectives – What is the purpose of this application?

6. Propose a solution – What are the proposed data structures? Reports? Queries? Applications? Tools?

7. Perform cost-benefit analysis – What will it cost? How will it improve the company's bottom line?

8. Perform risk assessment – What types of risks in terms of technology, complexity, integration, organization, project team, and financial investment are inherent in this project?

9. Write assessment report – What are your findings and recommendations?

ENTERPRISE INFRASTRUCTURE EVALUATION

Enterprise infrastructure evaluation has two components: technical infrastructure and non-technical infrastructure.

Technical Infrastructure Evaluation

The technical infrastructure evaluation step has four major activities, as shown in Figure 8.3. The arrows indicate common dependencies between the activities.

Figure 8.3 Technical Infrastructure Evaluation Activities

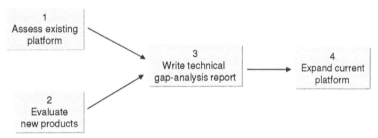

Business Intelligence Roadmap by Larissa T. Moss and Shaku Atre, ©2003. Printed and electronically reproduced by permission of Pearson Education, Inc., Upper Saddle River, NJ.

1. Assess existing platform – Are your current servers, network components, DBMS, tools, and utilities adequate to support the new EDW/BI service request?

2. Evaluate new products – What other products are on the market that you could use?

3. Write technical gap-analysis report – What are your findings and recommendations?

4. Expand current platform – Is it time to upgrade your current platform? Do you need to purchase new tools?

Non-Technical Infrastructure Evaluation

The non-technical infrastructure evaluation step has three major activities, as shown in Figure 8.4. The arrows indicate common dependencies between the activities.

Figure 8.4 Non-Technical Infrastructure Evaluation Activities

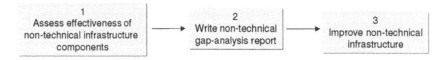

Business Intelligence Roadmap by Larissa T. Moss and Shaku Atre, ©2003. Printed and electronically reproduced by permission of Pearson Education, Inc., Upper Saddle River, NJ.

1. Assess effectiveness of non-technical infrastructure components – Do you have your methodology and standards defined and published? Are the standards complete? Are they effective? Are they being followed?

2. Write non-technical gap-analysis report – What are your findings and recommendations?

3. Improve non-technical infrastructure – Will you have requirements to improve your non-technical infrastructure?

REQUIREMENTS DEFINITION

The requirements definition step has eight major activities, as shown in Figure 8.5. The arrows indicate common dependencies between the activities.

1. Define requirements for technical infrastructure enhancements – Which hardware or network components need to be upgraded as part of this project? Do you need new tools or utilities?

2. Define requirements for non-technical infrastructure enhancements – Which standards, procedures, and guidelines need to be created or updated as part of this project?

3. Define reporting requirements – What are the functional requirements on the EDW/BI service request? Will it be a new BI application or just a set of reports?

4. Define requirements for source data – What source data will you need to support the EDW/BI service request? How many potential source systems do you have to analyze? What are the level of data quality and the level of metadata quality for each source?

5. Review the project scope – How large is the scope in terms of functionality and data? Is it achievable in the timeframe expected?

6. Create the logical data model – Has some of the data already been modeled on a previous project? Who will model the data from a business perspective? How much detail will be included?

7. Define preliminary service level agreements – What expectations do the users have in terms of data quality, timeliness, availability, security, history, etc.?

8. Write the application requirements document – How many total requirements are there? To what level of detail can each requirement be described at this point?

Figure 8.5 Requirements Definition Activities

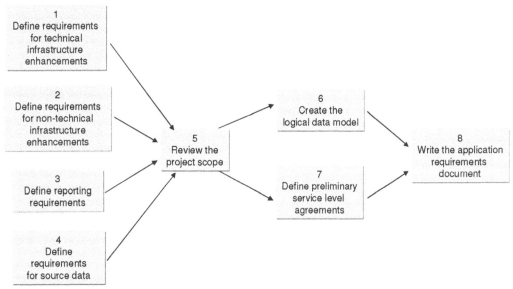

Business Intelligence Roadmap by Larissa T. Moss and Shaku Atre, ©2003. Printed and electronically reproduced by permission of Pearson Education, Inc., Upper Saddle River, NJ.

PROJECT PLANNING

The project planning step has eight major activities, as shown in Figure 8.6. The arrows indicate common dependencies between the activities.

Figure 8.6 Project Planning Activities

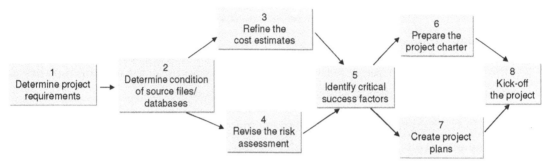

Business Intelligence Roadmap by Larissa T. Moss and Shaku Atre, ©2003. Printed and electronically reproduced by permission of Pearson Education, Inc., Upper Saddle River, NJ.

1. Determine project requirements – How many and what types of requirements do you have? Do you have technical and/or non-technical infrastructure requirements in addition to functional and data requirements?

2. Determine condition of source files and databases – How much data do you know or suspect to be dirty? Do you know of any data disputes among business people? Do you know who the data stewards and data owners are for this data?

3. Refine the cost estimates – Have you obtained new information that will change the cost estimates for this project?

4. Revise the risk assessment – Are there additional risks and assumptions that need to be added to the risk matrix? Do you have contingency plans?

5. Identify critical success factors – What items are absolutely required for this project to be successful? Do you have all the staff you need? Do they have the right skills?

6. Prepare the project charter – What items (e.g., constraints, assumptions, risks, skills) do you agree on with the user and the sponsors for this project?

7. Create project plans – *This activity is replaced by the seven steps of the Extreme Scoping planning process (Part III of this book).*

8. Kick off (initiate) the project – What type of kick off meeting do you plan to have?

DATA ANALYSIS

The data analysis step has six major activities, as shown in Figure 8.7. The arrows indicate common dependencies between the activities.

Figure 8.7 Data Analysis Activities

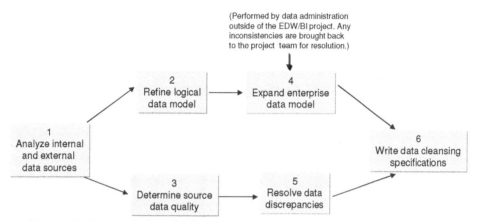

Business Intelligence Roadmap by Larissa T. Moss and Shaku Atre, ©2003. Printed and electronically reproduced by permission of Pearson Education, Inc., Upper Saddle River, NJ.

1. Analyze internal and external data sources – Will you have an external feed? What internal and external data sources have to be analyzed? Why was each source chosen?

2. Refine logical data model – What internal and external data sources must be modeled from a business perspective? Will you be able to fully attribute the logical data model? If not, why not? Have you identified the subject matter experts and other information consumers who can validate the logical data model?

3. Determine source data quality – What type of dirty data do you have? Are there data domain violations? Are there data integrity violations?

4. Expand enterprise data model – Who will merge the project-specific logical (business) data model into the enterprise data model?

5. Resolve data discrepancies – How will you resolve data discrepancies among business units? Who will be responsible for facilitating the resolutions?

6. Write data cleansing specifications – What type of dirty data has to be corrected before it is loaded into the EDW target databases? What are the allowable threshold percentages for dirty data? For example, all amounts have a 0% dirty data threshold, meaning no dirty amount data is allowed in the EDW.

APPLICATION PROTOTYPING

The application prototyping step has seven major activities, as shown in Figure 8.8. The arrows indicate common dependencies between the activities. Activities 5 and 6 are performed simultaneously and demonstrated repeatedly.

Figure 8.8 Application Prototyping Activities

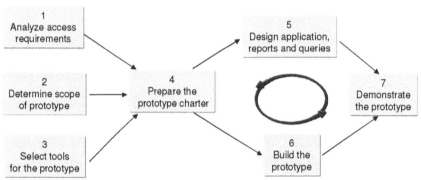

Business Intelligence Roadmap by Larissa T. Moss and Shaku Atre, ©2003. Printed and electronically reproduced by permission of Pearson Education, Inc., Upper Saddle River, NJ.

1. Analyze access requirements – What types of reports, queries, and/or applications have to be written?

2. Determine scope of prototype – What function will be prototyped? How much data is needed to support the function? Which users will participate in the prototype?

3. Select tools for the prototype – Do you already know which tool you will use for prototyping? Are the users trained in that tool?

4. Prepare the prototype charter – What items (e.g., function, data, user) do you agree on for this prototype?

5. Design application, reports and queries – Can your prototyping tool produce the final design documents? If not, why not? What is your option if the tool doesn't function as needed?

6. Build the prototype – Have you set a time-box for building the prototype? Can the prototype be expanded? Why or why not?

7. Demonstrate the prototype – To how many users and stakeholders will you demonstrate the prototype? Why was this audience chosen?

METADATA REPOSITORY ANALYSIS

The metadata repository analysis step has five major activities, as shown in Figure 8.9. The arrows indicate common dependencies between the activities.

Figure 8.9 Metadata Repository Analysis Activities

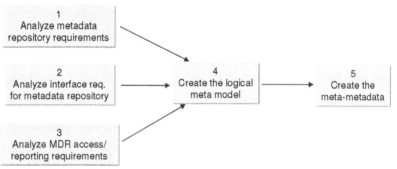

Business Intelligence Roadmap by Larissa T. Moss and Shaku Atre, ©2003. Printed and electronically reproduced by permission of Pearson Education, Inc., Upper Saddle River, NJ.

1. Analyze metadata repository requirements – What types of metadata will you capture in your metadata repository (e.g., data names, definitions, domains, business rules, technical names, process logic)?

2. Analyze interface requirements for metadata repository – With what tools will the metadata repository have to interface (e.g., data modeling tool, ETL tool, OLAP tool)?

3. Analyze metadata repository access and reporting requirements – Who will access the metadata repository? Will you produce metadata reports for business people?

4. Create the logical meta model – Who will capture the metadata requirements in a logical meta model?

5. Create the meta-metadata – Who will define metadata about metadata components? What meta-metadata is required for each metadata source (e.g., the name of the tool where metadata is originally captured)?

DATABASE DESIGN

The database design step has eight major activities, as shown in Figure 8.10. The arrows indicate common dependencies between the activities.

Figure 8.10 Database Design Activities

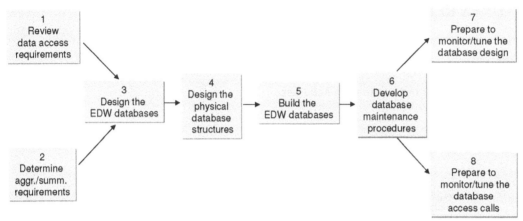

Business Intelligence Roadmap by Larissa T. Moss and Shaku Atre, ©2003. Printed and electronically reproduced by permission of Pearson Education, Inc., Upper Saddle River, NJ.

1. Review data access requirements – How will data be accessed by the BI application or reports? How should data be stored?

2. Determine aggregation and summarization requirements – Should the data be pre-aggregated and pre-summarized? Will summaries be stored?

3. Design the EDW target databases – What is the most appropriate database design schema based on data access paths (e.g., multidimensional, relational/non-multidimensional)?

4. Design the physical database structures – How will data and indices be distributed? What types of indices are most appropriate? Will you partition some of the tables?

5. Build the EDW target databases – How many new databases or tables will have to be created? Can you reuse some existing tables? How will the tables be loaded? Can you reuse any stored procedures?

6. Develop database maintenance procedures – Who will perform database maintenance procedures, how often, and when?

7. Prepare to monitor and tune the database design – Who will monitor and tune the databases? Will those routines be tested regularly?

8. Prepare to monitor and tune the database access calls – Who will monitor and tune the database access calls in the application, report, and query programs? Will those routines be tested regularly?

ETL DESIGN

The ETL design step has five major activities, as shown in Figure 8.11. The arrows indicate common dependencies between the activities.

Figure 8.11 ETL Design Activities

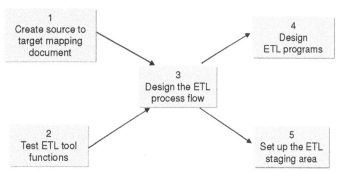

Business Intelligence Roadmap by Larissa T. Moss and Shaku Atre, ©2003. Printed and electronically reproduced by permission of Pearson Education, Inc., Upper Saddle River, NJ.

1. Create source to target mapping document – How many transformation and cleansing rules have to be applied? Can the ETL tool generate the final (official) source to target mapping document? If not, what is your alternative? Excel spreadsheet? Who will maintain it?

2. Test ETL tool functions – Will the ETL tool be able to handle all transformation and cleansing rules? Will additional code have to be written?

3. Design the ETL process flow – How many new ETL components have to be added to the existing ETL process flow? How many can be reused? How much will the existing ETL process flow have to be redesigned?

4. Design ETL programs – Do you have to design code modules for the historical load in addition to the initial and incremental loads? Will you be using the DBMS load utility?

5. Set up the ETL staging area – How will the existing ETL staging area have to be expanded? Should you have a dedicated ETL server?

METADATA REPOSITORY DESIGN

The metadata repository design step has four major activities, as shown in Figure 8.12. The arrows indicate common dependencies between the activities. Activities 1 and 2 are mutually exclusive. Activity 4 is not needed if you purchased a metadata repository product.

Figure 8.12 Metadata Repository Design Activities

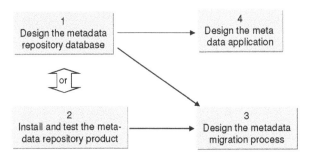

Business Intelligence Roadmap by Larissa T. Moss and Shaku Atre, ©2003. Printed and electronically reproduced by permission of Pearson Education, Inc., Upper Saddle River, NJ.

1. Design the metadata repository database – What type of database design schema will you choose? Fully normalized entity-relationship based or highly abstract object-oriented? Will the metadata repository serve the entire enterprise or only the EDW/BI environment?

2. Install and test the metadata repository product – Have you already purchased a metadata repository? Will you have to enhance it?

3. Design the metadata migration process – How many tools will you have to access to extract business, technical, process, and usage metadata?

4. Design the metadata application – Do you have to write a user interface for technicians and business people to access the metadata repository directly? If not, how will business people gain access to the metadata they need?

ETL DEVELOPMENT

The ETL development step has five major activities, as shown in Figure 8.13. The arrows indicate common dependencies between the activities.

Figure 8.13 ETL Development Activities

Business Intelligence Roadmap by Larissa T. Moss and Shaku Atre, ©2003. Printed and electronically reproduced by permission of Pearson Education, Inc., Upper Saddle River, NJ.

1. Build and unit test the ETL process – How many developers will be coding and unit testing the ETL process?

2. Integration and regression test the ETL process – How many changes will be made to the existing ETL process? How extensive will integration and regression testing be? Will additional testers be utilized?

3. Performance test the ETL process – Will you have to test complicated code modules that process very high volumes of data? Will you use a stress test simulation tool?

4. Quality assurance (QA) test the ETL process – Do you understand the process required by operations to QA test your ETL process, BI application, and reports before going into production?

5. User acceptance (UA) test the ETL process – How much have the users been involved throughout all other testing activities? Will it be necessary to go through a separate UA test with them?

APPLICATION DEVELOPMENT

The application development step has five major activities, as shown in Figure 8.14. The arrows indicate common dependencies between the activities.

1. Determine the final project requirements – What have you learned from prototyping that will affect the application scope or the reports?

2. Build and unit test the application programs – How many developers will be coding and testing the BI application and reports? What type of semantic layer exists or needs to be built between the application and the databases?

Figure 8.14 Application Development Activities

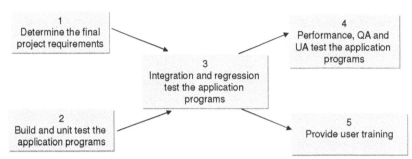

3. Integration and regression test the application programs – How extensive will integration and regression testing be? Will additional testers be utilized? Will the business representative participate?

4. Performance, QA, and UA test the application programs – Will you have to performance test any application or report programs that process very high volumes of data? Will you use a stress test simulation tool? What are the requirements for QA testing? How much have the users been involved throughout all other testing activities? Will it be necessary to go through a separate UA test with them?

5. Provide user training – How many users will be trained? Who will train the users? What type of training material has to be prepared?

DATA MINING

The data mining step has eight major activities, as shown in Figure 8.15. The arrows indicate common dependencies between the activities.

Figure 8.15 Data Mining Activities

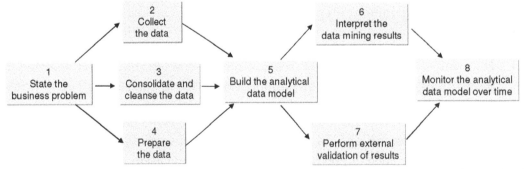

1. State the business problem – Is the purpose for data mining clearly understood?

2. Collect the data – What are the data sources for the data mining tool (e.g., source system, EDW database, exploration warehouse, data mart)?

3. Consolidate and cleanse the data – Who will consolidate and cleanse the data before it is used by the data mining tool?

4. Prepare the data – Will data be classified or reduced before it is used by the data mining tool? Who will prepare the data?

5. Build the analytical data model – Who will build the analytical data model?

6. Interpret the data mining results – Who will interpret the data mining results?

7. Perform external validation of results – Who will compare the data mining results to published industry statistics?

8. Monitor the analytical data model over time – Who will monitor and revise the analytical data model over time?

METADATA REPOSITORY DEVELOPMENT

The metadata repository development step has six major activities, as shown in Figure 8.16. The arrows indicate common dependencies between the activities. If you purchased a metadata repository product, activity 3 does not apply because it is supplied by the vendor.

Figure 8.16 Metadata Repository Development Activities

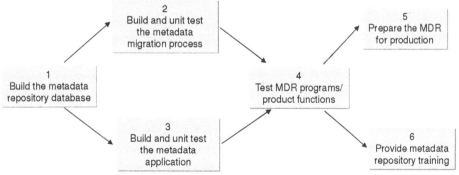

Business Intelligence Roadmap by Larissa T. Moss and Shaku Atre, ©2003. Printed and electronically reproduced by permission of Pearson Education, Inc., Upper Saddle River, NJ.

1. Build the metadata repository database – Who will build the metadata repository database? If you already have one, will you need to expand it with new metadata components? If you have a purchased product, can it be expanded with new metadata components?

2. Build and unit test the metadata migration process – Who will build and unit test the code that will extract metadata from the tools where it is captured and prepare it for the metadata repository?

3. Build and unit test the metadata application – Who will build and unit test the application that will give technicians and business people direct access to the metadata in the metadata repository?

4. Test metadata repository programs or product functions – What additional types of testing will be necessary (e.g., integration, regression, performance, QA, UA)?

5. Prepare the metadata repository for production – Will the metadata repository reside on the production platform? What is the process to move it there?

6. Provide metadata repository training – Who will train the users on how to use the metadata repository? What type of training material has to be prepared?

IMPLEMENTATION

The implementation step has six major activities, as shown in Figure 8.17. The arrows indicate common dependencies between the activities.

Figure 8.17 Implementation Activities

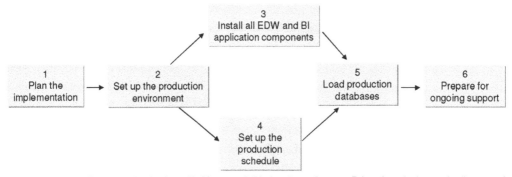

Business Intelligence Roadmap by Larissa T. Moss and Shaku Atre, ©2003. Printed and electronically reproduced by permission of Pearson Education, Inc., Upper Saddle River, NJ.

1. Plan the implementation – How long does it take at your company to move an application into production? Do you know the process?

2. Set up the production environment – How many new program libraries and databases will have to be created in the production environment? How many will need to be updated?

3. Install all EDW and BI application components – How many new ETL code modules will have to be moved to the production libraries? How many report programs? How many BI application programs?

4. Set up the production schedule – Who will set up the ETL jobs and the reports on the job scheduler?

5. Load production databases – How many EDW target databases will have to be loaded? ODS? EDW? One or more data marts?

6. Prepare for ongoing support – Who will perform the database maintenance activities (e.g., backups, restores)? Who will monitor performance, growth, and usage of the databases? Who will mentor the users?

RELEASE EVALUATION

The release evaluation step has four major activities, as shown in Figure 8.18. The arrows indicate common dependencies between the activities.

Figure 8.18 Release Evaluation Activities

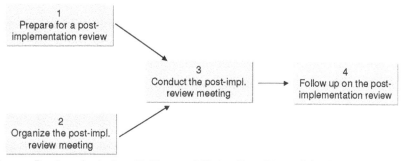

Business Intelligence Roadmap by Larissa T. Moss and Shaku Atre, ©2003. Printed and electronically reproduced by permission of Pearson Education, Inc., Upper Saddle River, NJ.

1. Prepare for a post-implementation review – Who will prepare the agenda? What topics will be reviewed?

2. Organize the post-implementation review meeting – Who will set up the meeting? Who will be invited to attend? What will each person be expected to contribute to this meeting?

3. Conduct the post-implementation review meeting – Who will conduct the meeting? Will there be a facilitator? Who will document the meeting?

4. Follow up on the post-implementation review – Who will document and track action items? When, how, and to whom will action items be assigned?

Completing the Third Step

I will use an example to demonstrate how to use this process. Let's assume:

- This is the 3rd release of a marketing data mart.
- There are two more releases scheduled after this one.
- The deliverables for this release are to add 20 new data elements from a new source file and to write two new reports. The data can be added to an existing database; in other words, no new database is required, but one table needs to be added and one table needs to be modified.
- The two reports will be written with the same report writer as the previous reports; therefore, no new report writing tool needs to be purchased.
- All standards and processes in place do not need to be revised for this release.
- Metadata has been spun off into a separate metadata project running in parallel. However, there is constant communication between the development track teams to stay informed of the other's activities and progress.
- An online help function is scheduled for the final release, and doesn't have to be considered at this time.
- Data mining is not on the radar screen for this company at all.
- Budget and resources are in place and are not an issue at this time.
- No post-implementation review is planned this time around because no problems are expected with this small release.

In our example from step one "speculation and scouting," the core team members had already eliminated the development steps of business case assessment, technical infrastructure evaluation, and data mining. As Figure 8.19 shows, now the core team members review the remaining development steps and decide which ones apply to the scope of this third release. They quickly agree that they can eliminate several more development steps that are not applicable to this release, namely non-technical infrastructure evaluation, metadata repository analysis, metadata repository design, metadata repository development, and release evaluation.

Figure 8.19 Selected Development Steps

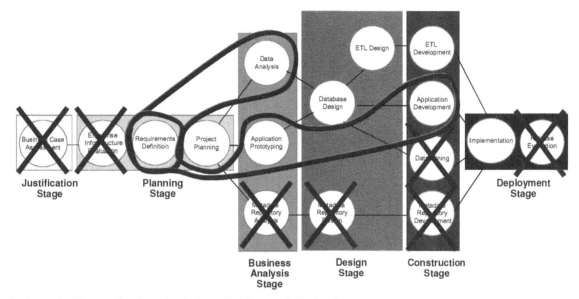

Business Intelligence Roadmap by Larissa T. Moss and Shaku Atre, ©2003. Adapted, printed and electronically reproduced by permission of Pearson Education, Inc., Upper Saddle River, NJ.

That leaves them with requirements definition, project planning, data analysis, application prototyping, database design, ETL design, ETL development, application development, and implementation. Of these steps, the core team members decide to fold activities from the requirements definition step into the data analysis step, seeing that the 20 new data elements have already been clearly defined. At the same time, the core team members fold the requirements definition step into the application prototyping step, and they decide to use the operational prototype to develop the two new reports, in which case applicable activities from the application development step can also be folded into the application prototyping step.

The next step is for the core team members to select the appropriate activities from the following development steps: project planning, data analysis, application prototyping, database design, ETL design, ETL development, and implementation. With red pen in hand, they review the high-level activities for these development steps and choose only those activities they deem necessary to complete this release.

PROJECT PLANNING

Figure 8.20 illustrates the selected activities for project planning.

Figure 8.20 Selected Project Planning Activities

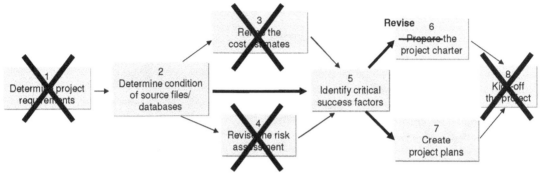

Business Intelligence Roadmap by Larissa T. Moss and Shaku Atre, ©2003. Adapted, printed and electronically reproduced by permission of Pearson Education, Inc., Upper Saddle River, NJ.

In the project planning step, the core team members decide that activities 1, 3, 4, and 8 are not applicable to this release; therefore, they delete them. Activity 6 is changed to *revise the project charter*. The activities selected for the project planning step are 2, 5, 6, and 7:

1. ~~Determine project requirements~~
2. Determine condition of source files and databases
3. ~~Refine the cost estimates~~
4. ~~Revise the risk assessment~~
5. Identify critical success factors
6. ~~Prepare~~ Revise the project charter
7. Create project plans
8. ~~Kick off (initiate) the project~~

DATA ANALYSIS

Figure 8.21 illustrates the selected activities for data analysis.

Since the core team members decided to merge the requirements definition step with the data analysis step, the applicable requirements definition activities are added to the data analysis activity diagram. There are only two activities that need to be added, namely activities 4 and 8 from the requirements definition step. The core team members will reuse the original application requirements document and revise it; therefore, activity 8 is changed to *revise the application requirements document*.

Figure 8.21 Selected Data Analysis Activities

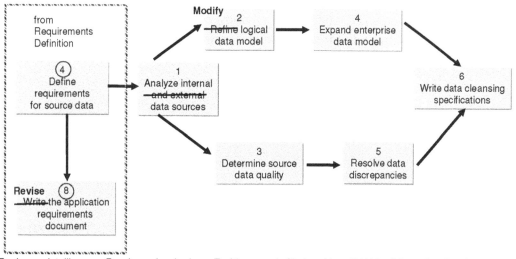

Business Intelligence Roadmap by Larissa T. Moss and Shaku Atre, ©2003. Adapted, printed and electronically reproduced by permission of Pearson Education, Inc., Upper Saddle River, NJ.

There are no external data sources; therefore, activity 1 is changed to *analyze internal data sources.* Since a logical data model already exists, activity 2 is changed to *modify logical data model.* The activities selected for the data analysis step are 1 through 6, as well as activities 4 and 8 from the requirements definition step added in front:

4. Define requirements for source data (from requirements definition step)
8. ~~Write~~ Revise the application requirements document (from requirements definition step)
1. Analyze internal ~~and external~~ data sources
2. ~~Refine~~ Modify logical data model
3. Determine source data quality
4. Expand enterprise data model
5. Resolve data discrepancies
6. Write data cleansing specifications

APPLICATION PROTOTYPING

Figure 8.22 illustrates the selected activities for application prototyping.

Similar to the data analysis step, there are two activities from the requirements definition step that are applicable and are added to the front of the application prototyping activity diagram. The two activities are 3 and 8 from the requirements definition step. Again, the core team members will reuse the original application requirements document and revise it; therefore, activity 8 is changed to *revise the application requirements document*. Since no new tools are selected for this project, prototyping activity 3 is deleted. Activity 5 is changed to *design reports* because the functional scope does not include an application or queries.

Figure 8.22 Selected Application Prototyping Activities

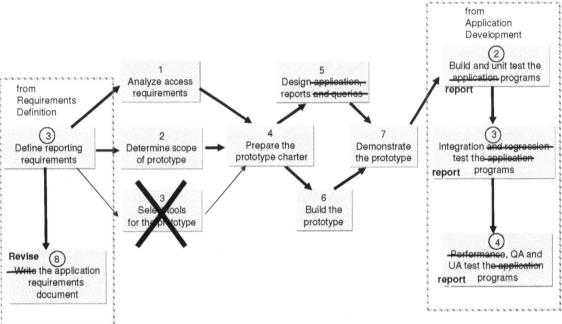

Business Intelligence Roadmap by Larissa T. Moss and Shaku Atre, ©2003. Adapted, printed and electronically reproduced by permission of Pearson Education, Inc., Upper Saddle River, NJ.

Since the project team members also decided to merge the application development step into the application prototyping step, three applicable activities are added to the end of the application prototyping activity diagram. These activities are 2, 3, and 4 from the application development step. Since these three activities only represent the final iteration of prototyping two reports, the three activities are simplified to *build and unit test the report programs, integration test the report programs* and *QA and UA test the report programs*. The activities selected for the application prototyping step are 1, 2, 4 through 7, as well as activities 3 and 8 from the requirements definition step added in front, and activities 2, 3, and 4 from the application development step added to the end:

3. Define reporting requirements (from requirements definition step)
8. ~~Write~~ Revise the application requirements document (from requirements definition step)
1. Analyze access requirements
2. Determine scope of prototype

3. ~~Select tools for the prototype~~
4. Prepare the prototype charter
5. Design ~~application,~~ reports ~~and queries~~
6. Build the prototype
7. Demonstrate the prototype
2. Build and unit test the ~~application~~ report programs (from application development step)
3. Integration ~~and regression~~ test the ~~application~~ report programs (from application development step)
4. ~~Performance,~~ QA and UA test the ~~application~~ report programs (from application development step)

DATABASE DESIGN

Figure 8.23 illustrates the selected activities for database design.

The EDW target database already exists and is being used, monitored, and maintained in production. Therefore, activities 6, 7, and 8 are deleted. To reflect the fact that the database is being enhanced, not designed and built from scratch, activity 3 is changed to *redesign the EDW databases*, activity 4 is changed to *modify the physical database structures*, and activity 5 is changed to *rebuild the EDW databases*.

Figure 8.23 Selected Database Design Activities

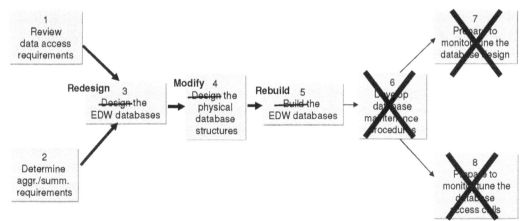

Business Intelligence Roadmap by Larissa T. Moss and Shaku Atre, ©2003. Adapted, printed and electronically reproduced by permission of Pearson Education, Inc., Upper Saddle River, NJ.

The activities selected for the database design step are 1 through 5:

1. Review data access requirements
2. Determine aggregation and summarization requirements

3. ~~Design~~ Redesign the EDW target databases
4. ~~Design~~ Modify the physical database structures
5. ~~Build~~ Rebuild the EDW target databases
6. ~~Develop database maintenance procedures~~
7. ~~Prepare to monitor and tune the database design~~
8. ~~Prepare to monitor and tune the database access calls~~

ETL DESIGN

Figure 8.24 illustrates the selected activities for ETL design.

The ETL process was also built during a prior release, and the ETL staging area is already in place; therefore, activities 2 and 5 are deleted. Since this project will add new data from a new source file, activity 1 is changed to *revise source to target mapping document*, and activity 3 is changed to *revise the ETL process flow*.

Figure 8.24 Selected ETL Design Activities

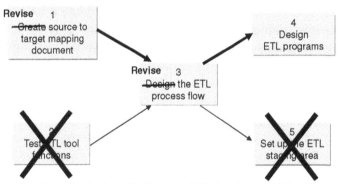

Business Intelligence Roadmap by Larissa T. Moss and Shaku Atre, ©2003. Adapted, printed and electronically reproduced by permission of Pearson Education, Inc., Upper Saddle River, NJ.

The activities selected for the ETL design step are 1, 3, and 4:

1. ~~Create~~ Revise source to target mapping document
2. ~~Test ETL tool functions~~
3. ~~Design~~ Revise the ETL process flow
4. Design ETL programs
5. ~~Set up the ETL staging area~~

ETL DEVELOPMENT

Figure 8.25 illustrates the selected activities for ETL development.

New code modules will be written to extract and transform the 20 data elements from the new source file and other existing ETL code will have to be modified and retested downstream in the ETL process. Therefore activity 1 is changed to *build & modify and unit test the ETL process*. The core team members delete activity 3 because they determine that these 20 new data elements will not significantly increase the size of the database and performance should not be impacted. The activities selected for the ETL development step are 1, 2, 4 and 5:

1. Build & modify and unit test the ETL process
2. Integration and regression test the ETL process
3. ~~Performance test the ETL process~~
4. Quality assurance test the ETL process
5. User acceptance test the ETL process

Figure 8.25 Selected ETL Development Activities

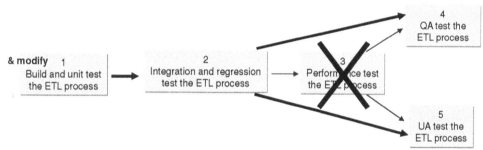

Business Intelligence Roadmap by Larissa T. Moss and Shaku Atre, ©2003. Adapted, printed and electronically reproduced by permission of Pearson Education, Inc., Upper Saddle River, NJ.

IMPLEMENTATION

Figure 8.26 illustrates the selected activities for implementation.

Figure 8.26 Selected Implementation Activities

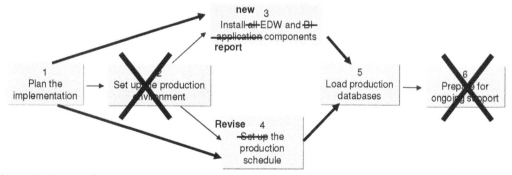

Business Intelligence Roadmap by Larissa T. Moss and Shaku Atre, ©2003. Adapted, printed and electronically reproduced by permission of Pearson Education, Inc., Upper Saddle River, NJ.

Since this is the third release of an application already in production, activities 2 and 6 are deleted. To reflect the fact that new data and new reports are being added, activity 3 is changed to *install new EDW and report components*, and activity 4 is changed to *revise the production schedule*.

The activities selected for the implementation step are 1, 3, 4, and 5:

1. Plan the implementation
2. ~~Set up the production environment~~
3. Install ~~all~~ new EDW and ~~BI application~~ report components
4. ~~Set up~~ Revise the production schedule
5. Load production databases
6. ~~Prepare for ongoing support~~

The changes made to the names of the activities are important because they will guide you in the task selection for these activities and in estimating the work effort. In other words, to match the intended scope of the activities you will select fewer tasks or estimate shorter timeframes for accomplishing the work.

Final Thought

The purpose of this step is to select only those activities that are needed to complete the first (or next) release. The core team members can also drop down another level in the methodology and select the more detailed tasks or even subtasks, if they prefer more details. After crossing out those activities that are not required for the first (or next) release, the remaining activities are used as a checklist to complete the next four steps in the Extreme Scoping planning process. This list of activities is ***not*** used as the final project plan because the selected activities (or tasks and subtasks) can be performed in any order, as many times as needed, and they can be dropped or amended whenever the core team members deem it necessary.

Chapter 9
Self-Organizing Project Teams

Because the scoping of EDW/BI releases are based on the BDTP Balance, it is of vital importance that the core team be made up of people who have the authority to represent the four perspectives of business value, data effort, technical considerations, and project constraints and interdependencies.

Extreme Scoping Project Team Structure

Figure 9.1 illustrates a three-tier project team structure in Extreme Scoping: core team, one or more development track teams, and extended team, in addition to the BI program manager and BI steering committee.

Figure 9.1 Project Team Structure

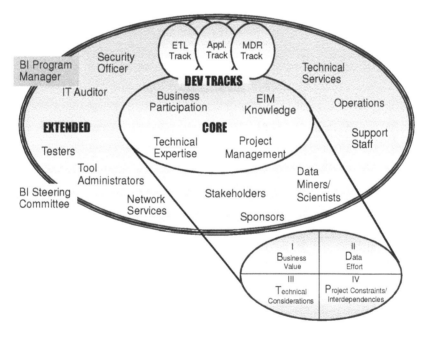

CORE TEAM

All core team members together comprise the project management team, which replaces the single project manager function. The core team members manage all releases of an EDW/BI service request, thus ensuring continuity and knowledge transfer. The core team should be staffed by:

135

- A business representative (user or subject matter expert) who has the authority to make business decisions, set policies, as well as determine and modify the project scope and deliverables.
- An EIM professional like a data administrator or enterprise data modeler who is trained in data administration disciplines, such as logical data modeling (business modeling), normalization rules, data standards (e.g., naming standards, definition standards), data quality management, data governance, etc.
- At least one senior technical person (lead developer, database architect, or technical architect) who has strong coding and technology skills.
- A seasoned project manager or project lead who will be a hands-on trouble shooter and the liaison person to management, other stakeholders, consultants, and vendors.

Core teams are ***self-organizing*** SWAT teams. A SWAT team is usually a "special weapons and tactics" group of highly trained police officers who deal with very challenging criminal situations. I call the core team a SWAT team because it is a group of highly trained EDW and BI professionals who deal with very challenging EDW/BI situations.

On a core team, all members of the team, together as a team, coordinate and assign tasks to each other and to members on the development track teams. They review each other's work, collaborate on project issues, and make project-related decisions. The entire core team meets every day for a status review, and the core team members make project-related decisions and take over each other's tasks when needed; for example, when a team member is out sick. It sounds like management by consensus, and to a degree it is. You are correct if you are thinking that it is rare for a group of people to always agree on everything. In order to avoid gridlock, one person on the team is designated to be the tie-breaker. This is a different person for different types of decisions. If it is a business decision, the business representative wears the lead hat. If it is a data-related decision, the EIM professional has the final say. If it is a technical decision, the senior technical person on the team makes it. If it is a project-related decision, the project manager is the tie breaker.

The core team must be very small; a team size of three to five people per project is optimal. Sometimes the EIM professional or a technical lead doubles as the project manager. Other times the technical leads from several development tracks are included in the core team. The makeup of the core team is entirely up to the program manager and the core team members themselves, as long as the core team does not exceed seven people.

DEVELOPMENT TRACK TEAMS

Development track teams are extensions or nodes of the core team. I jokingly call them the "polyps" of the core team because they are so tightly attached to the core team. The most common development tracks are back-end ETL development, front-end BI application development, and metadata repository. If metadata is not a deliverable, then at least two development track teams work in parallel, namely ETL development and BI application development. On the other hand, there could also be more than three development track teams, such as an additional data mining team or a permanent scouting team. The core team members organize the project in the most optimal way, and they may, at times, assemble two ETL track teams to work in parallel on the same release, as long as the two teams are not working on the same ETL code at the same time.

The development track teams are led by the technical expert from the core team, which could be the person who plays the role of ETL architect, database architect, or BI application lead, depending on how the core team is staffed. Alternatively, you may choose to have each development track team be led by a different track expert, if that better supports your organization and if you have the resources. In that case, the leads from all development track teams would represent the technical expertise on the core team. If you have a data mining track team, it is led by the data mining expert, and a permanent scouting team is led by an EIM professional, such as a data administrator, an enterprise data modeler, or a data quality analyst.

Development track team members are primarily developers or senior systems analysts who have the skills needed for their particular track. They only participate in track-specific tasks for the duration of their track activities. They do **not** participate in making day-to-day general project-related decisions, unless the decisions involve their own track.

A development track team is even smaller than a core team; a team size of two to three people per track/per project is optimal. Since most development track teams are coding teams, their team size should never exceed five people per track/per project.

EXTENDED TEAM

The extended team members play traditional roles and participate on the EDW/BI projects on an as-needed and as-scheduled basis, not on a full-time or daily basis. Members of the extended team may be heavily involved only at certain times during the project, or they may be called on intermittently for their expertise and contributions. Extended team members include technicians and business people who contribute in much the same way they do on operational system development projects. Extended teams include support roles such as technical support, operations, security officer, IT auditor, the sponsors, and other stakeholders.

The core team, the development track teams, and the extended team make up the complete project team structure.

BI PROGRAM MANAGER

The EDW/BI program management office is led by a BI program manager (director) who works directly with – if not for – the BI steering committee. If the company has a chief data officer (CDO), the BI program manager reports to the CDO.

The BI program manager periodically surveys the business community to measure the BI maturity level of the organization, to identify general information needs in all lines of business, and to find out if users like the EDW/BI environment. The BI program manager creates a strategy for the EDW/BI environment and ensures that the EDW/BI project teams adhere to the common architectural components in this environment. He or she also assists the BI steering committee to prioritize EDW/BI projects by making them aware of project interdependencies. The BI program manager also coordinates the project resources and sometimes the project activities.

BI STEERING COMMITTEE

A steering committee is an advisory body of business executives and senior business managers, who understand enterprise-class initiatives, such as EDW/BI, MDM, CRM, CDI, and so on. The BI steering committee is a group of business executives who provide collective sponsorship for EDW/BI projects specifically. The sponsors meet on a regular basis to discuss, plan, prioritize, staff, and fund EDW/BI projects. They also support enterprise-wide activities by funding an EIM group. They direct the business managers to adopt a cross-functional development approach and to identify data owners in their line of business. The BI steering committee is the ultimate tie breaker for BI-related disputes among business people.

Team Dynamics

The team dynamics are completely different in a self-organizing project team than they are in a traditional project team. The interaction and communication among the core team members and among the development track team members are not the same as the interaction and communication with the extended team members.

CORE TEAM DYNAMICS

Although the core team members have their assigned cubicles and offices, they do not spend most of their time in them. Instead, they collaborate, brainstorm, solve problems, and make decisions together in a "war room" dedicated to their project. If you saw the movie Apollo 13, think of the core team as being similar to the SWAT team at the National Aeronautics and Space Administration (NASA) in Houston, Texas. When the oxygen tank exploded on the Apollo 13 spacecraft, crippling the service module on which the command module depended, the lives of the astronauts were put in danger. The mission manager did not decide what to do or assign tasks to the ground crew to solve the problem. Instead, the ground crew huddled together with the mission manager in a "war room," bringing to bear their collective expertise to save the astronauts. They collaborated, brainstormed, and experimented with copies of items known to be on the spacecraft until they managed to jury-rig a carbon dioxide removal system that saved the astronauts.

The EDW/BI core team functions in a similar way to NASA. For example, the core team meets every day to review status and deliverables and to discuss roadblocks and solutions. Sometimes these meetings last ten minutes; other times working sessions could be scheduled for half a day to solve a critical problem. During these sessions, individual assignments are distributed to the appropriate team members on either the core team or one of the development track teams. The team members work on the assignments right after the meeting and report back the following day.

If a major roadblock is encountered, the core team members decide whether to solve it immediately, take the requirements affected by the roadblock out of scope, consider alternative solutions, or execute a contingency plan. If their decision affects the release deadline, the core team members must decide whether or not time lost in this release can be recovered in future releases. If the answer is no, and if the requirements affected by the roadblock cannot be permanently dropped from the service request, the project manager and the business representative must take the issue to the BI steering committee for a decision to extend the final project deadline. The core team members cannot make that decision themselves, because extending the final deadline affects other business people who are waiting in the queue with their EDW/BI service requests.

DEVELOPMENT TRACK TEAM DYNAMICS

The development track teams function similarly to the core team, only on a smaller scale. The development track team members also meet every day to review the status and deliverables within their own track. They collaborate, brainstorm, solve problems, and make decisions together on their track-specific issues. In fact, some development track teams function similar to Scrum and XP teams because their members are developers whose primary job is to write code using the prototyping approach where the activities of analysis, design, coding, and testing are merged into one.

Communication with the core team is automatically established through the technical expert on the core team, which could be the ETL architect, database architect, or BI application lead who is managing the development track teams.

EXTENDED TEAM DYNAMICS

In general, the extended team meets with the core team once a week, usually on the same day and same time of the week. The core team members set up the meeting schedule at the beginning of the project, and the sponsor sends out the notification to the extended team members. The meetings are scheduled for thirty minutes, but could be as short as ten minutes if no major issues are to be discussed. The purpose of the weekly meetings is to keep all extended team members current with activities, status, and issues of the project. It also serves as a forum for face-to-face interactions and exchanges between extended team members and core team members.

When members of the extended team are scheduled or called as needed to participate on project activities, they temporarily become part of that development track team for the duration of their participation.

Roles and Responsibilities

So far, we have discussed the project team structure and the team dynamics in terms of interaction and communication. In this section, we will look at the roles and responsibilities assigned to the core team members, the development track team members, and the extended team members.

CORE TEAM ROLES

There are a number of roles that are played by the members of a core team. Which specific role is applicable to a project depends on the scope of the work and the type of deliverable. Roles do ***not*** equate one-for-one to people. A person can, and probably will, play multiple roles in most organizations. For example, the database architect could double as the BI infrastructure architect, or the business representative could double as the subject matter expert, etc. Occasionally one role can also be played by multiple people. For example, a project with hundreds of new source data elements may require two EIM professionals to split the work of profiling, analyzing, modeling, standardizing, cleansing, and transforming the source data.

Some roles are IT roles, while other roles are business roles. Note that at least one business person should be an active full-time participant on the project (if possible) who will perform project activities. You might doubt that a business person can perform project activities. Not to worry, because nobody works alone. Instead, two people always share responsibility for work artifacts. The idea is very similar to pair-programming in Scrum and XP, only it is applied to all roles and not just developers. For example, the business representative teams up with the data administrator during data modeling activities, or the data administrator teams up with the database architect during database design, or the subject matter expert teams up with the ETL developer during ETL testing, and so on.

BI Application Lead (BI Solution Architect)

The application lead role is responsible for designing and delivering the front-end BI application, as well as the reports and queries. The application lead manages and mentors the other BI application developers on the project, and writes and tests the more complex code modules. This person could be in the role of technical expert on the core team.

BI Infrastructure Architect

The BI infrastructure architect role is responsible for the technical infrastructure components (configuration management), such as hardware, system software, tools, and network components. The infrastructure architect aligns the technical infrastructure components with the overall strategic IT infrastructure of the company. The architect also participates in the evaluation, selection, installation, and testing of purchased products (e.g., OLAP tool or report writer). He or she also monitors all platform components for usage, trends, and performance.

Business Representative

The business representative is the primary business person on the project. This person must be familiar with the requirements, as well as with the business policies and business rules. This can be a user, a business liaison, a subject matter expert, or a data steward, as long as this person is given the authority to make decisions about the data and the project requirements. The business representative should participate in the planning, business analysis, especially logical (business) data modeling, and prototyping activities, as well as in most testing activities.

Data Administrator

The data administrator role is the primary EIM role. This person is responsible for data standardization, data integration, logical data modeling, and normalization. Data administration is a cross-functional data governance function, and it is not to be confused with database administration, which is a technical function. To be clear, data administrators are trained in modeling the business, while database administrators (architects) are trained in modeling databases. Data administration is also known as data resource management, information resource management, enterprise information architecture, and enterprise information management (EIM).

Data Quality Analyst

The data quality analyst role is responsible for bottom-up source data analysis, finding the dirty data, and writing the data cleansing specifications. This person must have a technical background and must be able to easily navigate through the operational source systems, get data dumps, use a data profiling and data cleansing tool, and write simple reports. The data quality analyst must also have a good rapport with business people and with the operational IT staff. A data quality analyst is usually part of the EIM group.

Database Designer/Architect (DBA)

The traditional responsibility given to the DBA role is to maintain databases (e.g., take backups, perform database reorganizations, tune the databases, etc.). Many companies separate the important activity of designing the EDW target databases into a new role called database designer or database architect. This role also monitors and tunes the EDW target databases. This person could be in the role of technical expert on the core team.

> Sometimes the term *data architect* is used for this role. However, the term *database architect* is more accurate because the term data architect also refers to data administrators – and has for many decades. We must be careful not to create homonyms with our own terminology! After all, we are in the data management business.

ETL Architect

The ETL architect role is responsible for designing and delivering the back-end ETL process. The ETL architect manages and mentors the other ETL developers on the project, and writes and tests the complex ETL code modules. The architect also works closely with the database architect to create the ETL process flow. This person could be in the role of technical expert on the core team.

Metadata Administrator

The metadata administrator role is responsible for creating, loading, and maintaining the metadata repository. This person works closely with the ETL architect to capture load statistics, data quality statistics, and reconciliation totals (tallies) produced by the ETL process during the initial, historical, and incremental database loads. The metadata administrator also extracts, links (relates), and loads metadata from various metadata sources, such as the modeling tool, ETL tool, OLAP tool, DBMS system tables, EXCEL macros, and so on. This person is usually part of the EIM group.

Project Manager

As a member of the core team, the project manager role is responsible for enabling the core team and the development track teams to work on project activities with minimum interruptions. The project manager has to negotiate with the sponsor, report progress of the project to stakeholders, negotiate with vendors, resolve technical issues, and help with project activities wherever needed.

> This role is different from the traditional project manager role. Traditionally, a person with this title has a window office and manages several projects at a time – or more accurately, the staff of several projects report to this person. The traditional project manager is in meetings all day long and is occupied with administrative tasks, such as creating budgets, writing performance appraisals, etc. In my view, this position should be called project administrator, not project manager.
>
> The role of a project manager in Extreme Scoping is to be a hands-on, roll-up-the-sleeves trouble shooter and negotiator who works on project activities full-time every day and has no administrative duties. The primary task of this project manager is to shield the team members from all interference and to help them with their work in any way possible. If you have a different title for this position in your company, such as project lead, then use that title instead to avoid confusion.

Subject Matter Expert

The subject matter expert role provides in-depth business knowledge for a subject area or business domain, and participates in planning, business analysis, design, and testing activities. This is often staffed by a senior business analyst or a business liaison person who has a cross-functional view over many departments. Sometimes, this person is the lead data steward of the business domain. The subject matter expert can also help facilitate the resolution of data disputes among the business units.

DEVELOPMENT TRACK TEAM ROLES

The roles played on the development track teams are mostly technical roles specific to a track. Which specific role is applicable to a project depends on the scope of the work and the type of deliverable. As I mentioned earlier, the typical development tracks include back-end ETL, front-end BI application, and metadata repository. Depending on your project organization and available resources, one person may play multiple roles or one role can be assigned to multiple people.

BI Application Developer

Additional BI application developers join the project during the application prototyping, construction, and testing periods. They work under the direction of the BI application lead or whatever technical expert represents them on the core team. They are responsible for building the BI deliverables, such as reports, queries, scorecards, dashboards, BI applications, front-end portals, and so on.

ETL Developer

Additional ETL developers join the project during the ETL construction and testing periods. They work under the direction of the ETL architect or whatever technical expert represents them on the core team. They are responsible for building and maintaining the extract, transform, and load processes. ETL developers work closely with the metadata repository developers to collect and store load statistics, data quality statistics, and reconciliation totals.

Metadata Repository Developer

Additional metadata repository developers may join the project during the metadata repository construction and testing periods. They work under the direction of the metadata administrator. They build and maintain the metadata repository solution. They extract metadata from the various tools where it is collected. They link the business metadata with the technical metadata, process metadata, and usage metadata. They provide access to the metadata in the metadata repository to technicians, as well as to business people.

EXTENDED TEAM ROLES

Members of the extended team play a number of different roles. Again, which specific role will participate on a project depends on the scope of the work and the type of deliverable. Extended team roles usually equate one-to-one to a person.

Data Scientist

Data scientists are high-ranking professionals with the training to make discoveries in the world of big data analytics. Their skill set includes the ability to find and interpret big data, to manage large amounts of data despite hardware, software, and bandwidth constraints, to create visualizations to aid in understanding the data, and to build tools that enable others to work with the data. Data scientists should not be confused with EIM professionals. EIM professionals help define and prepare the data; data scientists use that data.

Data Miner

Data miners are usually statisticians who utilize methods of artificial intelligence, machine learning, statistics, and database systems to discover patterns in large datasets. Their skill set includes preprocessing the data, building analytical data models, interpreting data mining results, and creating visualizations to convey these results to business managers and executives. Data miners should also not be confused with EIM professionals. EIM professionals help define and prepare the data; data miners use that data.

IT Auditor or QA Analyst

IT auditors or QA analysts are tasked with identifying the risks and exposures of EDW/BI projects. Their skill set includes understanding the technology and SDLC methodology, as well as knowing the difference between operational systems and EDW/BI environments. Their audits determine if the new systems are safeguarding assets, maintaining data integrity, and operating effectively to achieve the organization's goals and objectives.

> It is imperative that auditors learn about agile methodologies and participate in the weekly review meetings. Auditors can no longer show up at the end of each phase with their book of tabs and look for traditional documentation inserted behind each tab. Agile projects are incongruent with traditional auditing methods.

Network Services

Network services staff members are responsible for installing, maintaining, and supporting computer communication networks within an organization or between organizations. Their skill set must include knowledge of local area networks (LAN), wide area networks (WAN), and global area networks (GAN). They manage email, anti-spam and virus protections, set up user accounts and passwords, and monitor network usage.

Operations

Operations staff members are responsible for running the scheduled EDW/BI application jobs, including the periodic ETL load cycles, as well as canned queries and reports. They maintain accurate IT asset inventories and up-to-date systems and operations documentation. They monitor, evaluate, and manage all system software, service pack updates, operating systems, and management tools.

Security Officer

Security officers are responsible for maintaining security and establishing external barriers such as firewalls and other security measures. Additionally, they review systems in order to identify potential security and privacy weaknesses, recommend improvements to reduce vulnerabilities, implement changes, and document upgrades.

Sponsors

Executive business sponsors on the BI steering committee spearhead the BI initiative and approve the direction and changes of the initiative. They evaluate EDW/BI service requests for their business value and prioritize EDW/BI projects accordingly. They are the ultimate tie breakers in disputes among business units.

Stakeholders

Stakeholders are individuals who are not directly involved with the EDW/BI project, but who are impacted by or interested in the EDW/BI project for their own current or future plans to participate in the organization's BI initiative. Stakeholders may be invited to attend post-implementation reviews, but they do not actively participate.

Support Staff (Helpdesk)

User support can be in the form of hotline trouble-shooting personnel or an individual designated to mentor the users. The support staff is responsible for diagnosing and resolving technical problems in a timely manner. They advise users on appropriate action. If they cannot help a user, they redirect the problem to an appropriate resource.

Technical Services

Technical services staff is responsible for preparing, testing, setting up, managing, and maintaining the technology platform components. They diagnose and resolve technical hardware and software issues.

Testers

Additional testers participate during system or integration testing, regression testing, and performance or stress testing activities. They create and execute test plans and scripts that will determine if a deliverable meets user requirements and functionality as designed.

Tool Administrator

Tool administrators are charged with evaluating, installing, testing, and maintaining developer tools (e.g., data modeling tool, data profiling tool, ETL tool) and BI tools (OLAP tool, report writer, query tool, dashboards, data mining tool).

Final Thought

You cannot go agile with your EDW/BI projects without converting your traditionally-organized project teams into self-organizing SWAT teams. The key is to keep your project teams small. The core team members collectively assume the project management role and perform project management activities together. Be sure there is a business representative on the core team. The core team members assign the various core team roles and responsibilities to each other and to those development track team members who have the most appropriate skills to play those roles. Your development track teams can have as few as one developer on each team (per project) or as many as three or four. Include the extended team members on your project on an as-needed and as-scheduled basis. And finally, be sure your teams are allowed to be self-organizing. That means they have the authority to create their own project plans, organize their own work, drop activities if they discover the activities are of no value, and repeat activities as often as they feel is necessary. Most importantly, shield the project teams from constant interruptions from users and IT managers, as well as administrative meetings.

Chapter 10
Staffing the Teams

Once the project activities for the first release are thoroughly understood, the core team members proceed to step four of the Extreme Scoping planning process, shown in Figure 10.1.

Figure 10.1 Extreme Scoping Step 4

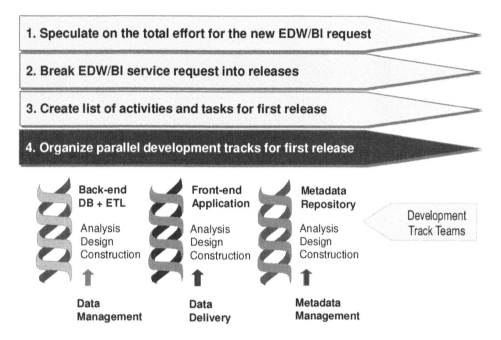

They self-organize into the appropriate number of development track teams or work groups. They also assign additional resources to the development track teams as needed. While all core team members are involved in all release activities, most development track team members only participate during the engineering stages of business analysis, design, and construction, as illustrated in Figure 10.2. Remember that one or more technical leads are part of the core team. They lead the development track teams, and they represent the development track teams on the core team.

Development track activities diverge significantly in terms of duration, repetition, and work organization for different tracks. The ETL team may spend more time on architecture before diving into coding the ETL processes, while the BI application team may combine the activities of functional analysis, design, and construction into one prototyping activity and execute that activity repeatedly.

Figure 10.2 Parallel Development Tracks

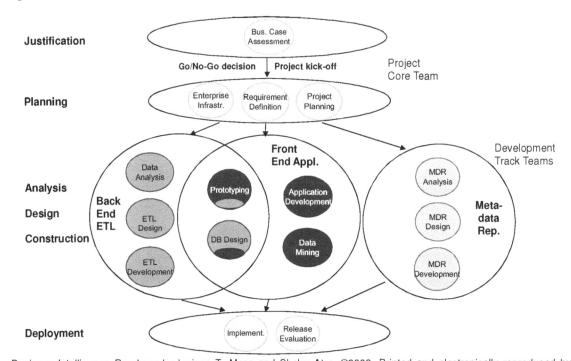

Business Intelligence Roadmap by Larissa T. Moss and Shaku Atre, ©2003. Printed and electronically reproduced by permission of Pearson Education, Inc., Upper Saddle River, NJ

The metadata repository track may be organized as a separate project, or it may simply involve buying and installing a metadata repository product. Some development tracks may start their work activities on a release earlier than others, but all tracks have to end by the same time for implementation.

EDW/BI Development Step Roles

The core team members discuss and choose only the roles of those development steps that apply to their first (or next) release. However, I will list all roles for all of the sixteen development steps in the Business Intelligence Roadmap methodology, which I am using again as an example. I will also indicate which role has the authority to make the final decision or be a tie breaker, when there is a dispute among core team members. In addition, I will point out the most significant BDTP Balance perspectives that apply to each development step.

BUSINESS CASE ASSESSMENT

The main roles participating in business case assessment are the business representative, the project manager, the sponsor, and potentially a subject matter expert and/or data quality analyst, as shown in Figure 10.3.

Figure 10.3 Business Case Assessment Roles

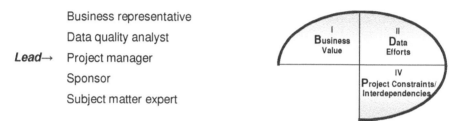

Business representative
Data quality analyst
Lead→   Project manager
Sponsor
Subject matter expert

Business Intelligence Roadmap by Larissa T. Moss and Shaku Atre, ©2003. Adapted, printed and electronically reproduced by permission of Pearson Education, Inc., Upper Saddle River, NJ

The business representative and project manager compile and process the information to produce the report. The subject matter expert and data quality analyst help research the current decision-support system solutions, the current data sources, and the current processes. The sponsor is the person who is the primary recipient of the report.

The project manager makes the final decision in case of a dispute. The main BDTP Balance perspectives for this step are business value, data effort, and project constraints and interdependencies.

ENTERPRISE INFRASTRUCTURE EVALUATION

As I stated previously, enterprise infrastructure evaluation has two components: technical infrastructure and non-technical infrastructure.

Technical Infrastructure Evaluation

The main roles participating in technical infrastructure evaluation are the BI infrastructure architect, the business representative, and potentially a database architect and/or tool administrator, as shown in Figure 10.4.

The BI infrastructure architect keeps up with the newest products and technologies in the EDW/BI space. The architect is assisted by the tool administrator or database architect, depending on what type of tool or DBMS is being evaluated. The business representative should always be involved in the selection of BI tools.

Figure 10.4 Technical Infrastructure Evaluation Roles

Lead→ BI infrastructure architect

Business representative

Database architect

Tool administrator

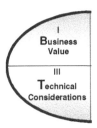

The BI infrastructure architect makes the final decision in case of a dispute. The main BDTP Balance perspectives for this step are business value and technical considerations.

Non-Technical Infrastructure Evaluation

The main roles participating in non-technical infrastructure evaluation are the business representative, the data administrator, and potentially the data quality analyst and/or metadata administrator, as shown in Figure 10.5.

Figure 10.5 Non-Technical Infrastructure Evaluation Roles

Business representative

Lead→ Data administrator

Data quality analyst

Metadata administrator

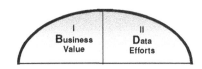

The data administrator works with the business representative to define the standards, procedures, processes, and guidelines for the organization. They are assisted by the data quality analyst and/or the metadata administrator, depending on what type of non-technical infrastructure components are being evaluated. Note that the business representative should always be involved in shaping the non-technical infrastructure because it pertains to standardizing the business data, as well as the development process.

The data administrator makes the final decision in case of a dispute. The main BDTP Balance perspectives for this step are business value and data effort.

REQUIREMENTS DEFINITION

The main roles participating in requirements definition are the BI application lead, the business representative, the data administrator, the data quality analyst, the metadata administrator, a subject matter expert, and potentially, the ETL architect, as shown in Figure 10.6.

Figure 10.6 Requirements Definition Roles

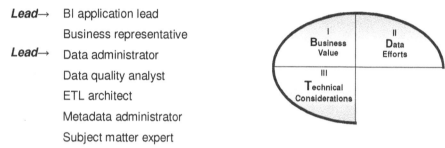

Lead→ BI application lead
Business representative
Lead→ Data administrator
Data quality analyst
ETL architect
Metadata administrator
Subject matter expert

Business Intelligence Roadmap by Larissa T. Moss and Shaku Atre, ©2003. Adapted, printed and electronically reproduced by permission of Pearson Education, Inc., Upper Saddle River, NJ

The BI application lead puts together the functional requirements. The data administrator and data quality analyst, in consultation with the ETL architect, compile the data requirements, and the metadata administrator prepares the metadata repository requirements. The business representative and the subject matter expert are assisting all of the technicians with gathering their respective requirements.

The authority to be the tie breaker for requirements definition is usually divided between the BI application lead for the functional requirements and the data administrator for the data and metadata requirements. The main BDTP Balance perspectives for this step are business value, data effort, and technical considerations.

PROJECT PLANNING

The main roles participating in project planning are all ten core team roles, as shown in Figure 10.7. That includes the BI application lead, the BI infrastructure architect, the business representative, the data administrator, the data quality analyst, the database architect, the ETL architect, the metadata administrator, the project manager, and potentially, a subject matter expert.

The entire core team (collectively) is responsible for planning the project, not just the project manager. The business representative and the subject matter expert assist the technicians in creating realistic estimates, or at least validate their estimates based on the business knowledge they have.

Figure 10.7 Project Planning Roles

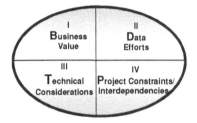

BI application lead

BI infrastructure architect

Business representative

Data administrator

Data quality analyst

Database architect

ETL architect

Metadata administrator

Lead→ Project manager

Subject matter expert

Business Intelligence Roadmap by Larissa T. Moss and Shaku Atre, ©2003. Adapted, printed and electronically reproduced by permission of Pearson Education, Inc., Upper Saddle River, NJ

The project manager makes the final decision in case of a dispute. The main BDTP Balance perspectives for this step are business value, data effort, technical considerations, and project constraints and interdependencies.

DATA ANALYSIS

The main roles participating in data analysis are the business representative, the data administrator, the data quality analyst, the database architect, the ETL architect, the metadata administrator, a subject matter expert, and potentially other stakeholders, as shown in Figure 10.8.

Figure 10.8 Data Analysis Roles

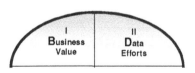

Business representative

Lead→ Data administrator

Data quality analyst

Database architect

ETL architect

Metadata administrator

Stakeholders

Subject matter expert

Business Intelligence Roadmap by Larissa T. Moss and Shaku Atre, ©2003. Adapted, printed and electronically reproduced by permission of Pearson Education, Inc., Upper Saddle River, NJ

The lead role for data analysis is always the data administrator, who is an EIM professional trained in logical data modeling, business metadata standards, normalization techniques, data domain rules, data integrity rules, and standardization methods. While the data administrator facilitates the top-down modeling sessions, the data quality analyst performs the bottom-up source data analysis. Both are assisted by the business representative and the subject matter expert. Other stakeholders, such as data owners, data stewards, information consumers, and data originators, are involved if their data is in the scope of the release.

The database architect and ETL architect should be involved in the logical data modeling reviews and must understand the complexity of cleansing the data because the cleansing algorithms must be incorporated into the ETL process. The metadata administrator needs to know what business metadata components are being collected because he or she has to extract the business metadata from the modeling tool and load it into the metadata repository.

The data administrator makes the final decision in case of a dispute. The main BDTP Balance perspectives for this step are business value and data effort.

APPLICATION PROTOTYPING

The main roles participating in application prototyping are the BI application lead, the business representative, the database architect, a subject matter expert, and potentially, additional BI application developers and other stakeholders, as shown in Figure 10.9.

Figure 10.9 Application Prototyping Roles

Lead→   BI application lead
BI application developers
Business representative
Database architect
Stakeholders
Subject matter expert

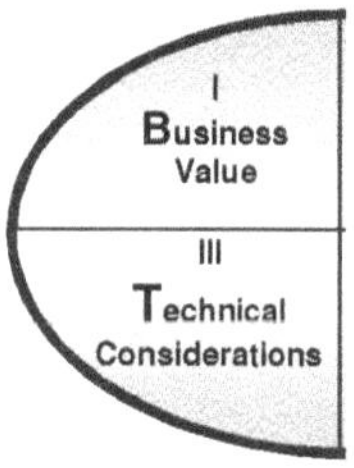

Business Intelligence Roadmap by Larissa T. Moss and Shaku Atre, ©2003. Adapted, printed and electronically reproduced by permission of Pearson Education, Inc., Upper Saddle River, NJ

The BI application lead is always assisted by the database architect to create the prototype database. Additional BI application developers may participate on an as needed basis. The business representative and a subject matter expert participate in the prototyping activities and in the prototype demonstrations to other stakeholders.

The BI application lead makes the final decision in case of a dispute. The main BDTP Balance perspectives for this step are business value and technical considerations.

METADATA REPOSITORY ANALYSIS

The main roles participating in metadata repository analysis are the business representative, the data administrator, the metadata administrator, and potentially a subject matter expert, as shown in Figure 10.10.

Figure 10.10 Metadata Repository Analysis Roles

Business representative
Data administrator
Lead→ Metadata administrator
Subject matter expert

I Business Value	II Data Efforts

Business Intelligence Roadmap by Larissa T. Moss and Shaku Atre, ©2003. Adapted, printed and electronically reproduced by permission of Pearson Education, Inc., Upper Saddle River, NJ

The metadata administrator always collaborates with the data administrator. The business representative, and maybe a subject matter expert, contribute their business knowledge and opinions in terms of metadata scope, metadata access, and metadata priorities.

The metadata administrator makes the final decision in case of a dispute. The main BDTP Balance perspectives for this step are business value and data effort.

DATABASE DESIGN

The main roles participating in database design are the BI application lead, the data administrator, the database architect, and the ETL architect, as shown in Figure 10.11.

Figure 10.11 Database Design Roles

BI application lead
Data administrator
Lead→ Database architect
ETL architect

Business Intelligence Roadmap by Larissa T. Moss and Shaku Atre, ©2003. Adapted, printed and electronically reproduced by permission of Pearson Education, Inc., Upper Saddle River, NJ

The database architect must be trained in designing the various types of EDW target databases. It is his or her responsibility to create the physical data models and subsequently, the physical database structures. The database architect works closely with the BI application lead, the ETL architect, and the data administrator.

> Designing and tuning EDW target databases is a highly specialized skill that requires extensive knowledge of how a DBMS engine functions internally. That is why companies hire database architects who have the specialized training and experience with their DBMS. Unfortunately, sometimes I see the BI application lead, ETL architect, data administrator, or even the user design the EDW target databases, and they design them poorly. This could have a catastrophic effect on performance. Therefore, the BI application lead, ETL architect, data administrator, or user should not be designing databases unless they have the required training and experience to do so, *and* there is no database person with the necessary skill set.

The database architect makes the final decision in case of a dispute. The main BDTP Balance perspectives for this step are data effort and technical considerations.

ETL DESIGN

The main roles participating in ETL design are the data quality analyst, the database architect, the ETL architect, and potentially, a subject matter expert, as shown in Figure 10.12.

Figure 10.12 ETL Design Roles

```
              Data quality analyst
              Database architect
    Lead→     ETL architect
              Subject matter expert
```

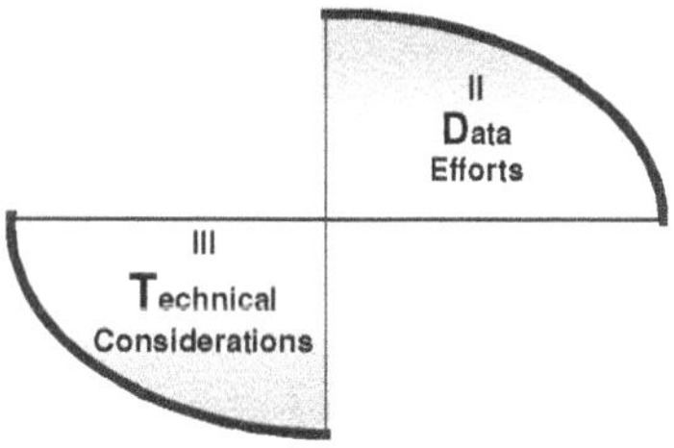

Business Intelligence Roadmap by Larissa T. Moss and Shaku Atre, ©2003. Adapted, printed and electronically reproduced by permission of Pearson Education, Inc., Upper Saddle River, NJ

The ETL architect is heavily assisted by the database architect, especially during the design of the ETL process flow. In addition, the ETL architect will get assistance from the data quality analyst, and maybe a subject matter expert, in regard to the data cleansing specifications.

The ETL architect makes the final decision in case of a dispute. The main BDTP Balance perspectives for this step are data effort and technical considerations.

METADATA REPOSITORY DESIGN

The main roles participating in metadata repository design are the data administrator, the database architect, the metadata administrator, and potentially, the BI infrastructure architect, as shown in Figure 10.13.

Figure 10.13 Metadata Repository Design Roles

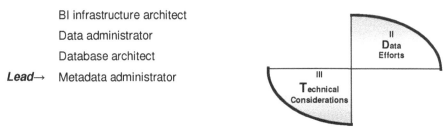

BI infrastructure architect
Data administrator
Database architect
Lead→ Metadata administrator

Business Intelligence Roadmap by Larissa T. Moss and Shaku Atre, ©2003. Adapted, printed and electronically reproduced by permission of Pearson Education, Inc., Upper Saddle River, NJ

The metadata administrator designs the metadata repository and its migration and application programs, unless the company chooses to buy a metadata repository product. In that case, the metadata administrator works with the BI infrastructure architect to evaluate, select, purchase, install, and test the metadata repository product.

The metadata administrator works closely with the database architect who creates the DDL and DCL statements for the metadata repository database. The metadata administrator collaborates with the data administrator on EIM topics, such as data standards, business metadata, the project-specific logical data models, and the enterprise data model.

The metadata administrator makes the final decision in case of a dispute. The main BDTP Balance perspectives for this step are data effort and technical considerations.

ETL DEVELOPMENT

The main roles participating in ETL development are the business representative, the database architect, the ETL architect, a subject matter expert, and potentially, additional ETL developers and/or additional testers, as shown in Figure 10.14.

ETL developers on the ETL development track team work under the supervision of the ETL architect. The database architect reviews and assists with the database calls in the ETL code. The testers (from the extended team), the subject matter expert, and the business representative all participate in the end-to-end testing activities, which include integration testing, regression testing, performance testing, QA testing, and UA testing.

Figure 10.14 ETL Development Roles

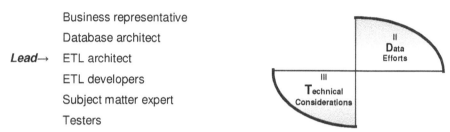

Business representative
Database architect
Lead→ ETL architect
ETL developers
Subject matter expert
Testers

Business Intelligence Roadmap by Larissa T. Moss and Shaku Atre, ©2003. Adapted, printed and electronically reproduced by permission of Pearson Education, Inc., Upper Saddle River, NJ

The ETL architect makes the final decision in case of a dispute. The main BDTP Balance perspectives for this step are data effort and technical considerations.

APPLICATION DEVELOPMENT

The main roles participating in application development are the BI application lead, the business representative, the database architect, a subject matter expert, and potentially, additional BI application developers and/or additional testers, as shown in Figure 10.15.

Figure 10.15 Application Development Roles

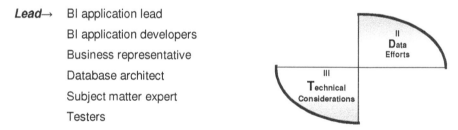

Lead→ BI application lead
BI application developers
Business representative
Database architect
Subject matter expert
Testers

Business Intelligence Roadmap by Larissa T. Moss and Shaku Atre, ©2003. Adapted, printed and electronically reproduced by permission of Pearson Education, Inc., Upper Saddle River, NJ

BI application developers on the BI application development track team work under the supervision of the BI application lead. The database architect reviews and assists with the database calls in the application code. The testers (from the extended team), the subject matter expert, and the business representative all participate in the end-to-end testing activities, which include integration testing, regression testing, performance testing, QA testing, and UA testing.

The BI application lead makes the final decision in case of a dispute. The main BDTP Balance perspectives for this step are data effort and technical considerations.

DATA MINING

The main roles participating in data mining are the business representative, the database architect, the data mining expert, and potentially, a subject matter expert, as shown in Figure 10.16.

Figure 10.16 Data Mining Roles

Business representative
Database architect
Lead→ Data mining expert (statistician)
Subject matter expert

Business Intelligence Roadmap by Larissa T. Moss and Shaku Atre, ©2003. Adapted, printed and electronically reproduced by permission of Pearson Education, Inc., Upper Saddle River, NJ

The lead role for data mining is always the data mining expert, who has a statistical background. The statistician is assisted by the database architect who will build the data mining database. The business representative, and maybe a subject matter expert, helps the data mining expert with identifying, retrieving, cleansing, and preparing the necessary data for the data mining database.

The data mining expert makes the final decision in case of a dispute. The main BDTP Balance perspectives for this step are business value, data effort, and technical considerations.

METADATA REPOSITORY DEVELOPMENT

The main roles participating in metadata repository development are the business representative, the database architect, the metadata administrator, and potentially, additional metadata repository developers, a subject matter expert, and/or additional testers, as shown in Figure 10.17.

Metadata repository developers on the metadata repository development track team work under the supervision of the metadata administrator. The database architect creates the metadata repository database and assists with the database calls in the metadata repository migration and application programs. The metadata administrator, the business representative, and maybe a subject matter expert and/or testers (from the extended team) all participate in the end-to-end testing activities, which include integration testing, regression testing, and UA testing. If the metadata repository is moved into the production environment, QA testing also applies.

Figure 10.17 Metadata Repository Development Roles

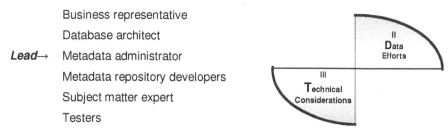

Business representative

Database architect

Lead→ Metadata administrator

Metadata repository developers

Subject matter expert

Testers

Business Intelligence Roadmap by Larissa T. Moss and Shaku Atre, ©2003. Adapted, printed and electronically reproduced by permission of Pearson Education, Inc., Upper Saddle River, NJ

The metadata administrator makes the final decision in case of a dispute. The main BDTP Balance perspectives for this step are data effort and technical considerations.

IMPLEMENTATION

The main roles participating in implementation are the BI application lead, the database architect, the ETL architect, and potentially, the data mining expert and the metadata administrator, as shown in Figure 10.18.

Figure 10.18 Implementation Roles

Lead→ BI application lead

Data mining expert

Database architect

Lead→ ETL architect

Metadata administrator

Business Intelligence Roadmap by Larissa T. Moss and Shaku Atre, ©2003. Adapted, printed and electronically reproduced by permission of Pearson Education, Inc., Upper Saddle River, NJ

The BI application lead, the ETL architect, and the database architect share the main responsibilities for going into production. If the deliverable includes data mining, the data mining expert participates in implementation activities for the data mining portion. If the metadata repository is moved into production, the metadata administrator is involved in implementing the metadata repository components. The other developers from the BI application development track, the ETL development track, and the metadata repository track may assist their technical leads during implementation.

The authority to be the tie breaker for implementation is usually divided between the BI application lead for the BI application and reports, and the ETL architect for the ETL process. The main BDTP Balance perspectives for this step are data effort and technical considerations.

RELEASE EVALUATION

The main roles participating in release evaluation are all ten core team roles, especially the project manager, as well as all development track team roles and all applicable extended team roles, especially the sponsor, as shown in Figure 10.19. It is also a good idea to have a third-party facilitator lead the meeting and a third-party "scribe" (documenter) keep a record of the discussions. These two additional roles should be assigned to individuals who did **not** participate on the project.

Figure 10.19 Release Evaluation Roles

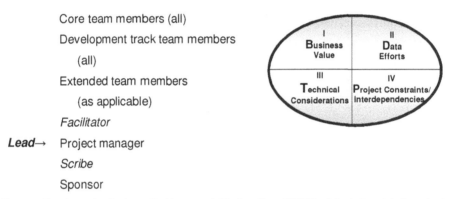

Core team members (all)

Development track team members
   (all)

Extended team members
   (as applicable)

Facilitator

Lead→   Project manager

Scribe

Sponsor

Business Intelligence Roadmap by Larissa T. Moss and Shaku Atre, ©2003. Adapted, printed and electronically reproduced by permission of Pearson Education, Inc., Upper Saddle River, NJ

The sponsor opens the meeting and gives a short introduction before turning the meeting over to the project manager. The project manager discusses the flow, the rules, and the expectations of the review before turning the meeting over to a skilled facilitator. The facilitator leads the group through the topics on the agenda and monitors the allocated time for each topic. The scribe documents the discussions and identified action items. At the end of the session, the sponsor closes the meeting. A nice touch to release evaluation meetings is to provide cookies or ice cream to all the participants.

The project manager makes the final decision in case of a dispute. The main BDTP Balance perspectives for this step are business value, data effort, technical considerations, and project constraints and interdependencies.

Completing the Fourth Step

At the beginning of a project, the BI program manager assembles the best qualified resources available for the core team, using the aforementioned guidelines for roles and responsibilities, and considering the BDTP Balance for each of the EDW/BI development steps. Since the core team is the project management team, it is important that the team members have sufficient expertise collectively to represent the four perspectives of business value, data effort, technical considerations, and project constraints and interdependencies. Additional characteristics of the team members include:

- Having leadership qualities
- Being innovative and self-confident
- Being self-motivated
- Having a positive disposition
- Being team players
- Listening to team members
- Enjoying brainstorming and solving problems

The objective of this step is for the core team members to organize the work in as many parallel tracks as possible in order to complete the work in the shortest elapsed time possible. Using the short list of selected activities from the previous project planning step as a reference or guide, the core team members self-organize themselves into the appropriate number of development track teams.

The core team members also obtain additional resources to staff the development track teams as needed. For example, the ETL architect on the core team may recruit one or more ETL developers to work on the ETL code. Another example might be that the EIM professional on the core team may want to get help from an experienced analyst who knows the source systems and can help with data profiling. The business representative may know of one or two subject matter experts to join in the work effort. Maybe the data modeling scope can be divided into multiple parallel business modeling tracks for different data subject areas, in which case additional information architects (data modelers) are organized into multiple data modeling tracks. The combinations of development tracks are broad and completely up to the core team to organize.

Another crucial concept in staffing the teams is that nobody works alone. If at all possible, you want two or more people sharing the responsibility for a release activity and artifact. Many times, the business representative is paired up with a technician or with a knowledgeable business analyst or data steward. Often two technicians pair up to work on an activity.

There are several reasons why sharing responsibility for activities and artifacts is desired:

- Two heads are better than one – the synergy between two people brainstorming on an activity generally produces more innovative solutions with higher quality.
- If one person gets sick, the work activity does not have to come to a halt because the other person can continue, albeit at a slower pace.
- Cross training and on-the-job training is automatic, without having to expend additional resources, time, and money.
- It is easy to enlarge the resource pool with new team members who already know how the process works and who become candidates for other core teams.
- If the business representative is involved in almost all work activities on a full-time basis, user acceptance testing can usually be dropped because the user will have participated in all rigorous integration, regression, and QA testing activities.
- The biggest benefit of pairing the business representatives with other team members is the tearing down of the "us versus them" wall that separates IT from the business in so many companies. They are in the boat together!
- Business people will learn about the complexities of enterprise-class data integration projects.
- Business people will feel the ownership of their projects much more than if they turn over their service request to IT and wait to be called for user acceptance testing.

Once again, the combinations of pairing team members are broad and completely up to the core team to decide. Much will depend on the number of resources available and their skills.

Final Thought

In Extreme Scoping, developers do not run the show on EDW/BI projects. Instead, they work under the direction of a core team that continuously balances all project decisions based on the perspectives of business value, data effort, technical considerations, and project constraints and interdependencies. Keep in mind this

BDTP Balance when staffing the development track teams. EDW/BI development steps and work activities require different perspectives and different skills than operational system development. Here is a summary of the main BDTP Balance perspectives to consider during the development steps:

Development Step	BDTP Balance Perspectives
Business Case Assessment	Business, Data, Project

Enterprise Infrastructure Evaluation
 	
    Technical Infrastructure
    Non-Technical Infrastructure
	
	Business, Technical
	Business, Data

Requirements Definition	Business, Data, Technical
Project Planning	Business, Data, Technical, Project
Data Analysis	Business, Data
Application Prototyping	Business, Technical
Metadata Repository Analysis	Business, Data
Database Design	Data, Technical
ETL Design	Data, Technical
Metadata Repository Design	Data, Technical
ETL Development	Data, Technical
Application Development	Data, Technical
Data Mining	Business, Data, Technical
Metadata Repository Development	Data, Technical
Implementation	Data, Technical
Release Evaluation	Business, Data, Technical, Project

Chapter 11
Planning – Where the Rubber Meets the Road

The last three steps of the Extreme Scoping planning process are where the rubber meets the road. This is where you find out whether or not your development track teams can comfortably deliver the first release in the original best-guess timeframe.

So far, your competent and balanced core team has reviewed the entire EDW/BI service request and has sized up its scope. The core team members agreed on whether the EDW/BI service request is the size of an elephant, a tiger, or a mouse. They also agreed on the best way to break the EDW/BI service request into smaller releases, the approximate scope of each release, and the most appropriate sequence of the releases. They spent some time studying the detailed requirements of only the first release, and they agreed on the necessary activities to build the deliverable for the first release. Finally, they determined how many development tracks they want and how to staff them. Taking into account the personalities, availability, skill sets, and shortcomings of all IT and business participants, they agreed on who should be paired up with whom. Now it is time to create the project plans.

Project Partitioning

In almost all methodologies, a project is typically partitioned into four levels, as shown on Figure 11.1. Traditionally, these levels are tracked and reported on Gantt charts. While Extreme Scoping uses these levels to identify the work effort for a release, it does **not** track and report these levels on a Gantt chart. In fact, Extreme Scoping does not use Gantt, CPM, or PERT charts.

1. The highest level is the definition of the project itself. With Extreme Scoping this would be the scope description of a release.

2. The second level is described in phases and milestones. With Extreme Scoping only milestones are used to report progress of a release to the sponsors and to management. I call this the macro plan. Note that phases (i.e., development steps) are not tracked and do not appear on any project plan.

3. The third level typically shows activities, which are any major work efforts that are measured in days or weeks. With Extreme Scoping this level is used only for selecting applicable activities for a release.

4. The fourth and lowest level contains tasks and subtasks, which are units of work that are measured in hours or days. With Extreme Scoping this level is used to create the internal and informal work plan, which is used solely by the core team members to manage their daily project activities. I call this the micro plan.

Figure 11.1 Project Partitioning

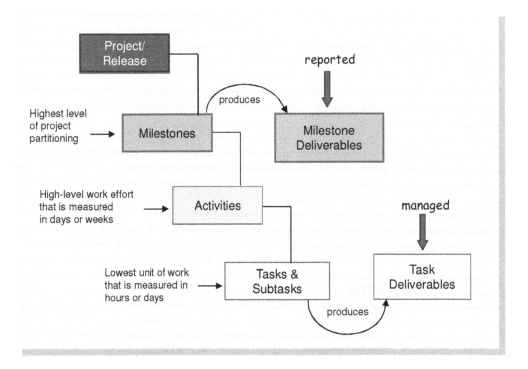

Reverse Milestones – Reality Check

Step five of the Extreme Scoping planning process, shown in Figure 11.2, is to validate your best-guess estimates and the assumptions you have made so far for the first release. How do you know that you can actually complete all the work activities that you have selected, with the number of work teams that you plan to have, in the timeframe you originally thought you could finish the first release? Up to this point, it is all speculation. Use the "reverse milestones" process as a reality check.

First, describe what you plan to deliver by the deadline. Is the release supposed to be running in the production environment by the deadline? Is the data (current and historical) supporting this release supposed to be loaded into the production databases by the deadline? Is this release ***not*** scheduled to go into production? What exactly is the agreed-upon deliverable at the deadline?

Figure 11.2 Extreme Scoping Step 5

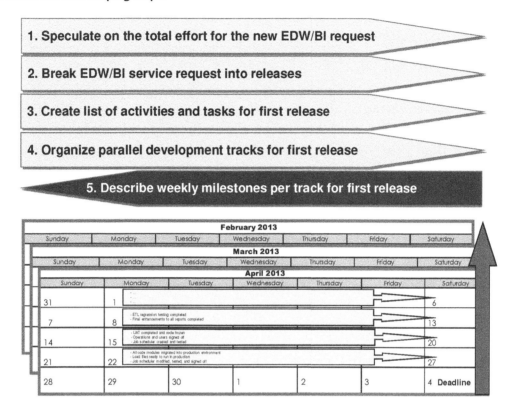

Starting with the deadline and ***working backwards***, the core team members describe the weekly milestones. Remember that your technical lead(s) are part of the core team and should be able to perform this activity on behalf of the development track teams. Alternatively, if you already have your development track teams staffed, you can delegate this activity to them. At the end, compile the milestones from each development track team into one milestone chart. It is important to work the milestones ***backwards*** from the deadline because the goal is to identify critical weekly check points at which certain progress must have been achieved in order to meet the deadline. Monitoring the weekly milestones will determine whether the project is on track or if it requires a course correction, such as a cut in scope.

The core team members, in consultation with the development track team members, describe how far along they must be the week before the deadline in order to make the deadline. To put it another way, they determine in what *state* the project or deliverable must be the week before the deadline. For example, in most companies, the operations staff has to sign off on QA testing before a project can go into production. Therefore, "signed off QA testing" might be a milestone. If it takes two weeks to go into production, "signed off QA testing" may be a milestone two weeks before the deadline. Another example might be: if business people are still arguing over data definitions the week before the deadline, then clearly you will never make the deadline, no matter how many hours you work. Therefore, "finalized data definitions" would be a milestone several weeks earlier.

The team members repeat this process by backing up another week and defining the state of the project or the state of an artifact two weeks before the deadline, then three weeks before the deadline, and so on. Hopefully they will end up at the project start date. If they pass the project start date, which happens more often than you might think, the team members must determine if the scope is too large for the release deadline, or if the work efforts between the milestones are overestimated. All team members must agree that the milestones are achievable without compromising quality, given the scope, deadline, and available resources.

These milestones are difficult to name because they represent the *state* of the release or the condition of an artifact each week. The easiest way is to number the weeks and to write a short description about the state in which the release must be at the end of each week. Figure 11.3 lists examples of milestones.

April 28, 2013 (deadline minus 1 week):
- All code modules migrated into production environment
- Load files ready to run in production
- Job scheduler modified, tested, and signed off

April 21, 2013 (deadline minus 2 weeks):
- UA testing completed and code frozen
- Operations and users signed off
- Job scheduler created and tested
- Production environment created

April 14, 2013 (deadline minus 3 weeks):
- ETL regression testing completed
- Final enhancements to all reports completed

And so on.

If you look up the dates on a calendar, you will notice that they fall on a Sunday rather than on a Friday. While it is customary to end a work week on a Friday, I like to use Sunday as the cut-off day for the week. The teams can often use the weekend to catch up if they are behind in their weekly milestones. After all, nobody looks at progress reports before Monday morning, anyway.

Figure 11.3 Describing the Milestones

Week 1: - Potential source files identified and profiled
        - Data cleansing specifications identified and reviewed with users
        - ETL architectural design changes identified
        - 8 report designs prototyped and demonstrated to users
Week 2: - New data modeled and data disputes among users documented
        - New table created and 3 existing databases modified
        - Undisputed data mapped from source to target
        - One new extract modules coded and 5 ETL modules modified
Week 3: - All data disputes among users resolved
        - Data cleansing specifications modified
        - All ETL code modules unit tested
        - 5 new reports coded based on approved designs using new table
        - 3 old reports from existing databases modified
Deadline -n weeks: ...
Deadline -3 weeks: - ETL regression testing completed
                   - Final enhancements to all reports completed
Deadline -2 weeks: - UAT completed and code frozen
                   - Operations and users signed off
                   - Job scheduler created and tested
                   - Production environment created
Deadline -1week: - All code modules migrated into production environment
                 - Load files ready to run in production
                 - Job scheduler modified, tested, and signed off

These milestones do *not* represent traditional phases, such as requirements, analysis, design, coding, and testing. These phases can be performed whenever needed, as often as needed, and in whatever sequence they are needed throughout the project. Never track phases!

I cannot overemphasize how important it is to start with the deadline and work **backwards** as you are describing the milestones. The purpose of this process is to understand the critical weekly checkpoints at which certain activities or artifacts must be in a certain state of completion in order to be able to finish the release on time. Think of it this way: "If we don't have X, Y, Z done by the week before the deadline, we'll never make the deadline." Then back up another week and say to yourselves: "If we don't finish U, V, W by this week, we will never make the next milestone." Working backwards forces you to think differently. It frees you from the psychological pressure to take shortcuts and make mental adjustments just to meet a deadline. If you don't work backwards, your milestones would reflect a "desired" state rather than a "necessary" state. If you start at the deadline, you will be less biased as you are thinking through the state of the project each week from its deployment back towards its beginning.

> ☞ If you like to experiment, and if you have some flexibility with staffing, consider switching steps four and five. I prefer to create the reverse milestones before having organized and staffed the development track teams. This allows the core team members to concentrate on what is doable purely from a work dependency point of view without thinking about resources. Once they have established the fastest path with as many parallel tracks as possible, they can ask for the resources they need to do the work. Unfortunately, I find that most companies have a limited number of resources available for EDW/BI projects. Therefore, creating the reverse milestones without taking staffing constraints into account is a futile exercise for them. But if you don't have such resource constraints, think about switching steps four and five. In fact, steps four and five used to be reversed in earlier versions of Extreme Scoping.

Micro Plan

The Extreme Scoping planning process produces two different project plans: the micro plan and the macro plan. In step six, shown in Figure 11.4, the core team members create an informal project plan that is only used by them to manage day-to-day project activities. It is a highly volatile plan that is adjusted daily. I call this the micro plan.

Knowing the selected activities for the first release (from step three), knowing the makeup of the development track teams (from step four), and knowing the milestones (from step five), the core team members together, in consultation with the development track team members, choose which selected activities and artifacts must be worked on each week between the milestones, based on the activity/task list (from step three). They also decide which tasks and artifacts are prepared by which development track team.

This informal detailed plan is used by the core team on a daily basis to guide their daily work activities, to manage their change control process, and to monitor their own progress. The reason this plan must be as informal and as easy to maintain as possible is because it will change every day as the team learns more about their project. These continuous minor daily changes are managed internally by the core team and are ***not*** reported to management.

Figure 11.4 Extreme Scoping Step 6

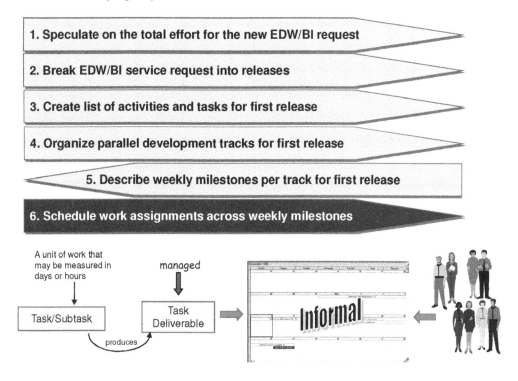

The core team members have complete control over the level of detail they want (or need) to track, since this informal project plan is for their internal use only. Some core teams may choose to track activities, while other core teams may feel more comfortable defining tasks and subtasks. Others may prefer to define the work effort by artifacts or by assigned resources. Yet others include requirement references, estimated and actual hours, and quality measures. Many core teams track all of the above.

The description of daily task assignments and artifacts can be documented on a variety of media. Any informal media is acceptable, as long as it can be modified quickly and easily! Here are some examples.

- If it is a short project, the weekly assignments might fit on an erasable white board with print capabilities. The core team members maintain the information on a daily grid on the white board, and all team members can print off a copy at will.
- Some core teams like using a flipchart, one page per week. The pages are then posted on the project room walls for everyone to see.

- Others prefer an Excel spreadsheet or even a project management tool because they are used to them. In my opinion, detailed project plans created with professional project management tools are too cumbersome to maintain – but to each his own!
- Some core teams prefer to use a large calendar to track who is working on what and when. The milestones are described in the weekend slots and the tasks are listed for all weekdays. In addition to documenting tasks and the names of assigned team members, some add hours estimated and hours burned (worked).
- Still other core teams like the visual effects of a task board. They create index cards in one color with the description of each week's milestones and in another color with the detailed assignments for each week, as shown in Figure 11.5. Alternatively, each development track team can use different color index cards for their detailed assignments for each week. These index cards can be as detailed or as vague as the core team decides. The index cards are then posted on the task board under the appropriate week. As the team members complete their milestones, they take off the index cards and store them with other project materials. An arrow on top indicates the current week.

Figure 11.5 Task Board

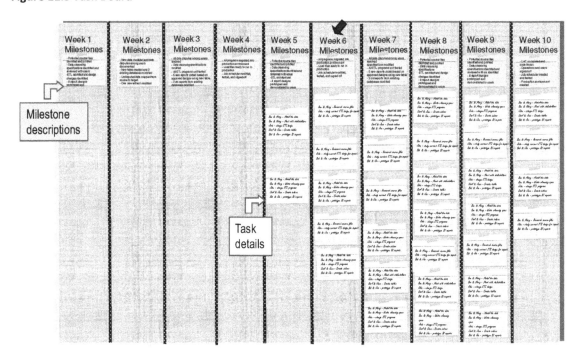

The idea for this micro plan is analogous to the whiteboards found at nurses' stations in hospitals. Those whiteboards list the patients, their rooms, their medications, their doctors, and the nurses assigned to them. If a nurse calls in sick, the hospital doesn't let her patients die. Instead, the other nurses quickly reorganize themselves and their tasks to cover the sick nurse's patients. In the same vein, if a team member gets sick or runs into unforeseen hurdles, the other team members can quickly reorganize themselves and their tasks to keep the project going. As we all know, this happens more often than we would like to admit, which is why "plan the work, then work the plan" has always been an idealistic and not very realistic expression.

SCRUM AND XP

In Extreme Scoping, the development track teams work under the direction of the core team or, more precisely, under the direction of the technical expert(s) on the core team. For those development track teams that are purely coding teams, each coding team is free to organize their internal coding activities in a way that is most comfortable for them. The coding teams that like using development-driven agile methods like Scrum or XP are free to do so, as long as their activities are folded into the overall micro and macro plans for the release. Burn-down charts used by the coding teams are internal to only their own development track. In addition, the coding teams are required to reject or work around any Scrum or XP rules that conflict with the way the work is organized by the core team. Scrum and XP are subordinate to Extreme Scoping.

Macro Plan

In step seven of the Extreme Scoping planning process, shown in Figure 11.6, the core team members create a simple milestone chart based on the milestones developed in step five. This chart is used only for weekly progress reporting. I call this the macro plan.

In contrast to the informal and internal micro plan, the macro plan is a formal project plan used to report progress to the sponsor and to management. This should be a simple one or two-page milestone chart with weekly milestones (from step five). It should not contain all the details from the informal micro plan because it is not appropriate to track progress by activities, tasks, resources, or artifacts. Activities and tasks can be performed by any skilled resource, in any order, out of order, multiple times, and any time during the project. The core team members may also decide to skip some activities, tasks, or artifacts, and they should not have to explain their decision. The only thing that is important for management to know is whether or not the weekly milestones are being met, and whether or not the project is in trouble. They do not need to know how the work is done. In other words, the milestone chart does not track completion of tasks like a typical Gantt chart does.

Figure 11.6 Extreme Scoping Step 7

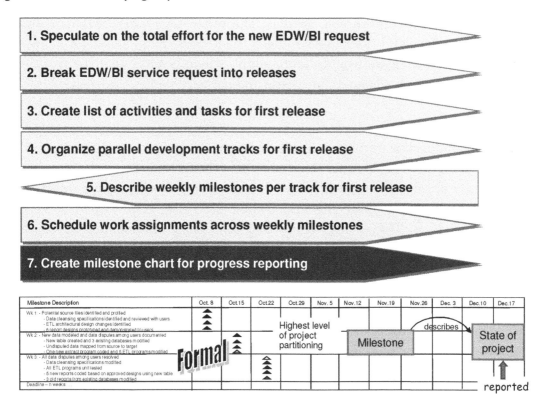

The descriptions in the left column on a milestone chart are not task names but descriptions of specific milestones that need to be achieved each week in order to meet the deadline. In addition, start and end dates are not shown because we do not report what tasks are currently being worked on. A milestone chart only shows whether or not milestones have been met to prove that the project is progressing. A simple legend, as shown in Figure 11.7, indicates whether a milestone was completed on time, completed with significant delay, not completed yet, or if it was modified in some major way, which is then explained on the next page of the progress report.

If a milestone is missed, it is not necessary to report it right away because it is entirely possible that the team can recover the following week. However, if the delay is unrecoverable, the core team members must renegotiate the scope of the current release and report the agreed-upon scope change to management. Remember that the business representative who has the authority to approve scope changes is a member of the core team.

Figure 11.7 Milestone Chart

Milestone Description	Oct. 8	Oct.15	Oct.22	Oct.29	Nov. 5	Nov.12	Nov.19	Nov.26	Dec. 3	Dec.10	Dec.17

Wk 1: - Potential source files identified and profiled
    - Data cleansing specifications identified and reviewed with users
    - ETL architectural design changes identified
    - 8 report designs prototyped and demonstrated to users
	▲
	▲
	▲
	▲										

Wk 2: - New data modeled and data disputes among users documented
    - New table created and 3 existing databases modified
    - Undisputed data mapped from source to target
    - One new extract program coded and 5 ETL programs modified
		▲
		▲
		▲
		△									

Wk 3: - All data disputes among users resolved
    - Data cleansing specifications modified
    - All ETL programs unit tested
    - 5 new reports coded based on approved designs using new table
    - 3 old reports from existing databases modified
			△
			▲
			▲
			▲
			▲								

Deadline – n weeks:											

Deadline – 2 weeks: - UAT completed and code frozen
    - Operations and users signed off
    - Job scheduler created and tested
    - Production environment created
										△
										△
										△
										△	

Deadline – 1 week: - All programs migrated into production environment
    - Load files ready to run in production
    - Job scheduler modified, tested, and signed off
											△
											△
											△

Legend: ▲ Completed on time
          △ Completed with significant delay
          △ Not completed yet
          ▲ Major modification to milestone (see detailed explanation on next page)

The core team members must also calculate the impact of folding the dropped requirements into an upcoming release to determine whether or not the overall project schedule (speculation from step one) is affected. If the total time set aside for this user's service request needs to be extended, the request for more time must be brought to the BI steering committee for approval. The business representative on the core team does not have the authority to monopolize the EDW/BI project team beyond the time allotted to his or her service request. Monopolizing the team would impact other business units who are waiting in the queue. Instead, the business representative needs to make a business case to the BI steering committee and argue why the business value of extending the overall timeframe for his or her service request is higher than the business value of the next project in the queue. After hearing the arguments from the sponsor of the next project in the queue, the BI steering committee decides whether or not to extend the allotted timeframe for the current project. If the answer is "no," the user will have to resubmit the dropped requirements with a new service request, which will then go through the regular prioritization process along with all other service requests from other users. This is the reason why the concept of one "product owner" who controls the requirements and priorities does not work on enterprise-class EDW/BI projects.

Planning the Next Release

If the first release was completed without any unanticipated problems (you wish!), the core team can start planning the second release. The core team members review the scope of the second release, which was originally carved out in step two. They pay close attention to the data requirements, and reaffirm that the scope of the second release is still doable in the timeframe initially allotted for it. This assumption will either be proven or disproven in the next steps as the core team goes through the planning process for the second release, as illustrated in Figure 11.8.

Figure 11.8 Planning the Next Release

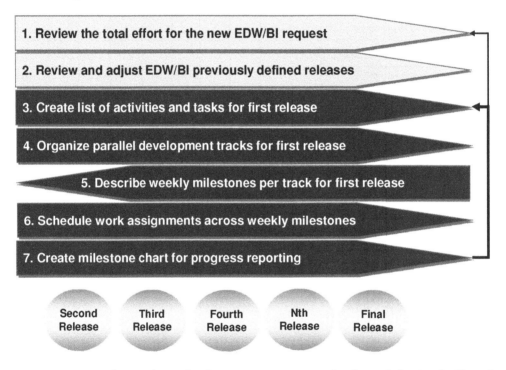

1. Review the total effort for the new EDW/BI request
2. Review and adjust EDW/BI previously defined releases
3. Create list of activities and tasks for first release
4. Organize parallel development tracks for first release
5. Describe weekly milestones per track for first release
6. Schedule work assignments across weekly milestones
7. Create milestone chart for progress reporting

Second Release   Third Release   Fourth Release   Nth Release   Final Release

The core team members (together) create a customized activity/task list for the second release (step three). After that, the core team members self-organize themselves into the appropriate number of development track teams or work groups (step four). Working backwards from the deadline for the second release, they establish the milestones - one week at a time (step five). Once the milestones are defined, they map out the detailed tasks, artifacts, and resources for each week between the milestones on an informal micro plan for themselves (step six). And finally, they create a macro milestone chart of the weekly milestones for formal progress reporting to the sponsor and management (step seven).

Many times, however, there are problems with the first release, such as underestimating time, dropped requirements, friction on the core team, constant adjustments to the scope, and so on. In that case, the core team members must go back to step one and review the high-level projections for the entire service request that they originally produced in step one. As shown in Figure 11.8, they revisit their speculations and their understanding of the overall effort, resources, cost, schedule, risks, and assumptions for the entire service request. Then they make the necessary adjustments to the remaining releases. That can include changing the scope for the second release, changing the number of releases, changing the deliverables for one or more releases, changing the time-boxes, reprioritizing and changing the sequence of the releases, and so on. Remember that the business representative is a member of the core team and participates in all deliberations and decisions.

If the core team decides that the overall effort for the entire service request was grossly underestimated and that the new estimates have an impact on other users waiting in the queue, the core team has two choices. The business representative on the core team either agrees to permanently cut the scope of the original service request, or the business representative submits the findings along with the new and more realistic time estimates to the BI steering committee for approval. Only then can the core team proceed with detailed planning of the second release, which means performing steps three through seven of the Extreme Scoping planning process.

Final Thought

An agile methodology should not only be agile in the way systems are developed or projects are managed, but the methodology itself must be flexible. I do not believe in prescriptive methodologies that must be followed to the letter to guarantee results. I do not believe in gimmicks and fads that so often creep into our industry. I recognize that policies and cultures vary in different companies, and that transitioning from old habits to new ones can be risky and slow. Even if the project teams are ready to experiment, their project management office or IT audit may not allow it. Extreme Scoping is a set of guidelines and steps that have helped many companies transition from a traditional big-bang approach to an agile release approach.

A different scenario exists in companies that have adopted Scrum as their one and only "real" agile methodology. I have seen numerous companies force their EDW/BI project teams to apply a development-driven methodology that was simply never designed for enterprise-class data integration projects. A stand-alone software development project is completely different from an enterprise-class data integration projects. Yet, their IT management has been brainwashed into believing that unless it is Scrum it is not "agile." This kind of dogma is harmful to enterprise-class BI initiatives because the EDW/BI project teams either fail completely or modify the agile methodology rules beyond recognition, which often earns them the wrath of Scrum activists.

I encourage project teams to follow their instincts, rely on their experience, experiment with new ideas, and only go as far as they are comfortable. The steps and guidelines of Extreme Scoping are not meant to be rigid. Adapt them in any way that fits your organization's policies and culture. If your first EDW/BI release takes six months instead of three or four, it does not mean you failed. Taking baby steps is OK as long as you try to apply the four principles of the Agile Manifesto.

1. "Individuals and interactions over processes and tools." The most valued assets on an EDW/BI project are the team members. I assume that you hire or promote people with the right skill sets and positive attitudes. Give them credit and respect as they work through the challenges of EDW/BI projects. Don't bog them down with over-regulating their projects.

2. "Working software over comprehensive documentation." Think of Olivia Newton John's song "Get Physical." Prototype everything. Documentation is important for communication, but most of it can be generated automatically from our EDW/BI development tools. With agile, we produce much of our documentation *after* our deliverables are built, rather than before.

3. "Customer collaboration over contract negotiation." With traditional and spiral methodologies, everything has to be signed off "in blood" before the project team can proceed to the next step. That reflects an "us versus them" mentality. Change that. Put the business representative in the boat with you – the boat being the core team. Deliberate and negotiate everything together on the core team.

4. "Responding to change over following a plan." Be flexible. Users don't always know what they want until they see it. Team members don't always know how something works until they do it. The only constant on EDW/BI projects – and in life – is constant change. Allow change, but manage its impact on other users.

Part IV
At the Program Level

An EDW/BI program is an enterprise-wide initiative based on a common development methodology, common enterprise standards, common ratified business rules, a common enterprise infrastructure (technical and non-technical), common ETL processes, a common metadata repository, and a common enterprise data model. All EDW target databases and BI applications in this program must be collectively architected and developed under the core competencies illustrated in Figure IV. I call the core competencies the *glue* that holds the EDW/BI environment together and prevents the development of customized stand-alone BI solutions.

Figure IV Core Competencies

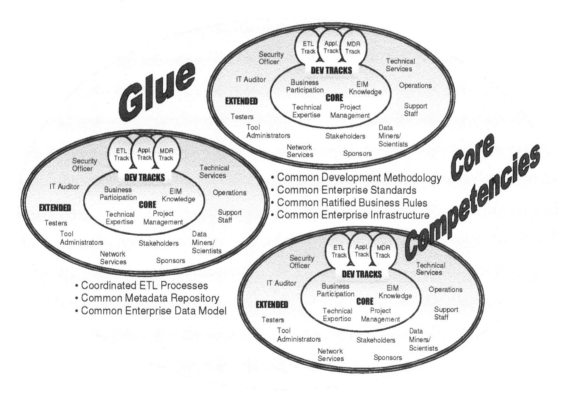

Chapter 12
Organizational Impact

Managing an EDW/BI program requires organizational changes, and implementing those changes must be systemic and holistic, not isolated and sporadic. The changes will eventually affect everyone in the organization, not just EDW/BI project teams. Changes must be planned, prepared, executed, reviewed, and revised, if necessary. That requires new leadership at the highest level in the organization.

BI Leadership

In today's information age, it is indisputable that data is a profitable commodity that companies can sell. Therefore, every company needs to elevate their data assets to the same level of importance as their other assets, such as financial assets or fixed assets. Data assets will eventually be reported on a company's balance sheet, and should therefore be managed at the C-level. Organizations need to create the position of a chief data officer (CDO) who is in charge of these profitable data assets.

CHIEF DATA OFFICER

A few organizations have already launched a CDO position. The collaboration between a CDO and chief information officer (CIO) is similar to the collaboration between chief financial officer (CFO) and chief operating officer (COO), as shown in Figure 12.1. The CFO is responsible for the financial health of the company. Similarly, the CDO is responsible for the data health of the company. In other words, the CDO has authority to exercise the same type of control and governance over data as the CFO does over money.

The most optimal reporting structure is for the CDO to report to the chief executive officer (CEO). A good alternative is to report to the CFO. Less optimal is a reporting structure to the COO. Clearly, the CDO position is not a technical position and should therefore not report to a CIO in IT.

Figure 12.1 Chief Data Officer

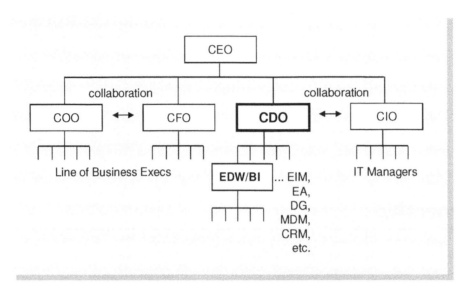

The organizational structure under the CDO is illustrated in Figure 12.2. Direct "solid line" reporting relationships to the CDO consists of enterprise architects, such as information architects (business data modelers) and database architects (database designers), EIM professionals, such as data administrators, data quality analysts, and metadata administrators, as well as data integrators/developers who deliver enterprise-class database solutions.

Figure 12.2 Direct and Indirect Reports to CDO

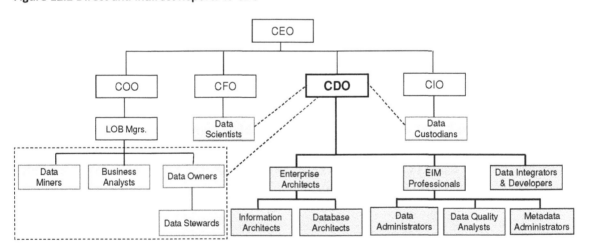

Indirect "dotted line" reporting relationships to the CDO exist from the business side, as well as from IT. They include data scientists, data miners, business analysts, data owners, and data stewards from the business side, as well as data custodians who are technicians in IT that create, modify, derive, or delete data.

The responsibilities of a CDO are extensive:

- Oversee the definition, management, and control of data policies and standards
- Oversee the definition, management, and control of metadata management policies and standards
- Oversee the definition, management, and control of procedures for sensitive data
- Oversee the definition, management, and control of programs for data governance and data stewardship
- Organize and lead a data governance (DG) council
- Oversee the leadership of enterprise architecture (EA) activities
- Oversee the management and development of data quality monitoring processes
- Serve as the executive for the enterprise information management (EIM) group
- Review business metrics to assure that business reports are representing the true state of the business
- Oversee the definition and publishing of measurement standards for master data analyses, statistics, and metrics
- Assure appropriate audit controls exist for all databases and files
- Oversee the management and development of enterprise-class data stores (e.g., EDW/BI, MDM, CRM, CDI, etc.)

BI PROGRAM MANAGER

The BI program manager is a director-level position that reports to the CDO. If the company does not have a CDO, the BI program manager reports to the CIO in IT and works directly with the BI steering committee. The BI program manager has the following responsibilities:

- Perform periodic readiness assessments to identify new information needs and to ascertain user satisfaction with the EDW/BI environment
- With the backing of the business executives and senior business managers, create a strategy for the company's BI initiative
- Enforce the common technical and non-technical infrastructure components in the EDW/BI environment
- Work with the BI steering committee to prioritize EDW/BI projects
- Determine the project interdependencies and coordinate the project resources and activities around these interdependencies

BI STEERING COMMITTEE

Successful BI initiatives are driven by business people, not by IT. That does not mean that non-technical business people should be making technical decisions, but it does mean that business people should take ownership of the EDW/BI environment. In other words, business people should co-manage the BI program with IT. The BI steering committee is composed of business executives and senior business managers who understand the benefits as well as the complexities of BI and EDW. Their responsibilities include:

- First and foremost, provide collective sponsorship for the EDW/BI program
- Prioritize EDW/BI projects based on highest business value to the company as a whole
- Support cross-functional activities, which means recognize the ROA derived from these activities, even if they impact the project delivery date
- Communicate enterprise-wide data integration principles to the company
- Establish and sustain a BI strategy that supports their business drivers
- Settle disputes among business people from different lines of business
- Fund an EIM group to perform enterprise-wide data governance activities together with data stewards and data owners
- Identify data owners and direct the data owners to identify data stewards in their line of business
- Release business people from their operational responsibilities so that they can participate as full-time core team members on EDW/BI projects

Culture Changes

The most obvious and also most difficult change will be to break down the barriers between IT and the business side. The current "us versus them" culture must be replaced with a "we're in the same boat" culture. At a minimum, that will require a collaboration and partnership between the business side and IT. Even more important, it will require a collaboration and partnership among the functionally divided lines of business, as well as between the EDW/BI teams and the operational systems teams in IT. Part of that culture shift will be the enforcement of a common architecture, common methodology, common enterprise standards, and cross-functional activities.

ARCHITECTURAL COMPONENTS

Since EDW/BI is an enterprise-wide initiative, it is necessary that all EDW/BI projects conform to architectural standards established for the EDW/BI environment.

You wouldn't allow 100 developers to use their own imaginations and preferences when designing Web pages for your Website. You would give them standards to follow so that all Web pages have a common look and feel. The same is true for an EDW/BI environment. At a minimum, you need to create a common technical and non-technical infrastructure, enterprise information architecture, also known as an enterprise data model, and a metadata repository. These infrastructure components do not have to be completed before embarking on EDW/BI projects. They can be built in iterations, as well. Infrastructure requirements can become their own projects, or they can be incorporated into EDW/BI releases as one of their deliverables.

Technical Infrastructure

Technical infrastructure refers to the components of configuration management. For example:

- Hardware components, such as servers, nodes, storage devices, and disk controllers
- Network components, such as servers, routers, switches, and network interface cards
- Database management systems, such as relational, columnar, and DW appliances
- Products, such as developer tools and BI tools for users

Non-Technical Infrastructure

Non-technical infrastructure refers to the components that constitute the policies and rules under which EDW/BI projects are executed. Examples are:

- A common cross-functional spiral DW development methodology that includes all tasks to build enterprise-class EDW target databases and BI applications
- A data strategy with enterprise standards and procedures for activities such as data modeling, data naming, data definitions, metadata capture, metadata maintenance, metadata usage, testing, reconciliation, and security
- Common business rules that have been ratified by all data owners and information consumers
- Roles and responsibilities for the core team, development track teams, and extended team

Enterprise Information Architecture

Enterprise information architecture is about attaining the proverbial "single version of the truth" for core business data. That applies to master data as well as transaction data. The reasons for creating an enterprise data model are to improve accountability for data, reduce information technology costs, reduce business process costs, improve productivity, improve data reusability, and manage data redundancy. In order to achieve these goals, data administration principles must be applied to standardize the data. For example:

- An enterprise data model is a pictorial representation of an organization's data assets. Its ultimate value comes from applying stringent data administration principles during the logical data modeling process.
- Formal rules for writing data definitions, for creating data names, and for defining valid data content (data domain) are essential for data standardization.
- Since metadata is the main vehicle for the documentation, navigation, and administration of data assets, you need to define metadata standards.
- Choose the level of data quality you want to attain and put processes in place to achieve it. Over time, this should be expanded into a permanent data quality improvement process.
- Data owners must be identified on the business side. They have the authority and responsibility to set business policies and create business rules for the data.
- Data stewards must be identified on the business side. They have the responsibility for auditing the data in their respective lines of business and reporting data quality problems to the data owners and to the operational systems owners. Data stewards work closely with EIM staff (i.e., data administrators, data quality analysts, metadata administrators) to improve the quality of the data.

Metadata Repository

A metadata repository is another major tool that supports enterprise-wide data standardization. It is a set of processes, technologies, and databases. Enterprise metadata management goes hand in hand with enterprise information management because it contains the detailed contextual information about the enterprise data model, as well as all the project-specific logical and physical data models. Maintaining a metadata repository includes five major processes:

1. Sourcing the metadata from the various tools where it is captured

2. Relating (linking) the business metadata with the corresponding technical metadata, process metadata, and usage metadata

3. Loading the metadata into the metadata repository database

4. Maintaining and administering the metadata repository

5. Making the metadata available to technicians and users

When creating a metadata strategy, the first decision to make is whether to buy a metadata repository product or to custom-build a metadata repository solution. The second decision to make is whether the metadata repository will be used exclusively for the EDW/BI environment or be expanded across the company to include other enterprise-class data integration solutions (e.g., MDM, CRM, and CDI) and even operational systems.

PORTFOLIO MANAGEMENT

Managing a BI application portfolio goes beyond managing a traditional IT systems portfolio.

Traditionally, IT portfolio management means that business people get together to prioritize IT projects. Based on priority, cost, and available resources, these projects are then distributed among various IT groups (like dealing cards) who independently build customized stand-alone solutions. There is no coordination of activities, and no attention is given to data integration, much less to business integration.

For enterprise-wide data integration initiatives, additional considerations go into BI application portfolio management. Business people (through the BI steering committee) must carefully prioritize their BI applications and decide which ones have the highest business value. Every service request has a high business value to the business person who is requesting it. However, when looking through an enterprise lens, replacing operational reports rarely – if ever – has a higher business value than delivering new analytical capabilities to executives who will use this new information to substantially increase the company's profitability. Without the BI steering committee being involved in prioritizing BI service requests, EDW/BI teams are often overwhelmed by a flood of low-value BI service requests from every corner of the company. I have seen prioritization by intimidation, meaning that the service requests from the business person who exerts the most power is put ahead of others, even though the business value of the other service requests are higher. Some EDW/BI teams fall back on the traditional "divide and conquer" principle in their desperation. They abandon cross-functional development and pump out as many customized stand-alone BI solutions as they can, just to appease the users at the expense of their enterprise data integration goal.

There are very strong interdependencies between all BI applications because they share the same EDW/BI infrastructure, the same pool of resources, much of the same data, and many of the same processes. Because of these interdependencies, fewer EDW/BI projects can be scheduled and managed (coordinated) at the same time. In addition, issues among interdependent projects have to be discussed and resolved.

POWER SHIFT

Some responsibilities clearly have to shift from IT to the business side, such as:

- BI program management
- Data ownership
- Data standardization and integration across the enterprise
- Enforcement of standards
- Dispute resolution among business units

This is uncomfortable for both sides, not only because it upsets the familiarity with the status quo, but also because it endangers the existing power structure. One of the most feared changes in all organizations is a shift in the existing power structure. IT managers do not want to readily give up authority and ownership of projects because they may be perceived as having slipped down a rung or two on the corporate ladder. Business managers do not want to readily accept authority and ownership of projects, because that authority and ownership comes with responsibility, which they had relegated to IT in the past.

CHARGE-BACK POLICY

System ownership implies that the person who owns the system also owns the data in the system, because a system is typically defined as an application with a database. Our old charge-back policies do not differentiate between applications and databases. The business person pays for the entire system, which, by definition, includes both. This gives system owners the authority to recreate any data at any time, and to name, define, and use the data any way they want without having to integrate, standardize, or coordinate any of their activities. The result is data chaos.

Information ownership separates ownership of the data from ownership of applications. Furthermore, data is a reusable asset, which is owned by the organization. That means that the data used by an application does not belong to the *system* owner of that application. System owners are no longer allowed to create any data at any time (with the exception of those data elements that are truly unique to their department or business function and will never be shared with anyone else). Since data belongs to the organization as a whole, data owners are identified and empowered to establish policies and set standards for the data assets in the same way that policies and standards are set for financial or other assets. Therefore, ownership of a BI application must be separated from ownership of the data that is used by the application. It means that system owners no longer have to pay for the creation, standardization, and maintenance of common data, which is most data in the company. The cost for developing the BI application must be calculated differently and charged back separately from the costs of enterprise data management.

A more appropriate name for system ownership is *application* ownership. But even the cost of developing BI applications must be shared by all those business units that subscribe to that application. Remember, we want to reuse and share as much of the data and the BI applications as we possibly can. That means that an application may be developed for one business unit, but will end up being shared by several other business units over time. A new charge-back policy has to be able to spread the total cost of ownership across all those business units.

INCENTIVE PROGRAM

Maybe the most profound change is the one that has to be made to the reward policies of the organization. Today, the most valued key performance indicator for all staff members, regardless of title, rank, or tenure, is *speed*. People are rewarded first and foremost for delivering quickly; and the timeframe describing "quickly" appears to be getting shorter every year. For BI applications, that timeframe can be as short as one to four months. In this scenario, the business value is defined by the time it takes to realize ROI from the deliverable. In reality, business value is diminished by poor quality. For example, would you rather have a Corvette going 175 miles per hour for two miles and then needing a valve job or have a Honda Civic going 70 miles per hour for 100,000 miles before needing a valve job? We have to temper speed with accuracy, reusability, and repeatability.

The change that has to occur is to make the most valued key performance indicator for all staff members, regardless of title, rank, or tenure be *quality* for the purpose of reusability. People must be rewarded first and foremost for delivering quality, no matter what their deliverables are. For BI applications, that means data and functionality. In this scenario, the business value is defined by the ROA realized from reusing data, processes, and technology components to assemble new deliverables (e.g., new data marts and reports).

Final Thought

After over 20 years of data warehousing, long-time EDW/BI practitioners have learned a thing or two about the critical success factors for implementing an enterprise-wide BI program. It is of primary importance to have strong collective sponsorship and support from a BI steering committee in order to get over the many hurdles and challenges of EDW/BI. New leadership at the strategic as well as tactical levels is needed. Strategic leadership is at the C-level through the CDO, or at least at the executive level through the BI steering committee. Tactical leadership is in the hands of a seasoned BI program manager who is equally knowledgeable in data management as well as in technology. Business people must be involved in almost all EDW/BI project activities because EDW/BI is not an IT initiative; it is a business initiative and the business must own it. Organizational impact is not to be underestimated. Business people are now expected to work across lines of business in order to standardize the company's data. They also have to lead other cultural changes, such as:

- Conform to enterprise architectural standards
- Enforce data standards on the business side
- Create data stewardship positions in their business units
- Perform periodic data audits
- Reward their staff for quality rather than for speed

Chapter 13
BI Maturity

EDW/BI projects are complex, with wide ranging functional disciplines across their development lifecycle. When I perform EDW/BI assessments, I use fifteen focus areas associated with success factors that produce best practices. Once I review the combined assessment results, I ascertain the client's BI maturity level. My focus areas are:

1. Organization and culture
2. Strategic direction (roadmap)
3. Business value (portfolio management)
4. Enterprise standards and governance
5. Spiral DW methodology
6. Requirements (data, functional, infrastructure)
7. EDW architecture (databases and ETL processes)
8. Data quality (sources and targets)
9. Modeling (enterprise, logical, physical)
10. Database design schemas (multidimensional, relational/non-multidimensional)
11. Database performance
12. Metadata management
13. Delivery modes (OLAP, reports, dashboards)
14. BI applications and tools
15. Vendor management

Another example of assessing BI maturity is a survey that was developed in 2004 by Wayne Eckerson in his capacity as research director at TDWI. The survey had 40 questions in eight categories, which were used to evaluate a company's BI maturity. (The survey and model have since been revised by TDWI.) The categories are:

1. Scope
2. Sponsorship
3. Funding
4. Value
5. Architecture
6. Data
7. Development
8. Delivery

Some companies and consulting firms use more detailed assessment criteria, while others use fewer. For example, many companies consult the Functional Framework of DAMA-DMBOK (*Data Management Body of Knowledge*) to ensure that data management practices are incorporated into their development lifecycle.

All evaluation methods and guidelines seem to come down to four fundamental factors: organization, people, technology, and data. Based on the assessment results, a company can be placed on a BI maturity model. Different versions of BI maturity models exist in the industry, and most of them follow the five levels of a capability maturity model (CMM), which are generally described as initial, repeatable, defined, managed, and optimized. In other words, maturity is related to stability and repeatability.

> The origins of CMM date back to the 1980's when the Department of Defense sponsored the Software Engineering Institute, located at Carnegie Mellon University in Pittsburgh, Pennsylvania, to develop a tool for assessing the processes of government contractors to determine their ability to perform a software project.

TDWI BI Maturity Model

Wayne Eckerson, currently director of BI leadership at TechTarget and president of BI Leader Consulting, made another important contribution to the industry while working at TDWI. His contribution was the TDWI BI Maturity Model. The model consists of five stages: prenatal/infant, child, teenager, adult, and sage. These stages indicate the architectural decision-support evolution from producing operational reports to using sophisticated BI services. The model also has two sticking points called the gulf and the chasm. The bell curve in Figure 13.1 shows that, as of 2010, most organizations have reached the child and teenager stages, which Wayne Eckerson calls the adolescent phase of BI. Only a few are still stuck in the first prenatal/infant stage or have advanced to the highly mature stages of adult and sage.

Companies that are still stuck in the prenatal/infant stage do not deploy any BI technology in their decision-support function. They still use hundreds, if not thousands, of hand-coded operational reports and Excel spreadsheets. Some companies are inching their way into BI by creating hundreds of customized stand-alone spreadmarts (Wayne Eckerson calls them spreadsheets on steroids) or private databases to replace some of their paper reports and spreadsheets. Other than replacing the underlying technology, these companies are not advancing on the BI maturity scale. On the contrary, they continue to add to their existing data chaos.

Figure 13.1 BI Maturity Model

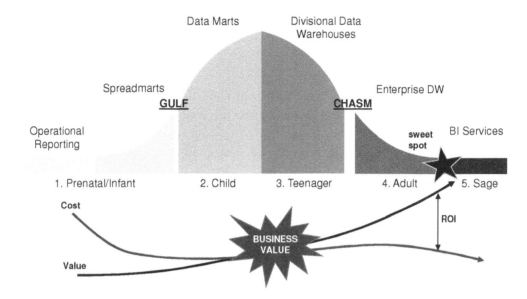

Based on the original TDWI BI Maturity Model, © 2005–2013 by TDWI. Used by permission of TDWI (tdwi.org).

The first hurdle, or sticking point, occurs when companies want to take the plunge into the BI world. That means acquiring BI tools, investing in BI training, attending BI conferences, and so on. That costs money and requires a sponsor. Sponsorship at this level often turns out to be at a departmental level or even lower. In order to solicit sponsorship, the benefits of BI solutions are often oversold and the complexities of BI are often understated or not mentioned at all. The result is a plunge into the child stage.

Companies in the child stage recognize the need for comprehensive departmental reporting and analysis capabilities. They utilize BI tools and technologies to create departmental data marts, such as one for marketing, one for sales, one for finance, another for human resources, and so on. Sometimes this process results in replacing and retiring some of the individual spreadmarts. Other times, the new data marts coexist with the spreadmarts and private databases. Each data mart has its own extract/transform/load (ETL) process, its own database, its own data quality rules, its own data definitions, and so on. Companies in the child stage are still developing independent decision support solutions the "Sinatra way."

When companies are starting to drown in dozens or hundreds of customized data marts, they begin to consider data mart consolidation, which is the teenager stage. The goal is to minimize the number of different and inconsistent reporting environments. As a first step, companies try to reduce the number of ETL processes and databases by creating a staging area that consolidates the data at a divisional level before feeding all the data marts. The next step is for the database architects to create shared dimensions, facts, and hierarchies and consolidate many of the data marts. Companies in the teenager stage have begun the architectural work toward the proverbial "single version of the truth."

At that point, companies hit the big chasm, and many never make the leap to the next stage. The effort for consolidating all reporting and analytical requirements into one collectively architected enterprise data warehouse seems too large. Some companies question whether it is worth it. They have experienced the level of disintegration and disagreements among business units when they moved from child to teenager stage. Standardizing data definitions, data names, data domains, data usage, and data security seems like an insurmountable hurdle. Some companies wonder how long it will take to affect changes to such a complex environment. At this point, many look for new technologies that support "virtual" integration solutions.

Companies who successfully overcome the challenges of the chasm enter the adult stage. Here they consolidate their divisional data warehouses into one collectively architected enterprise data warehouse with dependent and shared data marts and BI applications. There is strong collective sponsorship from business executives, and business people drive the BI program instead of IT. The EDW is recognized as the indispensable engine for BI reporting and analytics. This is a sophisticated environment where data management practices are applied on every EDW/BI project. Companies who achieve the adult stage often spawn other enterprise-wide initiatives, such as master data management, customer relationship management, data governance practice, and enterprise-wide data quality improvement processes.

At the sage stage, companies make their BI solutions available to their customers and suppliers. By providing only their personal account data through extranet BI applications, customers and suppliers can better manage their business operations and interactions with your company. Internally, the BI team embeds BI solutions into the core operational applications, and thus into the business processes that drive the company. Self-service BI becomes standard practice. Data scientists and analysts must be trained in the EDW target databases, the BI applications, the BI tools, the standard metrics, the metadata repository, and business policies and rules. This is the stage of maximum ROI, as well as maximum ROA.

In his research, Wayne Eckerson noticed that companies evolve at different rates through the five stages and may even exhibit characteristics of multiple stages at a given time. He observed that while it is possible to skip stages, it is unlikely, because companies must learn critical lessons at each stage before they can move to the next. The companies that successfully skip stages have strong senior leadership, considerable funding, and experts with extensive EDW/BI experience.

POSITIONING AGILE ON THE BI MATURITY MODEL

In the first two stages of the BI maturity model, the prenatal/infant stage and the child stage, are the development-driven projects. Whether creating paper reports, spreadsheets, spreadmarts, or customized stand-alone data marts, the focus is on functionality and not on data integration. As Figure 13.2 indicates, using development-driven agile methodologies like Scrum and XP will work just fine in these stages. These projects have only one user who can prioritize and control the backlog of his or her requirements. Most of the work effort is writing software, not data standardization. All agile principles that are followed by Scrum and XP teams on operational systems can be followed here.

Figure 13.2 Agile on the BI Maturity Model

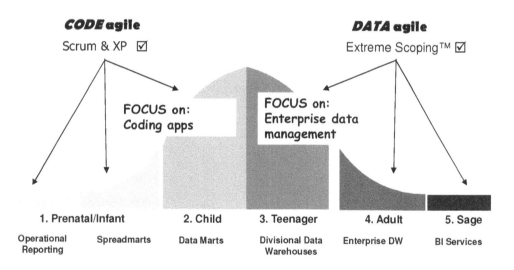

Based on the original TDWI BI Maturity Model, © 2005–2013 by TDWI. Used by permission of TDWI (tdwi.org).

Significant data consolidation begins at the teenager stage, which requires that cross-functional data management activities be performed. This is especially true for the adult and sage stages. EDW/BI project teams must have extensive experience with data management activities and must rely on a robust spiral data warehouse methodology to guide their data integration and development work. In order to be *data agile*, Extreme Scoping will provide the necessary guidelines for the EDW/BI project teams to know which agile principles apply and which ones do not.

Final Thought

I hope that EDW/BI project teams who struggle with today's popular development-driven agile methodologies will find my data-driven Extreme Scoping methodology a suitable alternative for their projects. Extreme Scoping goes beyond managing development activities. It embraces and includes the indispensable data management activities that usually slow down enterprise-wide data integration initiatives, and it makes the entire "data in" process more agile. Extreme Scoping recognizes that EDW/BI projects need to be run by a project management team that has the collective wisdom of business value, data effort, technical considerations, and project constraints and interdependencies. It is based on a solid soup-to-nuts spiral data warehouse methodology, the Business Intelligence Roadmap, but can be adapted to any other data-driven methodology. Finally, Extreme Scoping should satisfy all IT audit and project management office requirements for a robust methodology, while still being agile in its execution.

Appendices

A: Business Intelligence Roadmap Methodology – Things to Consider

If you do not have your own soup-to-nuts spiral data warehouse methodology, read this appendix to learn about additional things to consider in the sixteen development steps that I listed as examples in Chapter 6. Use this appendix during step one of the Extreme Scoping planning process, before you decide which development steps to select or drop.

B: Business Intelligence Roadmap Methodology – Activities

This appendix provides more details about the high-level activities in the sixteen development steps that I listed in my examples in Chapter 8. If you are using your own spiral data warehouse methodology, compare the activities in this appendix to your methodology to ensure that you are not omitting important activities. Then use this appendix during step three of the Extreme Scoping planning process to decide which activities to select or drop.

C: Glossary

In order to avoid any misunderstandings of the terms, titles, and acronyms that I use in this book, look up my definitions and explanations of them in this glossary.

As you review your methodology, consider and discuss all aspects of every development step before you decide whether or not a development step is applicable to your new EDW/BI service request. Following are additional things to consider in the sixteen development steps of the Business Intelligence Roadmap methodology.

Business Case Assessment

Executive sponsorship is mandatory for all successful BI initiatives. The sponsors must be from the business side, not from IT. The sponsors should be well connected, be willing to provide an ample budget, and be able to get other resources for the project, when needed. The sponsors should be accepting of problems as they occur and not use those problems as an excuse to either kill the project or withdraw support.

☞ The most significant thing to consider about sustained executive sponsorship is that it is *collective* sponsorship from the business side, usually represented as the BI steering committee.

Information requirements refer to the data that must be turned into information to be used by business people to make decisions in response to the business drivers. Enterprise data warehousing turns data into information and BI applications deliver that information to the business people who will take actions based on it.

☞ The most significant thing to consider about information requirements is that they must provide business value through integration and standardization.

Business value is calculated in four different ways.

1. Return on investment (ROI) is expressed by comparing the benefits (business value received) to the costs of developing the BI application.

2. Return on asset (ROA) is expressed by comparing the benefits (business value received) to the value of the existing assets that are used to support a new EDW/BI service request. These assets are hardware, software, people, and

data. Data is typically the most underutilized and underappreciated of all assets. Moreover, it is an asset with the least investment.

3. Total cost of ownership (TCO) refers to all of the costs for an initiative or application, from its inception and development through ongoing maintenance.

4. Total value of ownership (TVO) refers to all of the benefits derived from an initiative or application, from inception through the present.

☞ The most significant thing to consider about business value is to include the ROA calculation in your cost/benefit analysis.

Risk management is essential on all EDW/BI projects. There are risks with new technology, project complexity, integration, organization, staffing, etc.

☞ The most significant thing to consider about risks is early identification of mitigating tasks.

Readiness assessment is one method for identifying some of these risks. Always perform a readiness assessment at the beginning of a BI initiative. It is also a good idea to repeat such an assessment periodically to see how fast the EDW/BI environment is maturing. Enterprise-class initiatives require a culture shift and a new approach to developing applications. That is an evolutionary process and the readiness assessment is a measuring tool for monitoring how fast the BI maturity level is growing in the organization.

☞ The most significant thing to consider about a readiness assessment is its use in monitoring the learning (maturity) of the organization regarding EDW/BI and the increased willingness to adopt best practices.

Enterprise Infrastructure Evaluation

Enterprise infrastructure evaluation has two components: technical infrastructure evaluation and non-technical infrastructure evaluation.

TECHNICAL INFRASTRUCTURE EVALUATION

Hardware refers to processors, disk drives, and other physical devices. The hardware must have sufficient "horsepower" to handle complex reporting requirements against large volumes of data. It has to support not only predefined, simple queries on summary data, but also ad-hoc complex queries on detailed data.

☞ The most significant things to consider about hardware components are scalability and cost.

Network components refer to local area networks, wide area networks, broad-band lines, Internet protocols, etc. The network must be able to support many users in different locations.

☞ The most significant things to consider about network components are network traffic and response time.

Middleware refers to runtime system software, which is the layer between the application and the operating system or DBMS. It is a bridge between software components in an environment with multiple network nodes and several operating systems and software products.

☞ The most significant thing to consider about middleware is the DBMS gateway.

The required DBMS infrastructure may change with the size of the overall EDW/BI environment which, in turn, influences the selection of the DBMS. A small departmental data mart may reside on a local file server, but an enterprise-class EDW/BI solution may need the infrastructure support of an enterprise server.

☞ The most significant things to consider about the DBMS are parallelism and performance.

Tools and utilities refer to products for developers, such as an ETL tool or a DBMS backup utility, as well as products for users, such as an OLAP tool or a report writer.

☞ The most significant things to consider about tools and utilities are functionality and ease of use.

NON-TECHNICAL INFRASTRUCTURE EVALUATION

Data modeling and metadata management are very effective methods for managing data assets across the enterprise. Data modeling is recognized as a function of the enterprise architecture practice, where it is called enterprise information architecture. Enterprise information architecture is typically comprised of five types of data models or schemas. Your standards should specify which schemas must be consulted or created during EDW/BI projects.

1. Business schemas mirror the operational data sets that hold un-normalized transactions, which means the data was never normalized or de-normalized.

Un-normalized schemas store all data elements that are necessary to support a specific process in one "flat" file or one "flat" table.

2. Conceptual schemas are high-level normalized business views of master data and the data relationships among the master data. Transaction data at this level is hidden in the data relationships.

3. Logical schemas are refined, normalized, and fully attributed business views of both master data and transaction data. This schema is called a logical data model.

4. Physical schemas are de-normalized database views of either master data or transaction data, or both. Physical schemas can be multidimensional or relational/non-multidimensional. This schema is called a physical data model.

5. Integrated enterprise schema is an integrated, refined, normalized, but not necessarily fully attributed, enterprise view of all master data and most transaction data. This schema is called an enterprise data model (EDM) – and there is only *one*! It is developed from the conceptual and logical schemas. You can develop it top-down as a separate project, as it is done in the enterprise architecture practice, or you can let it grow over time from project-specific logical schemas, one BI application at a time.

☞ The most significant thing to consider about data modeling is to acknowledge that business models are just as important as database models.

Metadata is contextual information that turns data into information. Examples of metadata are data names, data definitions, data domains, data types, data lengths, data relationships, and data-related business rules.

☞ The most significant thing to consider about metadata is to capture business metadata, not just technical, process, or usage metadata, and to link (relate) the different types of metadata together.

Organizations must establish architectural standards for their EDW/BI environment in the same way they set up standards for their Websites. A company would never consider building its Website with a different look and feel for each Web page. In the same vein, a company should never build an EDW/BI environment where EDW target databases store data redundantly and under different names, or with inconsistent domain values for the same unique business data element.

☞ The most significant thing to consider about architecture is that all EDW/BI projects within an organization must adhere to the same architectural standards.

Standards should include a uniform and repeatable data-driven SDLC methodology. EDW/BI projects are too complex to build by the seat of your pants. You are integrating data from multiple legacy source systems that were never designed with integration in mind. Therefore, dirty data, duplicates, and inconsistencies are everywhere and add to the complexity. The Business Intelligence Roadmap methodology contains 900 tasks that are potentially applicable to EDW/BI projects. Of course, not all tasks are pertinent to all projects, but you must consider them and either select or reject them, depending on the nature of the project.

☞ The most significant things to consider about methodology are that nobody can remember hundreds of potential tasks without the help of a methodology, and nobody should ever commit to a deadline without having first reviewed the tasks to understand the effort that may be required for the entire project.

There also needs to be a standard for testing. Business people should establish data defect thresholds for the most significant data and have data quality improvement standards tied to those thresholds. Testing standards apply to all code segments that extract, merge, sort, move, copy, modify, update, and delete data.

☞ The most significant thing to consider about testing is that it applies to both the ETL "data in" side, as well as to the BI application "data out" side.

Not all data has the same requirements for security and privacy. For example, data that is available on the organization's Website is exposed to the whole world and is classified as "public." On the other hand, the financial information with data on profit for the next quarter needs to be secure to avoid insider trading and trading by others outside the company who would profit from knowing about extraordinary profits and losses. If confidential patient information, which is secured under the HIPAA Privacy Rule, is breached, it will result in regulatory fines and public relations erosion.

☞ The most significant thing to consider about security is to work closely with the organization's security office and with the owners of data to determine the required level of data security.

Requirements Definition

Functional requirements are about data delivery, such as reports, queries, OLAP applications, business analytics, scorecards, dashboards, and other access or delivery methods.

☞ The most significant thing to consider about functional requirements is that they must clearly define the expected business value to be delivered.

Data requirements not only refer to what source data elements are needed for the BI application, but also extend to standardizing and integrating that data.

☞ The most significant things to consider about data requirements in this step are to model them from a business perspective (not a database perspective) and to profile the source data early on.

Historical requirements refer to consolidating snapshots of historical data with current data so that both can be accessed together.

☞ The most significant thing to consider about historical requirements is whether you have to back-load historical data into the EDW target databases. If you do, you will have to write additional ETL code.

Security requirements refer to protecting the data from unauthorized access for security or privacy reasons.

☞ The most significant thing to consider about security requirements is to ensure that the security parameters set on the tools are synchronized and at the same level as the security parameters set on the DBMS.

Performance requirements for an EDW/BI environment will rarely match the performance requirements of operational systems. However, speed of data delivery does contribute to the business value. You have to understand what performance levels would *not* be acceptable for the ETL process and the BI application.

☞ The most significant thing to consider about performance requirements is that your technical infrastructure must be scalable enough to support these requirements into the near future.

Project Planning

In addition to organizing the work effort, you have to consider additional things when planning a project. For example, user involvement has two aspects: (a) strong sponsorship, and (b) hands-on participation by at least one business representative.

> ☞ The most significant thing to consider about business involvement is to have a business representative assigned full-time to the core team to co-manage the project.

Cost-benefit analysis, if performed during a prior business case assessment step, should be reviewed and adjusted. In addition, consider and justify the business value of the service request.

> ☞ The most significant thing to consider about cost-benefit review is to ensure that the project will still deliver the expected business value and ROI.

Infrastructure enhancements are often incorporated into the deliverables of new BI applications. Therefore, consider and include the infrastructure related requirements.

> ☞ The most significant things to consider about infrastructure improvement are to schedule sufficient time for them and to coordinate the infrastructure deliverables with the new BI application.

Project scope and deliverables must be doable within the expected time frame with the available staff. Unrealistic expectations of what can be delivered with any kind of quality have killed more than one BI initiative.

> ☞ The most significant thing to consider about project scope and deliverables is to put quality before time.

Staffing and skills have a tremendous influence on a project. If you are short on either, you should consider getting outside help. However, if you hire contractors and consultants, be sure that they take the time to mentor the employees and transfer their knowledge to them.

> ☞ The most significant thing to consider about staffing and skills is to supplement both with contractors and consultants whenever needed so as not to slow down the project or jeopardize its success.

Every project has risks, and you need to prepare a risk mitigation plan. This plan should indicate the likelihood of the risk materializing and the impact it would have on the project. Furthermore, the plan should list triggers, which are situations that point to a potential and perhaps imminent materialization of a risk, and what alternative actions the core team can take to prevent project failure. Finally, identify the mitigation tasks and include them in the project plan.

☞ The most significant thing to consider about risks is to have a contingency plan.

An assumption is anything taken for granted. For example, if you must have a specific database architect on your project in order to meet a deadline, and the database architect has already been assigned to your project, you can probably assume that staffing this critical position is a "done deal." However, were that database architect to quit all of a sudden, your project could be in jeopardy.

☞ The most significant thing to consider about assumptions is to show a counterpart risk for every critical assumption.

Business people always have four basic questions:
- What will you build for me?
- When can I have it?
- What is it going to cost me?
- Who is going to do the work?

These translate into the constraints of expected scope, expected schedule, expected cost, and expected resources (people). Many people don't consider quality to be a "constraint" because they see it as a measure of how well the deliverable meets the requirements. However, I believe that quality should be treated like a fifth constraint during negotiations, because it needs to be balanced against the other four constraints.

☞ The most significant thing to consider about constraints is to include quality as a fifth constraint.

Data Analysis

Business data models, also known as logical data models, represent the business view of data and its data relationships. They are completely process independent, which means they are not database models. The enterprise data model, part of the enterprise information architecture, evolves over time from the project-specific logical data models, and may never be completed. It does not need to be completed because the objective of this process is not to produce a finished model, but to discover and resolve data discrepancies among *different* views and implementations of the *same* data. These data discrepancies exist en masse among operational systems, and are the root causes for the inability to provide consistent information to the business community.

☞ The most significant things to consider about business data models are to discover, discuss, and resolve the data disputes among different business units.

Source data is more often than not stored redundantly and inconsistently on heterogeneous platforms, and selecting the most appropriate sources for the EDW target databases can be a challenge. Many EDW/BI project teams make the mistake of not researching all available source files. Too often, they simply accept the source files their user wants them to use without getting approval from other information consumers of the same data. As a result, they often choose a sub-optimal source file that ends up being unacceptable to other users of the EDW/BI environment. Every potential source file should be evaluated in terms of its:

- Availability
- Understandability
- Stability
- Accuracy
- Timeliness
- Completeness
- Granularity
- Point of origin
- System of record

☞ The most significant things to consider about source data are defining the business rules and identifying the data owners.

Data quality refers to the accuracy of a data element in relation to its own domain or to the domain of other related data elements. It is quite common that existing operational data does not conform to the stated business rules and business policies. Many data elements are used for multiple purposes or are simply left blank.

☞ The most significant thing to consider about data quality is defining the level of data defects that is acceptable for each data element.

Data cleansing refers to correcting the data defects discovered during data analysis. It is important to recognize that data cleansing is a labor-intensive, time-consuming, and expensive process. Cleansing all the data is usually neither cost-justified nor practical, but cleansing none of the data is equally unacceptable. It is therefore important to analyze the source data carefully and to classify the data elements as critical, important (but not absolutely critical), or insignificant to the business. Concentrate on cleansing all of the critical data elements, keeping in mind that not all data is equally critical to all business people. Plan to cleanse as many of the important data elements as time allows, and move the insignificant data elements into the EDW target databases without cleansing them. Look for the following data conditions in your source files:

- Dummy or default values (0 or 9999)
- Intelligent dummy values (an age of 777 means "corporation")
- No data values (missing)
- Multi-purpose fields (overloaded columns)
- Cryptic fields (non-intuitive codes like A, B, C or 1, 2, 3)
- Free-form address lines
- Contradicting data (state NY with zip code 75261 < not a NY zip code)
- Violation of business rules
- Reused primary identifiers (keys)
- Non-unique identifiers
- Missing data relationships
- Inappropriate data relationships

☞ The most significant things to consider about data cleansing are that you don't need to cleanse all the data and you don't need to do it all at once.

Application Prototyping

Prototype objectives describe *why* you are building the prototype and how the project or the business people will benefit from prototyping.

☞ The most significant thing to consider about prototype objectives is to be really clear about the reason for prototyping.

Prototype deliverables describe *what* you are building as a prototype.

☞ The most significant things to consider about prototype deliverables are to clearly define them, to keep them small, and to know whether or not they will be throwaways.

The small scope and tight schedule of a prototype force you to write minimal code, i.e., deliverables with the barest number of features possible to satisfy the objective of the prototype.

☞ The most significant thing to consider about prototype scope is to keep it extremely small; and the most significant thing to consider about prototype schedule is to keep it to only a few days or weeks.

You cannot prototype in a procedural language because it would take too long to change and retest the code. You also cannot serially perform the activities of system analysis, design, coding, and testing. Instead, those activities are all intertwined as you are iteratively refining the deliverable.

☞ The most significant thing to consider about tools and methods is that they must be extremely flexible and easy to use.

Business participation should start with a small set of users, and then slowly include more and more business people from different business units or departments. Observe the business people during prototyping to determine their business and technical skills. This will allow you to hone the final deliverable to meet their specific needs.

☞ The most significant thing to consider about business participation is that it is mandatory.

Metadata Repository Analysis

Metadata capture refers to the method and place where business metadata, technical metadata, process metadata, and usage metadata are first stored.

☞ The most significant thing to consider about metadata capture is to determine whose responsibility it will be.

Metadata repository usage refers to metadata delivery to the technicians and business people. That can be done through metadata reports, an online help function, or direct access to the metadata repository.

☞ The most significant thing to consider about metadata repository usage is to understand how metadata can help the business people navigate through the EDW/BI environment.

Metadata integration refers to the process of linking or associating business metadata with technical metadata, process metadata, and usage metadata to establish data lineage.

☞ The most significant thing to consider about metadata integration is to link business metadata with technical metadata, and technical metadata with process and usage metadata.

Metadata requirements refer to a prioritized list of metadata components that must be captured as part of your project.

☞ The most significant thing to consider about metadata requirements is to know which metadata components would be the most valuable to have for the business people.

Metadata repository security refers to protecting the metadata inside the metadata repository. Only certain people should have the authority to populate the metadata repository or to change any metadata in it.

☞ The most significant thing to consider about metadata repository security is that update authority must be limited.

Metadata delivery refers to providing metadata to the business people as part of the BI application.

☞ The most significant things to consider about metadata delivery are to know what metadata components can be helpful to the business people and how they will use them.

Metadata repository staffing refers to the requirement for one or more metadata administrators with the proper skill set to maintain the metadata repository.

☞ The most significant thing to consider about metadata repository staffing is that you will need at least one full-time metadata administrator.

Database Design

During database design you have to decide whether the data will be stored in a relational/non-multidimensional schema or a multidimensional star or snowflake schema. A database design schema is called a physical data model. Visually, a physical data model looks similar to a logical data model, but there is a big difference. The physical data model represents a de-normalized process-dependent *database* view, while the logical data model represents a fully normalized process-*in*dependent **business** view. Process dependency refers to such things as how the data will be accessed, how many tables will have to be joined for how many queries and in what way, how many people will access the database at the same time and during what times of the day, etc. Using those types of questions, the database architect determines if the best design would be relational/non-multidimensional or multidimensional.

- A relational/non-multidimensional design gives you maximum flexibility at the expense of performance. If you are building an ODS or an EDW database you need to design for flexibility, because most of the time the data will be accessed through indices, and most queries will return small answer sets.
- A multidimensional design gives you maximum performance at the expense of flexibility. If you are building data marts that are tailored toward specific reporting patterns or a BI application that must read large tables for an analytic report, the multidimensional design is optimal.

☞ The most significant thing to consider about design considerations is performance.

Performance considerations also affect the physical components of database design. During physical database design you have to decide how to cluster the tables, whether and how to partition tables, what type and how many indices to use, etc. Relational DBMS engines are based on intricate internal sets of rules. These rules must be understood and followed if performance in the EDW/BI environment is not to suffer. Here are some implementation options.

- Physical Dataset Placement: Methods for achieving fast response time by storing frequently referenced data on fast devices, storing different aggregation levels on different platforms, positioning data so that lengthy seeks are avoided, separating indices from data and putting them on separate disks, etc.
- Partitioning: Large tables should be partitioned across multiple disks. Partitioning enables backing up and restoring one partition of a table without impacting the availability of other partitions of the same table.
- Clustering: This is a useful technique when you are facing table scans. Using this technique, you can store rows sequentially in a table, which can dramatically improve performance.

- Indexing: DBMSs provide a number of index methods to choose from, using any of the many well-known indexing algorithms, such as B-tree, hash, inverted file, sparse, and binary.
- Reorganizations: From time to time, it will be necessary to reorganize the EDW target databases because incremental loads fragment the datasets over time. This fragmentation may result in long data retrievals, and users may notice a big drop in performance.
- Backup and Recovery: DBMSs provide backup utilities for full backups and incremental backups. Disaster recovery requires the backup tapes or cartridges to be stored offsite to enable recover after a disaster.
- Parallelism: To improve performance, a query or a load process should be broken down into components that can run in parallel. There are many products that offer transparent parallel execution.

☞ The most significant thing to consider about performance considerations is how to deal most optimally with huge data volumes.

Database administration staffing is critical for ongoing support of the EDW/BI environment. Not only do the database administrator and database architect have to be experienced with the optimizer of your DBMS, but they also must know advanced techniques for multidimensional database design.

☞ The most significant thing to consider about database staffing is to employ a skilled senior database architect who understands the differences in design philosophies.

ETL Design

Tools and utilities are essential for the ETL process. Writing all the ETL code modules in a procedural language would be very difficult to maintain because the code is constantly modified with each release.

☞ The most significant thing to consider about tools and utilities is their functionality.

ETL staging refers to the process of extracting data from multiple operational sources, transforming, cleansing, and filtering the data, and finally loading the data into one or more EDW target databases.

☞ The most significant thing to consider about ETL staging is that all ETL processes for all BI applications are coordinated in one [logical] ETL staging process.

ETL process flow refers to the sequence of executing code modules, sort and merge utilities, and ETL tool functions that extract data from the source files/databases, transform and cleanse it, and then load it into the EDW target databases.

> ☞ The most significant things to consider about the ETL process flow are that its design must be expandable and that it will have to be redesigned periodically.

Performance considerations for the ETL process involve using parallelism, dropping and rebuilding indices, and turning off referential integrity (RI) on the databases.

> ☞ The most significant thing to consider about performance considerations is that the ETL process must fit into a finite batch window.

Load statistics refer to process related metadata, such as:

- Start and end date and timestamp of the ETL process
- Number of records extracted
- Number of records rejected
- Rejection reasons
- Number of records loaded

> ☞ The most significant thing to consider about load statistics is to make them available as metadata in the metadata repository.

Reconciliation refers to verifying that all counts and amounts tally up between processes. Every code module that manipulates data in any way should produce reconciliation totals. This can be in the form of input and output record counts, specific domain counts, or amount counts.

- Record counts are adequate for extract, sort, and merge modules.
- Domain counts are appropriate for more complicated transformations, such as separating data values from one source data element into multiple target columns.
- Amount counts are usually performed on all amount data elements, whether they are moved as is, transformed into a new format, or used in a calculation.

> ☞ The most significant thing to consider about reconciliation is that the tallies must be accessible to the users, preferably as metadata in the metadata repository or in the form of a report.

Loading the EDW target databases has three processes: initial load, historical load, and incremental load. All three types of loads require three sets of programs: extract, transform, and load.

- Initial load is very similar to a system conversion run. The main task is to move the selected source data elements to the target columns. Transformation specifications include logic to resolve duplicate records, match the primary keys, and truncate or enlarge the length of the data elements.

- Historical load is a process that could be viewed as an extension of the initial load process. However, this set of specifications will be slightly different because historical data has typically been archived to offline storage devices. Since the record layouts of the files and databases usually change over time, the code for the historical load has to accommodate those changes.

- Incremental load refers to the ongoing daily or hourly updates (inserts) to the EDW target databases after the databases have been populated with initial and historical data.

When designing the load process, there are two additional things to consider:

- The first is referential integrity (RI). Because of the huge volumes of data, many organizations prefer to turn off RI to speed up the load process.

- The second is indices. For performance reasons, it is necessary to build many indices on the EDW target databases. However, indices slow down the load process. Therefore, many organizations drop all indices before running the load process.

☞ The most significant things to consider about database loading are to understand the historical data requirements and to benchmark the load performance.

Metadata Repository Design

Very few organizations have a mature metadata environment with an existing metadata repository. If your organization already has a metadata repository, you have to review its metadata components and its functionality, then determine whether to expand them.

☞ The most significant thing to consider about the existing metadata repository is expandability.

Metadata repository products are available and popular. Most of the products are expandable.

☞ The most significant thing to consider when you buy a metadata repository product is to know your metadata requirements and to verify that the product you are buying meets all of your mandatory requirements.

Metadata repository interfaces come in two categories: one category is an interface for people, such as business people or technicians, and the other category includes an interface to tools, such as the ETL or OLAP tools or the DBMS dictionary.

☞ The most significant thing to consider about the metadata repository interfaces is that it will require some effort to understand the interface requirements in order to design the appropriate solutions.

ETL Development

Source data dependencies are very important to understand, since the schedule of the ETL processes has to be coordinated with the completion of the update cycles of operational systems.

☞ The most significant thing to consider about source data dependencies is to know the safest time at which you can extract the source data.

There are ETL process dependencies to consider. One is reusing already existing ETL code modules, which may need to be expanded or may need to be connected to the new ETL module. The other is a dependency between target tables that will influence in what sequence they can be loaded.

☞ The most significant thing to consider about ETL process dependencies is to schedule as many ETL processes in parallel as the dependencies allow.

ETL testing refers to unit testing, integration or regression testing, performance (stress) testing, quality assurance testing, and user acceptance testing. ETL testing is usually guided and controlled by a test plan, which should specify:

- What is being tested (purpose)
- Sequence of program executions (schedule)
- Input criteria for test cases
- Expected output results for the test cases

In addition, document the detailed results of the test runs in a test log. After correcting the code, retest the entire flow again, not just the code module that was fixed. Unfortunately, testing is often done very poorly on EDW/BI projects.

☞ The most significant thing to consider about ETL testing is that, with the exception of unit testing, all testing activities must be managed with a formal test plan.

ETL technical considerations refer to the server(s) on which the ETL process will execute. The decision of where to run the ETL process will largely depend on where your ETL tool is able to run and where your source data resides.

☞ The most significant thing to consider about technical considerations is to run the ETL process on a platform that will maximize performance.

One of the most common user complaints about BI applications is that the data in the EDW target databases does not match the data in the operational source systems. As a result, business people often do not trust the EDW data. Ironically, most of the time, the data in the EDW target databases is more accurate than the data in the operational source systems, because the data has been reformatted, standardized, and cleansed according to business rules given by the users. However, without proof, this trust cannot be restored.

☞ The most significant thing to consider about data accuracy is to provide reconciliation totals as metadata in the metadata repository.

Application Development

Reuse as many of the prototyping results as you can.

☞ The most significant thing to consider about prototyping results is to use the operational prototype to finish developing the BI application and reports.

Development considerations refer to the technology components you use during development.

☞ The most significant thing to consider about development considerations is to beware of any technology differences between the development environment, the test environment, and the production environment.

Scope and requirements are revisited for the last time to see if any adjustments should be made to the project charter and the application requirements document. These final adjustments are not unusual, especially if you prototyped extensively.

☞ The most significant thing to consider about scope and requirements is that changing the scope – especially cutting it – is quite acceptable when you are using the release concept, provided you renegotiate the other project constraints of time, budget, resources, and quality.

Skills and training, in this context, refer to the business people who will be using the BI application.

☞ The most significant thing to consider about skills and training for business people is to provide a support function (and even mentors) to them after the training.

Business analytics applications are tailored to supply the metrics necessary to support business performance management (BPM), business activity monitoring (BAM), customer relationship management (CRM), partner relationship management (PRM), and supply chain management (SCM). The two most popular types of business analytics applications are dashboards and scorecards.

☞ The most significant thing to consider about business analytics applications is to build the appropriate solution for your target audience (e.g., dashboards for executives and scorecards for financial analysts).

Data Mining

Data considerations refer to the quality and meaning of data that will be used by the data mining tool.

☞ The most significant thing to consider about data considerations for data mining is that if the underlying data is inaccurate, the data mining results will also be inaccurate, which, if acted upon, could have dire consequences for the organization.

Data mining tools work with BI applications and can sift through vast amounts of data. Once you build your analytical data model, the data mining operations will return results based on patterns, associations, and relationships among the data.

☞ The most significant things to consider about a data mining tool are to understand the tool's algorithms and to know how to interpret the data mining results.

Staffing considerations refer to the technicians who will build the data mining application, as well as to the statisticians who will run the application and interpret the results.

☞ The most significant thing to consider about staffing is that the data mining expert must have a statistical background.

Metadata Repository Development

Buying a metadata repository product may seem like an easy solution, but it is not "plug and play". You still have to develop a process to extract metadata from its current sources and populate the metadata repository product.

☞ The most significant thing to consider about a purchased product is to ensure that you will get superb vendor support.

Custom-building a metadata repository may take some effort, but you have complete control over metadata components, their storage, and their delivery.

☞ The most significant thing to consider about custom-building a metadata repository is to build it in iterations, not all at once.

Whether you buy or build a metadata repository, you need staff to support it.

☞ The most significant thing to consider about staffing is to realize that after the development work or the installation of the product is completed, you need at least one full-time metadata administrator to maintain and enhance the metadata repository.

Only four types of testing are usually required when developing a metadata repository: unit testing, integration and regression testing, and user acceptance testing. Performance testing is not required, because metadata repositories rarely become big enough to be concerned about performance. In addition, metadata repositories are used less frequently than EDW target databases, so access contention is not an issue for performance. QA testing may or may not be required, depending on whether or not the metadata repository will reside in the production environment. In that case, it is governed by the same production rules as other applications.

☞ The most significant thing to consider about metadata repository testing is to test it as rigorously as any other EDW/BI deliverable built for the business community.

Implementation

Preparing for production refers to setting up program libraries on the production server; setting up the ETL process, the BI application and the regular reports on the job scheduler; preparing the support staff, and training the business people.

☞ The most significant thing to consider about preparation for production is to know the procedures for going into production. In some large organizations, the process of going into production can take a few weeks because you have to follow a very strict process.

Security considerations are sometimes given superficial attention on EDW/BI projects. Keep in mind that the data in the EDW target databases is the same data as in the operational systems. Most EDW target databases store a lot of detailed data.

☞ The most significant thing to consider about security is to understand the privacy issues and regulations in your industry, such as HIPAA in the health care industry.

Database maintenance procedures have to be scheduled. That includes database backup and recovery, disaster recovery, and reorganizing, monitoring, and tuning of databases.

☞ The most significant thing to consider about database maintenance is to understand the service level agreements pertaining to availability, timeliness, and performance.

Training and support for the business people are important critical success factors. The business people will need time and assistance to become familiar with the new technology, the new tools, the new databases, the new BI application, the metadata repository, etc.

☞ The most significant thing to consider about training and support for business people is to give them "just enough" training "just in time".

Prepare to monitor your utilization of resources, such as hardware, network, and staff.

☞ The most significant thing to consider about utilization of resources is to keep an eye out for potential shortages and shortfalls, so as not to affect the EDW/BI environment.

Prepare to manage growth of your EDW/BI environment. As data volumes increase, you need a strategy for summarizing data as it ages. Users rarely require the same level of detail for very old data as they do for current data. Another area to watch is usage. As BI becomes popular, more and more business people will use the EDW/BI databases and applications.

☞ The most significant thing to consider about growth management is to design a flexible architecture that is easy to expand or modify.

Release Evaluation

Conducting a post-implementation review after every major release is critical. It is important that lessons learned are explicitly stated and documented in order to improve the quality and the speed of the development process for future releases.

☞ The most significant things to consider about post-implementation reviews are to schedule each review no later than one week after implementation and to let a trained facilitator lead the session.

Measures of success can be expressed in economic, political, and technical terms. Economic success means that ROI was achieved. Political success means that business value is realized and business people are using the BI applications. Technical success means that the technology components work well together and that the applications perform adequately.

☞ The most significant things to consider about measures of success is that you have to collect metrics to substantiate your success, and you must report on these metrics regularly to prove the value of BI and to sustain your funding requests.

Before you make plans for the next release, review and reprioritize the functions and data that were dropped from the current release. Decide which of the functions and data to bundle with the new requirements for the next release, and which ones to defer and for how long.

☞ The most significant thing to consider about planning the next release is to have the business representative involved in the planning discussions.

Appendix B
BI Roadmap Methodology – Activities

As you review your methodology, consider and discuss all activities (or tasks) of every selected development step before you decide whether or not an activity/task is applicable to your release. Following are detailed descriptions of high-level activities in the sixteen development steps of the Business Intelligence Roadmap methodology.

Business Case Assessment

The business case assessment step has the following nine major activities.

DETERMINE BUSINESS NEED

Some people say it is hard to justify EDW/BI projects. That may be true if you are replacing existing operational reports with a fancy and costly BI application; but it is not true if you are building a solution for a painful business problem that your executives are currently struggling with. Business executives do not hesitate to fund and support projects that solve their business pain.

ASSESS CURRENT DECISION SUPPORT SYSTEM (DSS) SOLUTIONS

Review your current reporting solutions and find out why they don't provide the information the users need. Maybe there are not enough resources in IT to write reports, or maybe the data elements the users need do not exist in operational systems. Another reason could be that it is difficult to access and merge the data because of different key structures or missing keys, or because of data redundancy and inconsistencies.

ASSESS OPERATIONAL SOURCES AND PROCESSES

While you are reviewing your current reporting solutions, take a good look at the operational source data and operational processes. The business problem could exist because the business community does not trust the data they get. Maybe the data is dirty because of poor data entry practices, lack of edits, defective code, or lack of training. There is a possibility that the business problem can be solved inexpensively by tightening the data entry edits.

ASSESS COMPETITORS' BI INITIATIVES

You want to stay ahead of your competition in today's economy. In order to stay ahead, you must know what the competition is doing; for example, if they are achieving higher sales volumes or introducing new innovative products. You don't want to lose your precious customers to your competition.

DETERMINE BI APPLICATION OBJECTIVES

Be sure to align the objectives of the BI solution to critical strategic objectives in the company. The business driver for your BI solution must be new business opportunities, regulatory compliance, or some business problem that cannot be solved without your BI solution. In any case, clearly state the BI application objectives by specifying expected concrete benefits, such as "$5,000,000 increase in revenue within 12 months due to new cross-selling ability."

PROPOSE A SOLUTION

Understanding the business pain and knowing why the current reporting solutions are deficient, propose a BI solution. Be sure to start educating your sponsors and users about a new iterative release approach. If this is not the first EDW/BI release, review any unfulfilled requirements from previous releases and decide whether or not they can be or should be included.

PERFORM COST-BENEFIT ANALYSIS

How much will it cost to build a robust EDW/BI solution for the business problem? What are the projected costs for new hardware, software, and tools? How about ongoing maintenance fees and training costs? Remember to account for the costs of new employees if you need to hire more staff. Then determine the benefits of the new BI application, both tangible and intangible. How will the BI application solve the business problem and save the company money or increase the profit margin? Calculate ROI and indicate the timeframe in which it will be realized.

PERFORM RISK ASSESSMENT

Can you identify all potential risks to the project? If you are unable to produce a detailed risk assessment matrix, use the six basic risk categories of technology, complexity, integration, organization, project team, and financial investment. For each risk, determine whether it is low, medium, or high, identify how likely it is for each risk to materialize, and describe what the impact would be on the EDW/BI project.

WRITE ASSESSMENT REPORT

Summarize all your findings into an assessment report. Include the results of the costs-benefit analysis and the risk assessment. Also include any other information you received from users that might help you make your business case.

Enterprise Infrastructure Evaluation - Technical

The technical infrastructure evaluation step has the following four major activities.

ASSESS EXISTING PLATFORM

With every new service request, review your existing platform in terms of hardware, middleware, DBMS, and tools, as well as your network architecture. Input/output (IO) was the bottleneck of the last century; today it is bandwidth, coupled with a limited capacity for network growth.

EVALUATE NEW PRODUCTS

Every few months, new BI products and vendors seem to make headlines. Better products with more sophisticated capabilities hit the market continuously. While you may not apply every upgrade or buy every new product, you must stay informed about what is available in the market. When evaluating BI user tools, engage the business people and stakeholders in the decision making process.

WRITE TECHNICAL GAP-ANALYSIS REPORT

Compile all findings about your platform into a gap-analysis report. Explain the strengths and weaknesses of your current technical infrastructure, and list any missing infrastructure components that are necessary to meet the project requirements.

EXPAND CURRENT PLATFORM

After you have decided which new products you need to purchase or upgrade, start planning the process of evaluating, selecting, purchasing, installing, and testing those products.

Enterprise Infrastructure Evaluation - Non-Technical

The non-technical infrastructure evaluation step has the following three major activities.

ASSESS EFFECTIVENESS OF NON-TECHNICAL INFRASTRUCTURE COMPONENTS

You need policies, procedures, guidelines, and standards to assist in the coordination and management of the EDW/BI environment. You may already have policies, guidelines, and standards for the operational systems, which may or may not be appropriate for your EDW/BI environment. Review them and decide if you can adopt them or if you need to change them.

WRITE NON-TECHNICAL INFRASTRUCTURE GAP-ANALYSIS REPORT

Compile all findings about your non-technical infrastructure into a gap-analysis report. List any missing or ineffective non-technical infrastructure components that need to be added, revised or replaced. Prioritize which ones to include in the next EDW/BI project, and which ones to defer.

IMPROVE NON-TECHNICAL INFRASTRUCTURE

Be sure to include time estimates for adding or improving non-technical infrastructure components in the project plan. If a lot of the non-technical infrastructure needs to be created or changed, you may want to consider spinning off a separate project.

Requirements Definition

The requirements definition step has the following eight major activities.

DEFINE REQUIREMENTS FOR TECHNICAL INFRASTRUCTURE ENHANCEMENTS

The technical gap-analysis report should point out whether your current technical infrastructure is able to support the new EDW/BI project or if it needs to be changed. Requirements for upgrading or adding new technical infrastructure components could include one or more of the following: hardware, network, DBMS, development tools, reporting tools, query tools, data mining tools, and metadata repository.

DEFINE REQUIREMENTS FOR NON-TECHNICAL INFRASTRUCTURE ENHANCEMENTS

The non-technical gap-analysis report shows whether your current non-technical infrastructure is able to support the new EDW/BI project or if it needs to be changed. Requirements for upgrading or adding new non-technical infrastructure components could include one or more of the following: standards and guidelines, roles and responsibilities, and procedures for the use of methodology, change control, issues management, security, prioritization, testing, service level agreements, user support functions, dispute resolution, metadata capture and delivery, data quality improvement, and communication.

DEFINE REPORTING REQUIREMENTS

Methodologies usually require that report layouts and sample queries are collected or created during the interview process. This can also be accomplished with a prototyping tool. Also define and document the business rules for deriving data and for creating aggregations and summaries.

DEFINE REQUIREMENTS FOR SOURCE DATA

Identify what source data you need and select the most appropriate source files and source databases from the potential list of source systems. Review the potential source systems so that you have a better understanding of the data scope and the data effort.

REVIEW THE PROJECT SCOPE

Compare the detailed requirements to the high-level scope outlined in the service request. Review your existing EDW target databases, the ETL process, and your current BI applications. Can any of it be partially reused? Based on your prior experience with EDW/BI projects and also based on how much code and data can be reused, guess how large this project is. Does it look like an elephant, a tiger, or a mouse?

CREATE THE LOGICAL DATA MODEL

Using the information gathered during this requirements process, create a high-level logical data model with entities, data relationships, and the most important attributes for the data requirements in the service request. This model will be further refined during data analysis.

DEFINE PRELIMINARY SERVICE LEVEL AGREEMENTS

Many technicians may argue that it is too early to commit to service level agreements, and that is true. However, most business people will ask for them because to some extent, they define their acceptance criteria.

☞ Hint: Don't ask the users what their expectations are for availability, timeliness, security, performance, cleanliness, and ongoing support.

Ask them for the outermost acceptable limits; what would *not* be acceptable in terms of availability, timeliness, etc.? At what point would they stop using the EDW/BI environment? This approach accomplishes two things: you get a broader range of expectations to work toward, and the users will have more realistic expectations.

WRITE THE APPLICATION REQUIREMENTS DOCUMENT

The application requirements document should itemize the requirements for functions, data, cleansing, security, performance, availability, and so on. In addition, list the requirements for technical and non-technical infrastructure during the EDW/BI project.

Project Planning

The project planning step has the following eight major activities.

DETERMINE PROJECT REQUIREMENTS

Be sure you understand all of the requirements for data, functionality, and infrastructure in sufficient detail to start the planning process. Remember that you can use prototyping to flesh out many of these requirements.

DETERMINE CONDITION OF SOURCE FILES AND DATABASES

The project schedule cannot be completed and a delivery date cannot be committed to without a good understanding of the condition of the source files and databases. Take some time to perform some cursory data profiling on suspected poor quality data in the operational files and databases. If you see a lot of dirty data, identify the responsible data stewards and data owners so that you know who to work with during data analysis.

REFINE THE COST ESTIMATES

Prepare detailed cost estimates and be sure to include hardware and network costs, as well as the purchase price and annual maintenance fees for utilities and tools. In addition, ascertain the costs for contractors, consultants, and training. A more indirect cost is associated with the learning curve for the business people and IT. Try to estimate it and be sure to factor it into your cost and time estimates.

REVISE THE RISK ASSESSMENT

Perform a project-specific risk assessment, or review and revise it if one was performed during a prior step. Rank the risks on a scale of 1 to 5 according to the severity of their impact on the EDW/BI project, 1 being low impact and 5 being high impact. Also indicate the likelihood of the risks materializing on a scale of 1 to 5, 1 being "it will probably never happen," and 5 being "you can almost count on it."

IDENTIFY CRITICAL SUCCESS FACTORS

Critical success factors are conditions that must exist for the project to be successful. Some common critical success factors are: supportive sponsorship, full-time involvement of the user, realistic budgets and schedules, realistic expectations, and team members with the right skills.

PREPARE THE PROJECT CHARTER

A project charter is often called a scope agreement, a document of understanding, or a statement of work. Traditionally, it is often no more than a three or four-page general overview of project requirements, resources, cost, and schedule. However, an EDW/BI project charter is a 20-30 page document that is developed by the core team with the participation of the business representative. It represents the baseline agreement about requirements, scope, resources, cost, schedule, constraints, assumptions, critical success factors, roles and responsibilities, methodology, project organization, and other agreed-upon items the core team members want to document.

CREATE PROJECT PLANS

This activity is replaced by the seven steps of the Extreme Scoping planning process (Part III of this book).

KICK OFF (INITIATE) THE PROJECT

Initiating a project usually begins with an orientation meeting for the entire team, which includes the core team members, the development track team members, as well as the extended team members. At this meeting, the project manager describes the project organization, discusses the project team dynamics, and sets up communication channels to the rest of the organization to keep stakeholders and interested parties up-to-date on the progress of the project.

Data Analysis

The data analysis step has the following six major activities.

ANALYZE INTERNAL AND EXTERNAL DATA SOURCES

Many BI applications need data from external sources, such as Dun & Bradstreet. Merging external data with internal data has its own challenges. External data is often dirty and incomplete, and it usually has a different format and key structure than internal data. It may take some time to resolve these differences.

REFINE LOGICAL DATA MODEL

If you're lucky, some of the internal and external data will have been modeled on a previous project and may already be part of the enterprise data model. In that case, extract and expand the portions you need and refine them with new data entities, new data relationships, and new attributes. Otherwise, create a new logical data model for the data scope of this EDW/BI service request.

> A project-specific logical data model is a fully normalized *business* model, *not* a database model.

DETERMINE SOURCE DATA QUALITY

At the same time as you are working on the project-specific data model, extensively profile the source files and databases. Don't expect the source files and databases to conform to the stated business rules and business policies on the logical data model. It is quite common for data elements in operational systems to be used for multiple purposes. It is equally common for many data elements to be left blank or set to a default value. These and other data anomalies have to be addressed in the logical data model.

EXPAND ENTERPRISE DATA MODEL

The enterprise data modeler from the EIM group typically manages the enterprise data model. Once the project-specific data model is relatively complete and stable, it is sent back to the enterprise data modeler, who then merges it into the enterprise data model. During this merge process, additional data discrepancies and inconsistencies may surface, which will be returned to the EDW/BI project team for resolution. At this point, managers, users, and the project team often panic because it is seen as an unexpected stumbling block on the project. Knowing the data chaos most companies have, this should be expected to happen and time should be built into your project plan to address situations like this.

RESOLVE DATA DISCREPANCIES

The data discrepancies discovered during data analysis often involve business people from other projects or other lines of business. In that case, it is the responsibility of the other stakeholders and the data owners to work out their differences and standardize the inconsistencies.

WRITE DATA CLEANSING SPECIFICATIONS

Based on your logical data modeling results, document the specifications for how to cleanse the data. Send these specifications to the users, the data owners, and other stakeholders for validation.

Application Prototyping

The application prototyping step has the following seven major activities.

ANALYZE ACCESS REQUIREMENTS

Determine the data access requirements for the BI application, reports, and queries. Prototyping is a proven way to discover detailed requirements. In addition, prototyping is the perfect activity during which you can assess the technical and business skills of the users participating in the prototype activities.

DETERMINE SCOPE OF PROTOTYPE

Break down the scope of the prototype so that it is small enough to be built and tested in a matter of days. Work with only a subset of data; just enough to support the selected function(s) of the prototype. Prototyping, by definition, is iterative; which means that more functions and data are added in iterations. Document the scope in the prototype charter.

SELECT TOOLS FOR THE PROTOTYPE

Evaluate the existing suite of tools at your company and use them for prototyping, if you can. People are already trained on those tools and feel comfortable using them. If new tools are selected, schedule training sessions as soon as possible.

PREPARE THE PROTOTYPE CHARTER

Create a short and informal document that describes the purpose of the prototype, its scope, on which platform it will be built, the time-box, and list the business people who will participate.

DESIGN APPLICATION, REPORTS, AND QUERIES

Design the prototype database based on the data access requirements. That will be either a multidimensional schema or a relational/non-multidimensional schema. In addition, design the selected functionality, such as reports, queries, or Web portal. Map the necessary source data to the prototype database. Remain in communication with the data quality analyst to exchange information about data quality problems.

BUILD THE PROTOTYPE

Build the first iteration of the prototype based on the initial design of the database, reports, queries, and Web portal. Refine the prototype in subsequent iterations. Try to get the users to participate in the prototyping activities. If you have time, use prototyping to test various tuning techniques.

DEMONSTRATE THE PROTOTYPE

Demonstrate the prototype to the users and solicit their feedback frequently. Think of the demonstrations as a marketing activity, in addition to being a good way to validate the requirements.

Metadata Repository Analysis

The metadata repository analysis step has the following five major activities.

ANALYZE METADATA REPOSITORY REQUIREMENTS

If you already have a metadata repository, review it and determine if you need to expand it. Identify and prioritize the new metadata requirements for your specific EDW/BI project. Update the latest version of the application requirements document to include the new metadata repository requirements.

ANALYZE INTERFACE REQUIREMENTS FOR METADATA REPOSITORY

Whether a metadata repository is bought or built, it must accept metadata from the different tools in which it is captured. Business metadata is captured in modeling tools, word processing documents, or spreadsheets. Technical metadata is captured in DBMS dictionaries. Process metadata is captured in ETL tools, OLAP tools, report writers, and data mining tools. Usage metadata is not captured by all DBMS vendors. Check with your DBMS vendor to find out whether and where usage metadata is captured.

ANALYZE METADATA REPOSITORY ACCESS AND REPORTING REQUIREMENTS

Define the requirements for accessing, querying, and reporting from the metadata repository. Remember that you have two audiences: technicians and business people. Consider building two different portals for them. Decide whether you want to build a help function (wizard) for the metadata repository.

CREATE THE LOGICAL META MODEL

A logical meta model is the best way to document metadata repository requirements. It is drawn as an entity-relationship diagram to explicitly show the relationships between metadata components (e.g., entity related to table, attribute related to column, data relationship related to foreign key). Many people just call this the *meta model* because generally, the logical meta model is identical to the physical meta model, if the database is implemented as a fully normalized structure.

CREATE THE META-METADATA

No, I did not make up this term. Meta-metadata refers to metadata collected about metadata. It describes the metadata components in detail (e.g., definition of `ENTITY`, its relationship and cardinality to `TABLE`, its physical location in the system table `MDRSYSENT`).

Database Design

The database design step has the following eight major activities.

REVIEW DATA ACCESS REQUIREMENTS

The database architect works closely with the ETL architect and the BI application lead to determine the most appropriate design schema for the EDW target databases. (If the database architect was actively involved in the prototyping activities – as he or she should have been – this review is not necessary.)

DETERMINE AGGREGATION AND SUMMARIZATION REQUIREMENTS

It is very important for the database architect to understand the data aggregation and summarization requirements before committing to the final design schema for the EDW target databases. These are based on the aggregation and summarization needs of the application, reports, and queries.

DESIGN THE EDW TARGET DATABASES

A lot of developers, and some users, think that BI applications are only about multidimensional analysis and multidimensional reporting. They are not! For example, financial analysts, statisticians, and data scientists need historical detailed data for ad-hoc reporting. They are willing to give up performance, even if it means that their queries will run for hours or overnight. These types of analysts are in the minority, but they do exist, and their data access requirements are probably more important than those of casual users. Therefore, the design of most of your data marts will indeed be multidimensional, but some data marts, as well as the EDW and ODS databases, will be based on a relational/non-multidimensional schema. Database designs are documented as physical data models.

DESIGN THE PHYSICAL DATABASE STRUCTURES

The most important characteristics of physical database design include clustering, partitioning, indexing, and placing the datasets in an optimal way, such as co-locating related tables.

BUILD THE EDW TARGET DATABASES

The database architect uses data definition language (DDL) to define the database structures (e.g. storage groups, database partitions, tables, indices) and data control language (DCL) to establish database security. The database architect grants create, read, update, and delete (CRUD) authority to individuals or to groups into which individuals are assigned.

DEVELOP DATABASE MAINTENANCE PROCEDURES

Once the databases are in production, you will have to run periodic maintenance procedures, such as taking database backups or reorganizing fragmented tables. The time to establish these procedures is during database design.

PREPARE TO MONITOR AND TUNE THE DATABASE DESIGN

You will also have to monitor and periodically tune the EDW target databases. In an EDW/BI environment, the databases continuously grow and access patterns constantly change. This leads to performance degradation over time. Most of the time, tuning the affected database will take care of performance problems, but be prepared to occasionally redesign a database.

PREPARE TO MONITOR AND TUNE DATABASE ACCESS CALLS

The same holds true for monitoring and tuning SQL database access calls. Consider parallel query execution as a solution to boost query performance.

ETL Design

The ETL design step has the following five major activities.

CREATE SOURCE TO TARGET MAPPING DOCUMENT

During data analysis, the data administrator documented the data cleansing requirements. Incorporate them now into your transformation specifications and map the combined specifications into a source to target matrix or spreadsheet. Since most companies use ETL tools, let the ETL tool produce the final documentation automatically.

TEST ETL TOOL FUNCTIONS

Be sure you understand what your ETL tool can and cannot do before designing the ETL process flow, and before deciding how to set up the staging area. Therefore, test the ETL tool functions early and determine if you have to write additional custom code for the more complicated and lengthy transformations that the tool was not designed to handle.

DESIGN THE ETL PROCESS FLOW

If you have a very complex ETL process, designing an efficient ETL process flow can be challenging. Consult with the database architect, who sometimes has a database solution for a tricky problem.

DESIGN ETL PROGRAMS

Expect to load several years of historical data, and remember that there are three sets of ETL programs to consider: the initial load, the historical load, and the incremental load. Break the ETL programs into the smallest possible code modules so that as many modules as possible can be executed in parallel. Design the code modules with reusability in mind.

SET UP THE ETL STAGING AREA

When designing the staging area, consider the type and location of source files and databases, as well as the functions and capabilities of the ETL tool. Decide if you want a centralized staging area on a dedicated server, or if it would be better to implement a decentralized staging area in your environment.

Metadata Repository Design

The metadata repository design step has the following four major activities.

DESIGN THE METADATA REPOSITORY DATABASE

If you are building your own metadata repository solution, design the metadata repository database. Your choices are a fully normalized entity-relationship design, or a more abstract object-oriented design. Create (or enhance) the physical meta model, which is the database design schema for the metadata repository. If you choose to implement a fully normalized entity-relationship design, then your physical meta model will look identical to your logical meta model. If you choose to implement an abstract object-oriented design, then the explicitly identified metadata components on your logical meta model will be reduced to three metadata tables on the physical meta model:

1. Metadata Object
2. Metadata Object Type
3. Metadata Object to Object Relationship

INSTALL AND TEST THE METADATA REPOSITORY PRODUCT

If you are buying a metadata repository, install and test it thoroughly. Be sure that you get adequate support and training from your vendor.

DESIGN THE METADATA MIGRATION PROCESS

Identify all metadata sources from which business, technical, process, and usage metadata will be extracted, such as the data modeling tool, ETL tool, OLAP tool, DBMS system tables, Excel spreadsheets, etc. Determine the import, export, and API capabilities of those tools. Design the code modules that will extract metadata from these tools, link it, and load it into the metadata repository.

DESIGN THE METADATA APPLICATION

Metadata repository products come with an application. Therefore, if you bought a metadata repository, you don't have to design a custom application. However, if you are building a metadata repository from scratch, design the metadata application, which will be used by technicians and business people to access the metadata repository. Don't forget an online help function (wizard).

ETL Development

The ETL development step has the following five major activities.

BUILD AND UNIT TEST THE ETL PROCESS

Write the ETL code for the three sets of load processes: initial load, historical load, and incremental load. Consider using a DBMS load utility for populating the EDW target databases. Be sure to unit test all ETL tool modules and all custom-written ETL code for compilation, functionality, and edits.

INTEGRATION AND REGRESSION TEST THE ETL PROCESS

Testing brand new code is called integration testing. Testing modified code is called regression testing. There will be a lot of regression testing with the ETL process! Both types of testing must be performed under a formal test plan.

PERFORMANCE TEST THE ETL PROCESS

Many – if not most – EDW target databases are very large databases. Therefore, it is important to stress test the code modules that read or write to high-volume tables and that perform complicated operations. It is common to simulate performance tests with stress-test simulation tools.

QUALITY ASSURANCE TEST THE ETL PROCESS

Usually, programs cannot be moved into production unless they have undergone rigorous quality assurance (QA) testing. These tests are usually run in a separate QA environment under the supervision of the operations staff.

USER ACCEPTANCE TEST THE ETL PROCESS

I always urge the users to participate throughout the development process, including integration, regression, performance, and QA testing. If the users participated, then user acceptance testing may not be necessary at all, because they will have already seen the test results from the other types of tests. However, if the users have not participated, then they must validate all functions of the ETL process and sign off on the test.

Application Development

The application development step has the following five major activities.

DETERMINE THE FINAL PROJECT REQUIREMENTS

Hopefully, you were able to finalize the requirements during prototyping. If not, this is your last opportunity. Maybe the user already requested changes or you had to log unresolved issues. In either case, you should have a good understanding of how stable the requirements are.

BUILD AND UNIT TEST THE APPLICATION PROGRAMS

After reviewing the prototyping results, code the remaining functions of the BI application, including the reports, queries, front-end interface, and online help function (wizard). Be sure the code modules and scripts are unit tested to prove that they compile error free.

INTEGRATION AND REGRESSION TEST THE APPLICATION PROGRAMS

Develop a test plan with detailed test cases and create the test data. All code modules and scripts should be integration and regression tested end-to-end, in the sequence in which they will run in the production environment. Load the databases with sample "live" data. Be sure to secure the live data appropriately! Rerun the tests until you get a clean run.

PERFORMANCE, QA, AND UA TEST THE APPLICATION PROGRAMS

Be sure to stress test some of the more complicated code modules, those that have many JOINs, and those that execute against high-volume tables. A simulated stress test will indicate how the BI application will perform in the production environment. Perform the QA test with operations, and the UA test with the users. Similar to ETL testing, if the users participate in all other testing, then user acceptance testing may not be necessary at all.

PROVIDE USER TRAINING

The help desk staff, power users, casual users, business analysts, and business managers will need training. Schedule the training sessions either in-house, or with a vendor. If you are conducting the training sessions yourself, create the training materials.

Data Mining

The data mining step has the following eight major activities.

STATE THE BUSINESS PROBLEM

Identify the goals for your data mining activities, such as increase profits, reduce costs, or expand the market share. You have to present these goals to management in order to get their commitment to invest in data mining.

COLLECT THE DATA

One of the most time consuming activities in data mining is collecting the right type of data. Identify all of the data that will be needed for analysis. This data can be from the operational databases or data from the EDW target databases. Once you decide what data to use, extract all pertinent data from these data sources, and load it into an exploration warehouse.

CONSOLIDATE AND CLEANSE THE DATA

Consolidate and cleanse the data from the various sources. Sometimes, internal data is supplemented with external data. If that is the case, resolve all data discrepancies between the two different data sources.

PREPARE THE DATA

Eliminate data with missing values or replace the missing values with *most likely* values. Business people often want to know the maximum, minimum, average, mean, median, and mode values. Also consider using data classification and data reduction techniques.

BUILD THE ANALYTICAL DATA MODEL

It is usually the statistician who builds, tunes, and maintains the analytical data model. The model has to be such that it continues to *learn* while it is repeatedly used by the data mining tool.

INTERPRET THE DATA MINING RESULTS

It is also the statistician who interprets whether the data mining results are actionable, and if they can be presented to business executives.

PERFORM EXTERNAL VALIDATION OF RESULTS

Periodically, the statistician will compare the data mining results with published industry statistics. If there are any deviations from the industry statistics, the statistician looks for the reasons. Maybe the selection criteria of internal data are different from that of the industry statistics. Maybe the time frame during which your data was selected is different from the time frame used by the industry statistics.

MONITOR THE ANALYTICAL DATA MODEL OVER TIME

Since industry statistics change over time, and some industries have seasonal changes, it is important that the statistician periodically adjusts the analytical data model.

Metadata Repository Development

The metadata repository development step has the following six major activities.

BUILD THE METADATA REPOSITORY DATABASE

If you are building your own customized metadata repository solution, generate the DDL and run it to create the metadata repository database structures. Also, generate the DCL and run it to establish CRUD authority on the metadata repository database. If you are buying a metadata repository product, set up CRUD authority on the metadata repository product to allow the metadata migration process and the reports to run, and to allow direct access to the metadata repository product.

BUILD AND UNIT TEST THE METADATA MIGRATION PROCESS

Metadata migration is the process that moves metadata into the metadata repository. If you are building your own metadata repository solution, code the metadata migration programs, including the tool interfaces. These code modules will extract metadata from the tools where it is collected and load the metadata into your metadata repository. If you bought a metadata repository product, test it to verify that its import/export functions work as expected.

BUILD AND UNIT TEST THE METADATA APPLICATION

The metadata application is the process that gets metadata out of the metadata repository. If you are building your own metadata repository solution, develop the metadata application functions, including the online help function, as well as metadata reports and queries. If you bought a metadata repository product, test the application functions (interfaces, reports, queries) that came with the product.

TEST METADATA REPOSITORY PROGRAMS OR PRODUCT FUNCTIONS

Perform integration testing and regression testing with a formal test plan. Subsequently, the users and the technicians perform a combination QA/UA test. If the metadata repository is not physically placed on a production server and is not accessed through the production environment, then there is no need for QA testing.

PREPARE THE METADATA REPOSITORY FOR PRODUCTION

If the metadata repository is going to be in production, then the server platform must be installed and tested. Write a reference guide for the help desk staff, and a training manual for the business people on how to use the metadata repository.

PROVIDE METADATA REPOSITORY TRAINING

Train the business people and the help desk staff how to use the metadata repository database and the online help functions, and how to extract reports and launch queries. Develop and schedule the training sessions in house, or arrange for training through the vendor.

Implementation

The implementation step has the following six major activities.

PLAN THE IMPLEMENTATION

Make sure that all the resources needed for the implementation are available. Plan to rollout your deliverable to a small group of business people first, and learn from the experience.

SET UP THE PRODUCTION ENVIRONMENT

If you work in a large organization, you will have to follow strict procedures to prepare the production environment, such as how to set up the production program libraries, create production databases, grant authority to those databases, set production security levels, etc.

INSTALL ALL EDW AND BI APPLICATION COMPONENTS

Move all ETL code, BI application code, and metadata repository code to their respective production libraries.

SET UP THE PRODUCTION SCHEDULE

Set up the job scheduler for all ETL programs and BI application programs that will run on a regular basis. Remember that some ETL jobs include metadata programs, such as capturing load statistics, reconciliation totals, and data quality errors.

LOAD PRODUCTION DATABASES

Run the initial load process, followed by the historical load process. Load the metadata repository with metadata from the various metadata sources (e.g. spreadsheets, data modeling tool, ETL tool, OLAP tool).

PREPARE FOR ONGOING SUPPORT

Begin to schedule regular backups for all production databases. Plan to use maintenance utilities provided by the DBMS vendor. Decide who will monitor performance, growth, usage, and quality on an ongoing basis.

Release Evaluation

The release evaluation step has the following four major activities.

PREPARE FOR A POST-IMPLEMENTATION REVIEW

Unless your release was very small and you encountered no problems whatsoever, it is usually a good idea to take some time to review your last release. You want to learn what worked well and what didn't.

ORGANIZE THE POST-IMPLEMENTATION REVIEW MEETING

Prepare an agenda with a list of topics and distribute the agenda to all project team members; include members of the core team, development track teams, and extended team. I recommend that you find a third-party facilitator and scribe, so that all project team members can fully participate in the review meeting. In addition, review any functional or data requirements that didn't make it into the last release and put them on the agenda.

CONDUCT THE POST-IMPLEMENTATION REVIEW MEETING

If this is a formal review, ask the sponsor to open and close the meeting. The project manager then reviews the agenda, and explains the rules of the meeting and the roles of the facilitator and scribe. The facilitator leads the meeting, and the scribe documents all discussion points and action items. Any dropped functional and data requirements are reprioritized and bundled into a future release.

FOLLOW UP ON THE POST-IMPLEMENTATION REVIEW

Someone on the project team is designated to follow up on all action items. Action items are such things as updating the standards or the methodology, resolving a data dispute, or correcting an urgent problem that cannot wait for the next release.

This glossary contains definitions and explanations of terms, titles, and acronyms *as I use them in this book*.

1NF. A data modeling term referring to first normal form: there are no repeating groups.

2NF. A data modeling term referring to second normal form: there are no partial key dependencies.

3NF. A data modeling term referring to third normal form: there are no non-key dependencies.

4NF. A data modeling term referring to fourth normal form: there are no independent multi-valued attributes. Beyond the scope of this book.

5NF. A data modeling term referring to fifth normal form: there are no dependent multi-valued attributes. Beyond the scope of this book.

Access path. Describes how records are retrieved from a database when a SQL statement is executed.

Actual test result. Describes the actual output a code module produced after running a test. It should match the expected test result.

Agile principles. A set of agile guidelines followed by agile practitioners. Most are used in Extreme Scoping, but not all.

Amount counts. Sum of amounts by source data elements or by original code values on the source files/databases, compared to the sum of amounts by target columns or by transformed code values on the EDW target databases. Usually performed on all amount data elements, whether they are moved as-is, transformed into a new format, or used in a calculation.

Analytics. The science of examining raw data with the purpose of drawing conclusions about it.

API. An application program interface is a set of commands, functions, and protocols that give a developer programmatic access to a proprietary software application.

Artifact. Used to be called task deliverable. A tangible output from an activity or task. For example, a logical data model, a requirements document, or a project plan.

Assumption. A supposition or presumption. Something you take for granted.

Attribute. A logical data modeling term referring to a data element. For example, *Customer Gender Code* is an attribute of the entity CUSTOMER.

Back-end. Refers to the 80% data management activities of EDW, such as data profiling, data modeling, and ETL processes.

Backlog. An agile term for a long list of user requirements. Not used in Extreme Scoping.

Bar chart. A graph using parallel bars of varying lengths to illustrate comparative values. Similar to a histogram, except the bars in the bar chart don't touch each other.

BCNF. A data modeling term referring to Boyce-Codd normal form; a variation of 3NF. Beyond the scope of this book.

BDTP™. B stands for business value, D stands for data effort, T stands for technical considerations, and P stands for project constraints and interdependencies.

BDTP Balance™. A balanced approach to planning and managing a project. The balance is between business, data, technology, and project perspectives.

BI application. A front-end deliverable from an EDW/BI project. For example, a dashboard.

BI initiative. A strategic business program for enterprise-wide analytics capabilities to help identify and develop new business opportunities.

BI program manager. A director-level position managing the company's EDW/BI environment. Should report to a CDO.

BI steering committee. A group of business executives who provide collective sponsorship for the company's BI initiative, prioritize EDW/BI projects, settle disputes among business people, and fund the EIM group.

Bottom-up source data analysis. Also known as data archeology, this refers to studying all the data elements in source files and operational databases, as well as analyzing the data declaration sections in programs for the purpose of understanding the semantic meaning of the data, determining its definition and proper business name, documenting its business rules, validating its domain values, and finding dirty data.

Burn-down charts. A graphical representation of work left to do versus time left in which to do it. It shows total effort (in hours or points) on the vertical axis and time remaining on the horizontal axis. A "burn down" line begins in the top left corner, indicating the greatest amount of work at the beginning of a project. The line then moves in the direction of the bottom right corner toward the deadline, as hours are spent (burnt) on project work. Not used in Extreme Scoping.

Business. I use this term for all types of companies and organizations, including for-profit, not-for-profit, government institutions, and non-governmental organizations.

Business analysis. Also known as integration analysis. I use the terms interchangeably. Focus is on understanding the requirements and finding opportunities for reusing/sharing data, applications, and business processes.

Business data model. Also known as logical data model. I use the terms interchangeably because this type of data model represents the business view of the data, not a database view.

Business domain. A specific operational area or functional responsibility in the organization. A line of business.

Business-focused activity. An activity performed with a business perspective instead of a technical perspective.

Business intelligence. A set of methodologies, processes, architectures, and technologies that transform raw data into meaningful and useful information for business purposes.

> *Not* to be confused with a BI application, which is a small subset of business intelligence.

Business metadata. Contextual information about business data. For example, business names for entities and attributes, business rules, business definitions, data domains, data types, data quality rules, and data integrity rules.

Business policy. Guidelines developed by an organization to govern the actions of its officers and employees regarding business processes and business data.

Business rule. A rule that defines or constrains some aspect of the business, such as an operational rule, a process rule, or a data rule. Business rules are documented as metadata.

Cadence. A rhythm for delivering something every X number of days, where X is a fixed, predetermined time period. Scrum has a cadence of 29 days, XP of ten days. Not used in Extreme Scoping.

Capability maturity model. The model describes a five-level evolutionary path of maturity. The levels are generally described as initial, repeatable, defined, managed, and optimized. Developed by the Software Engineering Institute (SEI) at Carnegie Mellon University in the 1980s.

Cardinality. The maximum number of times one entity can be associated with another entity. The choices are one time or many times.

CDI. See Customer data integration.

CDO. Chief data officer is responsible for enterprise information management and data governance. Reports to the CEO and is a peer of the CIO, CTO, COO, and CFO.

CEO. Chief executive officer is the highest-ranking officer in charge of total management of the company.

CFO. Chief financial officer is primarily responsible for managing the financial risk of the company.

Charge-back. The process of assessing and assigning the costs of project deliverables (e.g., operational systems and BI applications) to the departments that use them.

CIO. Chief information officer is responsible for information technology and the computer systems of the company.

> Many CIOs are actually CTOs, which is the reason for the new position of CDO.

CMM. See Capability maturity model.

Clustering. Storing data physically adjacent (in sequence) on a disk, based on a clustering index.

Code-centric. Technical activities that revolve around coding and building systems. Seen through a developer's eyes. Similar to development-driven.

Collective sponsorship. A group of business executives that sponsor a project, program, or initiative together (collectively). If one executive leaves the company, the project, program, or initiative continues uninterrupted.

Collectively architected. Architected with an enterprise view to avoid unnecessary and uncontrolled redundancy. Architectural components are meant to be shared and reused. Opposite of silo.

COO. Chief operating officer is responsible for the daily business operations of the company.

Conceptual data model. A high-level business data model (ER Diagram) that contains only kernel (fundamental) entities of an industry or a company, and where most data relationships are many-to-many. This model is refined into a more detailed logical data model.

Consultant. A person who is an advisor and who provides expertise when the company has none in house. The consultant tells the company what needs to be done, and the company's staff performs the work.

Contractor. A person who has a specific set of skills that the company does not have or needs more of. The company tells the contractor what needs to be done, and the contractor performs the work.

Core team. Also known as project management team. I use the terms interchangeably because core team members collectively manage EDW/BI projects. The team consists of a business representative, an EIM professional, a technical expert, and a project manager or project lead.

CPM. Stands for critical path method. Similar to a PERT chart. An algorithm to calculate the longest path to a project end date based on historical data about the duration of tasks and dependencies between tasks. Developed by Morgan Walker and James Kelley, Jr. in the late 1950s. Not used in Extreme Scoping.

CRM. See Customer relationship management.

CRUD. Access authority granted to a developer, a user, or a program to create, read, update, and/or delete records from a file or database.

CTO. Chief technology officer is focused on scientific and technological issues of the company.

Customer data integration. A comprehensive representation of a customer across multiple channels and lines of business. Customer data is typically integrated from multiple operational systems and databases.

Customer relationship management. Refers to all aspects of interaction that a company has with its customers, whether it is sales or service-related.

Daily stand-up meeting. An agile term for a very short daily team meeting to provide a status update. Rules: the meeting is usually time-boxed to 5–15 minutes, and is held standing up to remind people to keep the meeting short and to-the-point. Every team member answers three questions: What did you accomplish yesterday? What will you do today? What obstacles are impeding your progress? Used in Extreme Scoping with relaxed rules and sitting down.

Dashboard. An easy to read, highly visual display of meters, alerts, dials, trends, and forecasts. Single page, real-time user interface showing a graphical presentation of the current status and historical trends of a company's key performance indicators. Primarily used by executives.

Data administrator. A person responsible for the administration, control, and coordination of all data analysis activities. For example, logical data modeling, data definitions, data analysis, data standards, maintenance of data models, including the enterprise data model, and the metadata repository. I use this term interchangeably with EIM professional, although in the strictest sense, an EIM professional can be a data administrator, a metadata administrator, a data quality analyst, an enterprise data modeler, or any other functional title associated with data management activities.

> This is *not* a technical position and has nothing to do with databases! Data administrators do not care about buffer pools or any other database concepts.

Data administration. Also known as enterprise information management (EIM), information resource management (IRM), and data resource management (DRM).

The development and execution of architectures, policies, practices, and procedures that properly manage the full data lifecycle needs of an enterprise (DAMA-DMBOK).

Data administration principles. Refers to business data modeling, enterprise data modeling, applying formal rules to data definitions and data names, defining data domains, standardizing data domains, collecting business metadata, defining and applying class words, defining and applying approved abbreviations, and defining data quality thresholds.

Data analysis. The systematic study of data for the purpose of understanding its meaning, structure, relationships, business rules, usage, value, etc.

Data anomalies. Something abnormal or irregular about the data. Could be data errors, duplicates, inconsistencies, multiple semantic meanings for the same data, or domain outliers.

Data architect. A person who models business data from a business perspective. This role is part of data administration.

> This term is frequently used by database architects, which creates a homonym situation.

Data-driven. A methodology or activity that has a business data perspective to it. For example, data analysis, enterprise data modeling, metadata collection, and data quality improvement. Opposite of development-driven.

Data effort. The amount of time it takes to identify all potential data sources, profile the data sources, model the data sources, standardize the data, document the business rules, identify data quality problems, determine how to correct them, extract the data, transform and cleanse the data, and load the data into the EDW target databases.

Data governance. A strategic business program to manage data as an enterprise asset. Includes policies, procedures, organization, roles, and responsibilities. Three A's of DG: authority (data owner), accountability (data steward), and administration (data administrator).

Data integration. Combining (consolidating) data from different sources and providing users with a unified view of the data. In addition to consolidating data, integration enforces data uniqueness.

Data management. The development, execution, and supervision of plans, policies, programs, and practices that control, protect, deliver, and enhance the value of data and information assets (DAMA-DMBOK).

Data mart. A database customized for a specific pattern of reporting or analytics application.

Data mining. Data analysis using a specialized tool to discover unsuspected or unknown relationships, patterns, or associations of data.

This is *not* writing SQL queries.

Data mining database. A database used by a data mining tool. Usually an exploration warehouse, but can be the EDW database, data marts, the ODS, or an operational file or database.

Data originator. A person who enters data into the operational system of record, or a department where data is entered for the first time into an operational system. For example, a loan origination department creates (originates) a new loan and enters the loan data into the loan application system.

Data owner. A business executive or senior manager who has the authority to establish and enforce policies and business rules for business data.

Data resource management. See Data administration.

Data source. Can be internal or external. Usually an operational system, but can also be any other file or database from which data is extracted.

Data steward. A data analyst on the business side who is accountable for the quality of data under their control.

Data transformation. Manipulation of data to bring it into conformance with the business rules, domain rules, and integrity rules.

Data type. Classification of an attribute that indicates whether the attribute is an integer, a decimal, a character, etc.

Data warehouse. See Enterprise data warehouse.

Data warehouse appliance. An integrated set of servers, storage, operating system, DBMS, and pre-optimized software specifically pre-installed for data warehousing.

Database architect. Also known as database designer. A person who models data from a database perspective. This role can also perform other database administration (DBA) duties.

Database designer. See Database architect. I use the terms interchangeably.

DBA. Database administrators have traditionally performed all database activities, such as designing, maintaining, monitoring, and tuning databases. On EDW/BI projects, the responsibility for designing the EDW target databases is often separated into a distinct database architect role.

DBMS. Stands for database management system, such as Oracle, DB2, or Teradata.

DCL. Data control language is the SQL syntax used to control access to data in the database.

DDL. Data definition language is the SQL syntax used to define the database structures.

"Death march" project. An extremely frustrating and unreasonable development project.

Decision tree. A graph that uses a branching method (like a tree) to illustrate every possible outcome of a decision.

Deliverable. Refers to a physical object created for the user. Could be a report, a column on a report, a table loaded with data, or any other BI service.

De-normalized data model. A physical data model where two or more entities from the logical data model are collapsed into one table.

Development considerations. Configuration differences between development, test, and production environments.

Development-driven. A methodology or activity that has a technical development perspective to it. For example, converting requirements into a system design, then coding and testing. Opposite of data-driven.

Development step. Used to be called phases in traditional SDLC methodologies.

Development track. A small sub-project that focuses on a specific deliverable. For example, ETL, BI front-end applications and report writing, metadata repository, and data mining.

Development track team. Consists of two or more developers (and systems analysts) who work on track-specific tasks.

Dirty data. Data that has structural or domain value defects. For example, inaccurate data, incorrect data, duplicates, business rule violations, etc.

DG. See Data governance.

DNA. Refers to documentation, navigation, and administration. It describes the purpose for metadata.

Domain. A set of data values that represent the full range of allowable values for a given attribute (data element).

Domain counts. Total count of records by original code values on the source files/databases compared to total count of rows by transformed code values on the EDW target databases. Appropriate for more complicated transformations, such as separating data values from one source data element into multiple target columns, or combining data values from multiple source data elements into one target column.

Duplex. A building that is divided into two separate living quarters. Metaphor for the two DW objectives: data management (80%) and data delivery (20%).

EDW database. A relational/non-multidimensional database in the EDW/BI environment that feeds dependent data marts. It is one kind of EDW target database.

EDW target databases. A collection of standardized, integrated, consistent, and reconciled databases that store data, which is used by information consumers through BI tools, analytics applications, reports, and BI services. Can be an EDW database, data mart, ODS, or exploration warehouse.

EDW/BI environment. The entire configuration that contains all EDW and BI components. For example, ETL staging area files and databases, ETL programs, EDW target databases (EDW database, ODS, data marts, exploration warehouse), metadata repository, OLAP tools, report writers, BI applications, reports, queries, dashboards, scorecards, etc.

EIM. See Enterprise information management.

EIM professional. Used to be called data administrator, but has been expanded to include data quality analyst, metadata administrator, and any other role assigned to perform enterprise information management (data administration) and data governance activities. This term does not include data stewards and data owners.

Engineering stage. Common progression of system development from inception to implementation. Typical stages are justification, planning, analysis, design, construction, and deployment. Operational systems have an additional stage at the end called maintenance.

Enterprise-class. Any initiative, program, project, or activity that has an enterprise-wide perspective. Opposite of silo.

Enterprise data model. A logical data model of a single, integrated, non-redundant view of business data across the entire enterprise.

Enterprise data warehouse. The plumbing of BI; also known as the *data in* side of BI. It contains EDW target databases, a staging area database, and ETL processes.

Enterprise information architecture. The data portion of enterprise architecture; the what (data) column in the Zachman Framework.

Enterprise information management. Used to be called data administration. It is "data administration on steroids" because its functions have expanded to include data profiling, data analysis, data modeling, data quality improvement, data cleansing, metadata administration, and data governance.

Entity. A logical data modeling term referring to any real-world object, such as a person, place, concept, or event. For example, CUSTOMER, PRODUCT, SUPPLIER, and LOCATION.

ER Diagram. Entity-relationship diagram showing entities, data relationships among those entities, cardinality, and optionality. Developed by Dr. Peter Chen in 1976.

ETL. The extract/transform/load process in data warehousing.

ETL process flow. Data flow diagram showing in what sequence all ETL modules and utility runs (sort, merge) are executed, as well as temporary and permanent files and databases that are the sources and targets of the data in the ETL process.

Expected test result. Describes the expected output a code module should produce after running a test.

Exploration warehouse. A separate database that is designed and optimized for exploration analysis. For example, what-if analysis and data mining. It is a safe haven for exploratory and data-intensive ad-hoc processing that requires data to be reloaded many times and manipulated in different ways. It contains detailed and historical data that is sourced either from EDW target databases, or operational files and databases.

Exploration. An agile term for prototyping or iterative development. In Extreme Scoping, I use the term operational prototype.

Extended team. Consists of project participants who work on project activities intermittently, and who are not part of the core team or development track teams. For example, operations, security and audit, technical support, and other stakeholders.

External feed. Data received from a third party, such as Dun & Bradstreet.

Extreme Programming. A popular development-driven agile methodology.

Foreign key. A column in a table that is inherited from the primary key of another table. The physical implementation of a data relationship on a logical data model.

Front-end. Refers to the 20% data delivery activities of BI, such as coding BI applications, reports, and queries.

Gantt chart. A project plan that shows the start and finish dates of project activities, as well as resources and dependencies between these activities. Developed by Henry Gantt in the 1910s. Not used in Extreme Scoping.

Gap analysis. Analysis to determine the difference between what is needed and what is available.

Histogram. A bar graph showing frequency distribution. The width of the rectangles on the horizontal axis corresponds to class intervals, and the height corresponds to frequency. Similar to a bar chart, except the bars in the histogram actually touch each other.

Historical load. Process that loads old historical data from operational historical files and archival databases into EDW target databases.

Homonym. One name that is given to two or more different things. Opposite of synonym.

Incremental load. Process that periodically, and on an ongoing basis, loads new data from operational files and databases into EDW target databases. Periodicity could be monthly, weekly, daily, or hourly.

Information architect. See Data architect.

Information consumer. A user who utilizes databases for their operational and/or analytical work.

Information resource management. See Data administration.

Information services. Modes for delivering information. For example, OLAP tools, BI applications, dashboards, scorecards, and reports.

Infrastructure. Technical and non-technical architectural components. For example, physical hardware, network, corporate standards, methodology, etc.

Initial load. Process that loads current data, at the time of implementation, from operational files and databases into EDW target databases.

Integration analysis. See Business analysis. I use the terms interchangeably.

Integration testing. Also known as system testing and end-to-end testing. A test of the complete integrated process to evaluate its compliance with its specified functional requirements.

Lift chart. A graphic display that shows the effectiveness of a classification model. It is calculated as the ratio between the results obtained with and without the model.

Load statistics. Facts and figures about a load process. For example, number of records loaded, number of records rejected, rejection reasons, etc. Should be stored as metadata.

Logical data model. Also known as business data model. I use the terms interchangeably. A normalized and fully attributed data model in the form of an entity-relationship diagram, plus business metadata. It is process independent, which means it is fully normalized.

> This is *not* a data model of a database design.

Key performance indicator. A business metric used to measure a company's performance in critical areas. For example, number of calls taken per operator/per day, marketing expenditures per revenue, and percentage of returns per sold items or service. Usually displayed on actionable scorecards or dashboards.

KPI. See Key performance indicator.

Master data. Represents the participants to a transaction. For example, CUSTOMER and PRODUCT are participants to a sales transaction. Master data provides accurate and consistent views of core business entities and their core data elements across all systems in the company.

Master data management. The practice of defining and maintaining consistent definitions of business entities (e.g., customer and product) and attributes (data elements) about them across multiple IT systems.

MDM. See Master data management.

Metadata. Contextual information about system components, such as data, databases, applications, and processes. There are four types of metadata: business, technical, process, and usage metadata.

Metadata component. An entity on a meta model. For example, dataset, table, entity, column, attribute, source system, index, primary key, and foreign key.

Metadata repository. A database that is designed to store contextual information about data and processes, as well as other system components. Used to be called a data dictionary.

Middleware. A software layer that sits between the operating system and applications, or between the DBMS and applications.

Milestone. Markers during the execution of a project that measure its progress or state.

Multidimensional. A database design schema based on fact and dimension tables. Opposite of relational/non-multidimensional.

Normalization. A data modeling technique to organize data in a manner that eliminates redundancy. There are six normal forms: 1NF, 2NF, 3NF, BCNF, 4NF, and 5NF.

Normalized data model. Logical data models are normalized. They can be in 5NF, 4NF, 3NF, or BCNF.

Object-oriented. I use this term both conventionally and also to refer to a highly abstract meta model that has only three entities: object, object type, and object-to-object relationships.

ODS. Operational data store is similar to an EDW database, except that it contains only current data and is volatile (can be updated). It is designed to integrate data from multiple operational systems for additional operations and reporting.

This is *not* an operational (OLTP) database.

OLAP. Stands for online analytical processing. OLAP tools have the capability of drilling down and across on various data dimensions.

OLTP. Stands for online transaction processing and refers to operational systems that support the daily business operations.

Operational prototype. Similar to exploration. An iterative development method that combines analysis, design, coding, and testing activities to produce a production-worthy release.

Optionality. The minimum number of times one entity can be associated with another entity. The choices are one time (mandatory relationship) or zero times (optional relationship).

Partitioning. Dividing a large table into partitions for manageability, availability, or performance.

Performance testing. Also known as stress testing. I use the terms interchangeably. A test of code modules with complex logic run against high-volume databases to evaluate if they meet the specified performance requirements.

PERT chart. Stands for program evaluation review technique. Similar to CPM. A project plan showing three values for each activity: the shortest time, the most likely length of time, and the longest time. Developed by the US Navy in the 1950s. Not used in Extreme Scoping.

Physical data model. A de-normalized database model in the form of a modified ER diagram, depicting tables, columns, and keys. It is DBMS and process dependent, and can be multidimensional to provide maximum performance, or relational/non-multidimensional to provide maximum flexibility.

Pie chart. A circle divided into sectors, where the size of each sector corresponds to the relative size of the quantities represented.

Pivot table. A spreadsheet feature. Allows you to turn the data to view it from different perspectives.

Post-mortem. Old term for a post-implementation review at the end of a project to determine what went right and what went wrong on the project. In many companies, these reviews were only conducted if something went wrong.

Primary key. A column on a table that uniquely identifies a row of data on that table. The physical implementation of a unique identifier on a logical data model.

Process metadata. Contextual information about processes. For example, names, descriptions, business rules, and logic of programs and scripts for ETL, BI applications, and reports. Also includes data error statistics, load statistics, reconciliation totals, and process statistics generated during the ETL runs.

Process statistics. Facts and figures about a process. For example, number of records read, number of records processed, number of records filtered, etc. Should be stored as metadata.

Product owner. An agile term for user. Not used in Extreme Scoping.

Project charter. Also known as document of understanding, scope agreement, or statement of work. A document that describes the project and its cost, risks, assumptions, constraints, and other items the core team agrees on.

Project constraints. I use this term to mean conflicting priorities between scope, time, budget, people, and quality.

Project management office. The department responsible for establishing, maintaining, and enforcing project management processes, procedures, and standards.

Project management team. See core team.

Project retrospective. An agile term for a half-day "lessons learned" meeting. A smaller version of post-implementation review in Extreme Scoping.

Project-specific logical data model. A fully normalized and fully attributed logical data model with a data scope that is limited to the data requirements of a project.

Prototype charter. A document that describes the prototype and its purpose, scope, deliverable(s), and participants.

Prototyping. A dynamic, interactive, and iterative way of quickly developing an incomplete piece of an application for the purpose of refining requirements, demonstrating functionality, proving a concept, or showing feasibility. It combines the engineering stages of analysis, design, and construction.

QA testing. See Quality assurance testing.

Quality assurance testing. A test required by operations before a system can go into production, like a dress rehearsal. Ensures that the new application code conforms to company standards and has the desired level of quality for production.

Readiness assessment. A periodic survey, performed once a year, to determine user satisfaction with the EDW/BI environment and user understanding of EDW and BI (BI maturity level). Also used to find out what information needs are not being met yet.

Reconciliation totals. Tallies between processes, and between source and target databases. Example: record counts, domain counts, and amount counts. Ensures that data is processed correctly and is not dropped inadvertently.

Record counts. Number of records read, processed, and dropped. Adequate for extract, sort, and merge modules.

Refactoring. An agile term for redesigning, refining, enhancing, improving or simplifying a previously coded program module.

Regression testing. A test of old code that has been modified to ensure that previously working functions were not broken when the old code was modified.

Relational/non-multidimensional. A database design schema based on an entity-relationship diagram, either fully normalized or de-normalized. Opposite of multidimensional.

Release concept. Also known as iterative or agile development. An approach that produces a fully tested, fully documented, high-quality, but only partially-functioning application until the final release.

ROA. Return on asset refers to the additional value achieved from reusability of an existing asset.

ROI. Return on investment refers to the value achieved when the benefits of a new asset exceed its cost.

Scatter plot. A mathematical diagram with a set of points plotted on a graph that shows the correlation between two sets of data.

Schema. A database design documented as a physical data model.

Scorecard. A performance management tool in the form of a structured report used by business managers and financial analysts. Based on a long list of key performance indicators for comparing business performance to business goals. Primarily used by financial analysts.

Scrum. A popular development-driven agile methodology.

ScrumMaster. A person certified in the Scrum methodology who ensures that the Scrum process is used as intended by enforcing the Scrum rules. Not used in Extreme Scoping.

SDLC. Stands for system development lifecycle. Usually used in connection with a methodology.

Self-organizing project team. A team that has the authority to organize their work in any manner they please. They coordinate and assign tasks to each other, review each other's work, collaborate on project issues, and make project-related decisions without interference from management or the user.

Silo. A customized, stand-alone system or application. Not integrated. Opposite of collectively architected.

"Sinatra way". I use this term to mean developing customized silo solutions where each project team chooses their own preferred methodology, their own preferred standards, their own preferred designs, and their own preferred processes. Nothing is integrated or shared.

Single version of the truth. A logical or physical inventory of unique, clean, consistent, and non-redundant data. A ratified, common, "golden" copy of business data. Called logical inventory if it is limited to the enterprise data model; called physical inventory if it is implemented in the EDW database.

Source data. Data from internal operational systems or external third-party companies that feeds into the EDW target databases.

Source system. An internal operational system used as input to the ETL process.

Specifications. Instructions written in non-technical language and given to a developer, explaining what code has to be written. Contains input and output descriptions, as well as an explanation of the function the program has to perform.

Spiral data warehouse methodology. A DW-specific, data-driven development methodology that supports iterative development. Within each iteration, development steps are executed in sequential order, like in a traditional methodology.

Sponsorship. Financial backing of a project, program, or initiative. See Collective sponsorship.

Sprint. An agile term for a predetermined time-box and repeatable work cycle (iteration). Scrum is 29 days; XP is ten days. See Cadence. Not used in Extreme Scoping.

Staging area. The place where the ETL tool modules and custom-written ETL code modules run, and where the source data is prepared for the EDW target databases.

Stakeholder. A person who has a vested interest in a project.

Stand-up meeting. See Daily stand-up meeting.

Stovepipe. Also known as Silo. I use the terms interchangeably. Stand-alone process or system that cannot easily integrate with any other process or system. Opposite of collectively architected.

Stress testing. See Performance testing. I use the terms interchangeably.

Subject area. In logical data modeling, it refers to a data subject area, such as CUSTOMER, PRODUCT, ORGANIZATION, and EMPLOYEE. In multidimensional reporting, it refers to a functional (event) subject area, such as BILLING, ORDER, SALE, and SHIPMENT.

SWAT. A military term. Stands for special weapons and tactics.

SWAT team. I use this term to mean a small team of self-motivated, skilled, and experienced EDW/BI practitioners who do not tolerate political interference as they make decisions and take actions to complete a project.

Synonym. One thing that is known by two or more different names. Opposite of homonym.

System analysis. The study of functional requirements for the purpose of turning them into a system design. Focus is on finding a design solution.

Technical metadata. Technical names of databases, tables, columns, indices, primary and foreign keys, referential integrity rules, etc.

Test cases. A set of documented conditions reflecting the user requirements. Test cases are executed against a pool of test data to determine whether a code module functions as expected.

Time-box. A fixed amount of time allocated to a project, activity, task, or meeting. The time period is not predetermined; every time-box can have a different duration.

Top-down business data modeling. Starting with a high-level conceptual model and then refining it into a normalized and fully attributed logical data model. Business data modeling is done with business people in facilitated sessions.

Track-specific task. A task that only applies to a specific development track. For example, designing the ETL process applies only to the back-end ETL track; writing reports applies only to the front-end BI application track.

Traditional methodology. Also known as waterfall methodology. Developed in the 1970's to help developers with system development. Organized into phases that are executed in sequential order after the user has signed-off on the artifacts of the previous phase. This is the reason they are called waterfall methodologies.

Transformation. See Data transformation.

Unique identifier. A logical data modeling term that refers to the attribute(s) that identify a specific instance of data.

Unit testing. A test of individual code modules to ensure that they compile error-free and produce the correct output (results).

Un-normalized schema. The data was never normalized or de-normalized. Usually refers to a flat file or flat table. Operational transaction data was often stored this way in flat file structures.

Usage metadata. Refers to statistics related to database access and usage.

UA testing. See User acceptance testing.

User acceptance testing. A test performed with the users to demonstrate that the functionality and data of the deliverable meet their requirements, and to obtain their acceptance and sign-off on the deliverable.

User story. An agile term for user requirements. Not used in Extreme Scoping.

Vendor. A company that sells products.

"War room". Colloquial term for a dedicated project room.

Waterfall methodology. Also known as traditional methodology. I use the terms interchangeably.

What-if analysis. The process of changing the values in columns to observe how those changes affect the result of a report or query.

Work breakdown structure. Hierarchical decomposition of a project into phases, activities, tasks, and subtasks.

XP. See Extreme Programming.

"Yo-yo" methodology. I use this term to describe spiral data warehouse methodologies because of their iterative nature. You execute all phases – top to bottom – several times before you are done, just like a yo-yo.

Zachman Framework. An enterprise architecture framework for a system. A matrix of six columns and six rows. The six columns are what (data), how (process), where (location), who (people), when (time), and why (rationale). The six rows are scope, enterprise model, system model, technology model, physical components, and functioning system. Developed by John Zachman in 1987.

Zip code. US postal code.

References

Adelman, Sid. *Capitalizing the Data Warehouse.* EIMInsight Magazine, Volume 3, Issue 2, February 2009.

Adelman, Sid, Larissa T. Moss and Majid Abai. *Data Strategy.* Upper Saddle River, NJ: Addison-Wesley, 2005.

Adelman, Sid et al. *Impossible Data Warehouse Situations: Solutions from the Experts.* Upper Saddle River, NJ: Addison-Wesley, 2002.

Adelman, Sid and Larissa Terpeluk Moss. *Data Warehouse Project Management.* Upper Saddle River, NJ: Addison-Wesley, 1999.

Ambler, Scott W. *Agile Database Techniques.* New York, NY: John Wiley & Sons, 2003.

Ambler, Scott W. and Mark Lines. *Disciplined Agile Delivery.* Boston, MA: Pearson Education, 2012.

Augustine, Sanjiv. *Managing Agile Projects.* Upper Saddle River, NJ: Prentice Hall, 2005.

Beck, Kent. *Extreme Programming Explained: Embrace Change. Second Edition.* Upper Saddle River, NJ: Addison-Wesley, 2005.

Berson, Alex and Larry Dubov. *Master Data Management and Customer Data Integration for a Global Enterprise.* New York, NY: McGraw-Hill, 2007.

Brackett, Michael H. *Data Sharing.* New York, NY: John Wiley & Sons, 1994.

Brackett, Michael H. *The Data Warehouse Challenge.* New York, NY: John Wiley & Sons, 1996.

Brackett, Michael H. *Data Resource Quality.* Upper Saddle River, NJ: Addison-Wesley, 2000.

Buytendijk, Frank. *Performance Leadership.* New York, NY: McGraw-Hill, 2009.

Cabena, Peter et al. *Discovering Data Mining.* Upper Saddle River, NJ: Prentice Hall, 1998.

Cockburn, Alistair. *Agile Software Development.* Upper Saddle River, NJ: Addison-Wesley, 2001.

Cook, Melissa A. *Building Enterprise Information Architectures.* Upper Saddle River, NJ: Prentice Hall, 1996.

DAMA International. *Guide to the Data Management Body of Knowledge*. Bradley Beach: NJ, Technics Publications, 2010.

DeCarlo, Doug. *eXtreme Project Management*. San Francisco, CA: Jossey-Bass, 2004.

DeMarco, Tom. *Slack*. New York, NY: Random House, 2001.

DeMarco, Tom and Timothy Lister. *Peopleware*. New York, NY: Dorset House, 1999.

DeMarco, Tom et al. *Adrenaline Junkies and Template Zombies*. New York, NY: Dorset House, 2008.

Dyché, Jill. *e-Data: Turning Data into Information with Data Warehousing*. Upper Saddle River, NJ: Addison-Wesley, 2000.

Eckerson, Wayne. *Performance Dashboards, 2nd Edition*. New York, NY: John Wiley & Sons, 2011.

Eckerson, Wayne. *Secrets of Analytical Leaders*. Westfield, NJ: Technics Publications, 2012.

English, Larry P. *Improving Data Warehouse and Business Information Quality*. New York, NY: John Wiley & Sons, 1999.

Halpin, Terry. *Information Modeling and Relational Databases*. San Francisco, CA: Morgan Kaufmann, 2001.

Highsmith, Jim. *Agile Project Management, Creating Innovative Products*. Boston, MA: Pearson Education, 2004.

Hoberman, Steve. *Data Modeler's Workbench*. New York, NY: John Wiley & Sons, 2002.

Hoberman, Steve. *Data Modeling Made Simple, 2nd Edition*. Bradley Beach, NJ: Technics Publications, 2009.

Hoberman, Steve. *Data Modeling for the Business*. Bradley Beach, NJ: Technics Publications, 2009.

Huang, Kuan-Tsae, Yang W. Lee and Richard Y. Wang. *Quality Information and Knowledge*. Upper Saddle River, NJ: Prentice Hall, 1999.

Hughes, Ralph et al. *Agile Data Warehousing*. Bloomington, IN: iUniverse, 2008.

Imhoff, Claudia, Lisa Loftis and Jonathan G. Geiger. *Building the Customer-Centric Enterprise*. New York, NY: John Wiley & Sons, 2001.

Inmon, W.H., J.D. Welch and Katherine L. Glassey. *Managing the Data Warehouse*. New York, NY: John Wiley & Sons, 1997.

Inmon, W.H., John A. Zachman and Jonathan G. Geiger. *Data Stores, Data Warehousing and the Zachman Framework.* New York, NY: McGraw-Hill, 1997.

Inmon, W.H., Claudia Imhoff and Ryan Sousa. *Corporate Information Factory, 2nd Edition.* New York, NY: John Wiley & Sons, 2001.

Inmon, William H. and Anthony Nesavich. *Tapping into Unstructured Data.* Upper Saddle River, NJ: Prentice Hall, 2008.

Inmon, William, Bonnie O'Neil and Lowell Fryman. *Business Metadata: Capturing Enterprise Knowledge.* Burlington, MA: Morgan Kauffman, 2008.

Kimball, Ralph, Laura Reeves, Margy Ross and Warren Thornthwaite. *The Data Warehouse Lifecycle Toolkit.* New York, NY: John Wiley & Sons, 1998.

Kimball, Ralph and Margy Ross. *The Data Warehouse Toolkit, 2nd Edition.* New York, NY: John Wiley & Sons, 2002.

Ladley, John. *Making Enterprise Information Management Work for Business.* Burlington, MA: Morgan Kauffman, 2010.

Loshin, David. *Business Intelligence, The Savvy Manager's Guide.* San Francisco, CA: Morgan Kaufmann, 2003.

Loshin, David. *Enterprise Knowledge Management.* San Francisco, CA: Morgan Kaufmann, 2001.

Loshin, David. *Master Data Management.* Burlington, MA: Morgan Kauffman, 2009.

Maydanchik, Arkady. *Data Quality Assessment.* Bradley Beach, NJ: Technics Publications, 2007.

Marco, David. *Building and Managing the Meta Data Repository.* New York, NY: John Wiley & Sons, 2000.

McGilvray, Danette. *Executing Data Quality Projects.* Burlington, MA: Morgan Kauffman, 2008.

Moss, Larissa. *No Silver Bullets for Data Integration.* EIMInsight Magazine, Volume 3, Issue 7, July 2009.

Moss, Larissa. *Enterprise Data Modeling – Is It Worth It?* EIMInsight Magazine, Volume 2, Issue 1, April 2008.

Moss, Larissa. *Origins of Data Modeling...The Forgotten Story.* EIMInsight Magazine, Volume 1, Issue 12, February 2008.

Moss, Larissa. *We Don't Need No Stinkin' Methodology.* EIMInsight Magazine, Volume 1,

Issue 4, June 2007.

Moss, Larissa T., and Shaku Atre. *Business Intelligence Roadmap: The Complete Project Lifecycle for Decision-Support Applications.* Upper Saddle River, NJ: Addison-Wesley, 2003.

O'Rourke, Carol, Neal Fishman and Warren Selkow. *Enterprise Architecture Using the Zachman Framework.* Boston, MA: Thomson Course Technology, 2003.

Olson, Jack E. *Data Quality: The Accuracy Dimension.* San Francisco, CA: Morgan Kaufmann, 2003.

Redman, Thomas C. *Data Quality: The Field Guide.* Boston, MA: Digital Press, 2001.

Reingruber, Michael C. and William W. Gregory. *The Data Modeling Handbook.* New York, NY: John Wiley & Sons, 1994.

Schwaber, Ken. *Agile Project Management with Scrum.* Redmond, WA: Microsoft Press, 2004.

Schwaber, Ken, and Mike Beedle. *Agile Software Development with Scrum.* Upper Saddle River, NJ: Prentice Hall, 2002.

Simsion, Graeme. *Data Modeling Essentials.* Boston, MA: Thomson Computer Press, 1994.

Simsion, Graeme. *Data Modeling Theory and Practice.* Bradley Beach, NJ: Technics Publications, 2007.

Soares, Sunil. *The IBM Data Governance Unified Process.* Ketchum, ID: MC Press, 2010.

Soares, Sunil. *Selling Information Governance to the Business.* Ketchum, ID: MC Press, 2011.

Tannenbaum, Adrienne. *Metadata Solutions.* Upper Saddle River, NJ: Addison-Wesley, 2002.

The Data Warehousing Institute. *TDWI Business Intelligence Executive Briefing.* Renton, WA: TDWI, 2006.

Thomsett, Rob. *Radical Project Management.* Upper Saddle River, NJ: Prentice Hall, 2002.

Williams, Steve and Nancy Williams. *The Profit Impact of Business Intelligence.* San Francisco, CA: Morgan Kaufmann, 2007.

Yourdon, Edward. *Death March: The Complete Software Developer's Guide to Surviving "Mission Impossible" Projects.* Upper Saddle River, NJ: Prentice Hall, 1997.

Index

NOTE: Bold numbers indicate the pages where the term is defined.